The Blood-Stained Benders; More Evil Than You Know

The Dreadful Deeds of The Bender Family

Compiled, Edited, & Introduction By

Charles M. Province

Books by Charles M. Province

Pure Patton
Patton's Proverbs
Patton's Third Army
Patton's Punch Cards
The Unknown Patton
I Was Patton's Doctor
Japanese Assault Boats
General Patton's Medals
A Long Way From Flat River
Patton's One-Minute Messages
Adventures of the Flat River Kid
A Little Kid From Flat River (Vol. I)
A Little Kid From Flat River (Vol. II)
A Little Kid From Flat River (Vol. III)
A Little Kid From Flat River (Vol. IV)
General Walton Walker; Forgotten Hero
A Message to Garcia; The Complete Story
Tail-gunner: The Leonard E. Thompson Story
Patton'w Third Army in WWII (Juvenile Book)

Books Edited by Charles M. Province

Saber Exercise, 1914
Generalship; It's Diseases and Their Cure
A History of the St. Joseph Lead Company
*A Living History of Flat River, Elvins, Desloge,
& Farmington, Missouri*

CMP Publishing House — History Division
www.pattonhq.com/cmp.html
cmprovince@gmail.com

Table of Contents

Part One

Introduction.

I must have been around nine or ten years old when I first heard of *The Blood-Stained Benders* as Grandpa Province referred to them.

It was a Sunday afternoon and we were spending the summer — as we always did — on Grandpa's farm near Irondale, Missouri. That would be Grandpa, Grandma, my brother Harold, and me. My old man stayed in town where he worked in the Lead Mines.

Grandpa and I had finished listening to a "western drama" on our old Philco Console Radio. Being the size of a small bookcase, the thing was as much a piece of furniture as it was a radio.

If I remember correctly, the broadcast was an episode of the old radio version of *Gunsmoke*, starring William Conrad as Marshal Dillon. Before that, we had been entranced as *Boston Blackie* — Grandpa's favorite private-eye — tracked down a missing heiress, or some such story.

Anyway, the *Gunsmoke* episode portrayed an entire family of murderers who made a profession of slaughtering unsuspecting travelers who stopped at their "hotel" for a meal or to stay overnight. The evil mother and father had raised their children from birth to be murders and thieves. Nice people, indeed.

Switching off the radio, I made the comment about us being lucky there weren't families like that in Flat River, the small Missouri town where my, father, brother, and I lived with my Grandparents following my Mother's death.

I was quite taken aback when Grandpa said, "Yeah, at least they weren't in *this* part of Missouri, but it was so long ago they'd all be nothin' but bones by now anyways."

With furrowed brow, I contemplated Grandpa's remark for a few moments and I finally said, "I don't understand what you're talking about. Are you saying there was a whole family of murderers living in Flat River?"

Grandpa said, "Nah, not right here in the Lead Belt. From the stories my Pap told me, they lived in a cave somewhere near Ste. Genevieve and they murdered folks travelin' up and down the Mississippi."

I said, "Holy cow! You mean the family on *Gunsmoke* was a real, live family, living in Missouri, and they killed people traveling the Mississippi River?"

"Well," he said, "That there radio show wasn't the real story, of course. It was a watered down story of the family's murderous ways. The real family was called *The Blood-Stained Benders*. At least, that's what Pap told me."

"They was almost caught when they were running that so-called "hotel" over in Kansas, but they snuck away, like they always did. They bumped off a bunch of folks, though, 'afore they skedaddled down to Texas, or the Indian Territory, or some such place. I don't reckon they was here in Missouri fer that long."

"Accordin' to what Pap told me, they'd watch out from a cave over-lookin' the river for folks in small boats or on rafts. They'd have their little girl act like she was drownin' or somethin', and she'd yell for help to lure the suckers to shore. When they was close enough, the old man shot 'em, pulled the boat to shore with grapplin' hooks, and then he slit their throats to make sure they was dead 'afore robbin' 'em. Then they'd toss 'em back on the boat, push it off, an' watch the current carry away the evidence."

"Nobody knows how many folks they killed and robbed, but there was a whole camp setup in the cave where they must'a lived."

"When the heck did all this happen?" I asked.

Grandpa said, "I ain't rightly sure, but it was probably the 1850s or so, right 'afore the *War of Northern Aggression*, I think. I figure Pap was right aroun' twenty when all this went on . . . that would'a been in 1858 . . . yeah, would'a been right afore the War."

I said, "1858? And he was twenty? So he was born in 1838? When were you born Grandpa?"

Grandpa said, "Well, Pap popped out in 1838 and I was born in 1885 . . . he was forty-seven when I was hatched. February 14th . . . a Valentine's Day present for Mam. Pap's first wife died and he married my Mam. Toted up, he had all of eighteen young 'uns from both women. A feller needs a lot of hands on a farm, ya know."

As Grandpa would have said, "I did some naughts and ciphers in my head," and then I said, "Holy cow. Your Grandpa would have been around when Jefferson, Washington, Franklin, and all the others were alive." I *naughted* and *ciphered* on my fingers and said, "That's only four generations away from me. Gee Willikers."

I remembered what we were talking about and said, "Let's get back to that murder family. What was their name?"

Grandpa said, "Pap told me they were called *The Benders* in Kansas, but they moved around a bunch and used lots 'a names. They only stayed in a place until people started asking questions about 'em."

"And they never got caught here in Missouri?" I asked.

"Nope," said Grandpa,"they ran into a bit of bad luck one day. A couple of rafters was headin' down the river together but were a few minutes apart. The little girl started in with her act and when the first raft headed toward shore, the old man was just about to shoot when the second raft came up on 'em. The girl didn't know what to do, and the old man shot early and missed. The folks on both rafts shot back, and the whole family took to runnin'. They never went back to the cave, either, just took off. They was never heard of or seen in Missouri again."

I had taken in a lot of information for a little kid and I was sitting there, thinking about it all when Grandpa got out of his chair and said, "Well, I gotta take care of Dolly and Daisy. Horses don't feed themselves, ya know."

I said, "I'll go check on the pigs."

Grandpa said, "That'd be a help."

So Grandpa headed for the barn and I headed to the pig pen and we never got around to continuing our discussion of *The Blood-Stained Benders.*

Being a *good 'ole Missouri boy* I knew all about Missouri's reputation as a "cave state."

South of St. Louis — down the west side of the Mississippi River — the Missouri hills are well known for sinkholes and caves. There was a big sinkhole behind our house at 301 First Street in Flat River that had been filled in with tons upon tons of rocks from the Lead Mines. I've seen many a sinkhole in my time and I've been in a few caves.

From St. Louis down to Cape Girardeau — roughly a 125-mile stretch, three miles wide — there are more sinkholes and caves than have been counted.

I've heard claims that Jesse James and the Younger Gang hid in some of these caves but I don't believe them. If Jesse and the Youngers hid in all the caves they were supposed to, they would have had little time for robbing banks and trains, and for killing people.

There are verifiable claims that these caves have used over past centuries by pirates, counterfeiters, bushwhackers, and bald-knobbers.

One place I can confirm, is the Hildebrand Cave north of Bonne Terre, where Sam Hildebrand hid occasionally during the *War of Northern Aggression*. Sam was a large and dangerous thorn in the side of the Union troops throughout the War. The Yankees neither captured nor killed him.

I never found out from Grandpa Province precisely where the "Bender Cave" was supposed to have been, but knowing what I do about Missouri terrain along the Mississippi, I can certainly believe in the possibility of his Pap's story being true.

That comment brings us to some explanations about this book, which consists of three parts:

Part One is this Introduction.

Part Two is a reproduction of the first, original *Dime Novel* about "The Bender Family," constructed with all of the original illustrations and the Clarendon font, which was used for the original text. The dime novel is extremely relevant because the story it proffers confirms some distinctively pertinent elements of the life-long murderous career of the Benders..

The thirty year period reflected in *The Five Fiends* — from 1842 in Texas until 1872 in Kansas — gives credence to the possibility that the Benders had a long and successful career as a family of murderers and robbers. This scenario would certainly verify them living a nomadic lifestyle throughout the less populated territories in those days to avoid detection. It would also fit the time frame of the "Mississippi Murders" reported to me by my Grandpa.

The family of killers could have studied and adapted various means of extermination requisite upon their circumstances and with three sisters "married" to "Mr. Bender" they could have had numerous children who could have been reared in the methodologies of mayhem and crime. Acceptance of this theory would prompt one to wonder how many people were killed by the homicidal family; perhaps hundreds.

Part Three is a *Judicial Report* gathered by an attorney named J. T. James. Mr. James was one of the two lawyers who defended two innocent women charged and prosecuted for "being the Bender Women." Mr. James' report contains the basic "Bloody Bender" story, trial transcripts and testimony, newspaper reports of the Kansas murders, and interviews with people directly involved with the discovery of the victims' graves, the subsequent exhumation of those graves, and the Vigilance Committee's activities following the "flight of the Benders."

In essence, Mr. James' report is fraught with verbosity, repetition, and pure gossip pertaining the Bender affair in Kansas and the trial. Some of it is rather sticky and complicated reading, making it difficult to get through it all, but taken as a whole, it provides a good account of the Kansas murders and the subsequent trial almost twenty years later.

Further consideration must be applied to the prolific number of aliases used by the Benders; they never used the same name twice. Claims about the origins, the marriage, and the children of Old Man and Old Lady Bender are unsubstantiated. Nothing about them has ever been proven and no one really, absolutely, knows where they came from, what their true names were, or how many children they had. The Benders — to this day — remain a mystery which, I believe, will never be adequately solved.

Neither has the enigma of their death been satisfactorily solved. Stories of them being killed, either by firearms or rope, are unproven. No bodies were ever found. The Governor of Kansas put a price on their collective heads and the reward would have been paid had they been brought in dead or alive.

It is difficult to believe the Vigilance Committee sent forth would find them, kill them, bury them, and not claim the reward and — more importantly — not let the world know the despicable demons had been exterminated. If the Vigilantes did, in fact, find and kill them, it would be incumbent upon them to let everyone know that the family was no longer a threat to anyone. It would also have precluded the arrest and prosecution of the two women who were innocent of the charge of "being Bender Women" in the late 1880s.

If nothing else, the judicial report provides us with a view of the incompetence and lack of professionalism of the so-called "authorities" in Kansas at the time of the murders and the subsequent trial. It is apparent that no one involved with the inquiry into the murders had a clue as to how to direct or control a murder investigation.

Thousands of strangers, delivered by the nearby railroad, were allowed to wander and tramp around in the "graveyard" of victims. The house and barn were allowed to be dismantled by souvenir seekers. No one took control of anything. One of the first people on the scene stole some hammers and a knife suspected of being the murder weapons. The whole affair was nothing less than inept, incompetent, bungled, unskilled, and ineffective.

It's little wonder *The Blood-Stained Benders* were able to abscond, never to be heard of again.

They most probably separated, hid out for a while, and after things settled down, reassembled, and reinitiated their homicidal enterprises in another scarcely populated territory.

Part Four is a condensed digest of newspaper stories published during the relevant time period of the Bender Kansas Murders. The most pertinent and least repetitive portions of newspaper accounts of events have been extracted and edited together to create a "composite article" as an example of the sensational nature of the reporting provided by newspapers. In most cases, newspaper editors were more interested in building circulation than in reporting the truth.

As little editing as possible was done to these newspaper accounts. The aim is to display the quality — or rather, lack of quality — in the typical newspaper reporting of such sensational stories. A purposeful attempt has been made to leave in all of the mistakes, misspellings, lack of proof and factual corroboration, the general inaccuracies, and the outright falsehoods inherent in newspaper reporting at the time.

The problem with such poor reportage, of course, is that it not only imparts to the public incorrect and inaccurate information, it creates an environment in which the truth is almost impossible to ascertain.

The bottom line is that very little is factually known about the Bender Family and almost everything reported about them is nothing less than conjecture. No one will ever know who they really were, where they came from, what happened to them, and how many people they murdered.

'Tis, indeed, a pity.

Charles M. Province
CMP Publishing House
Oregon City OR
2019

Photograph of graves with notations of victim's names.

Open graves with an assemblage of "observers." The photographer
has blacked out the grave pits to better display their positions.

Stereopticon images of graves being exhumed at the Bender House. To view these in "3D" simply look in the middle of the photograph and cross your eyes until you see a third image appear between both images. It may take a little practice, but it's worth it.

Busybodies with nothing to do but investigate the scene of gruesome murders. The local railroad had to generate two additional train runs to accomodate the thousands of visitors to the Bender house. Many of them took home pieces of the house, clods of graveyard dirt, and anything else they could grab as a souvenir.

Stereopticon of the Bender House, with boards missing. By the time the thousands of busybodies came and went, the entire house had been torn apart and stolen for souvenirs. To see the image in "3D," look at the middle of the photograph and cross your eyes until you see a third image in the middle. It may take some practice, but it's worth it.

THE BENDER SHANTY.—[FROM A PHOTOGRAPH BY GEORGE R. GAMBLE.]

1, Grave of Dr. York. 2. Grave of M'Kenzie. 3. Grave of M'Croutly. 4. Grave of Brown. 5. Grave of unknown. 6. Grave of unknown. 7. Grave of Longcore and child. 8. Pit or cellar in which bodies were cast.

SCENE OF THE BENDER MURDERS.—[FROM A SKETCH BY JOHN W. DONLADY.]

THE GRAVE OF DR. YORK.—[FROM A PHOTOGRAPH BY GEORGE R. GAMBLE.]

THE BENDER MURDERS NEAR CHERRYVALE, KANSAS

Artist Renderings of the Bender Family murder site;
From an issue of Harper's Magazine, 1873.

Kate Bender lecturing on Spiritualism.

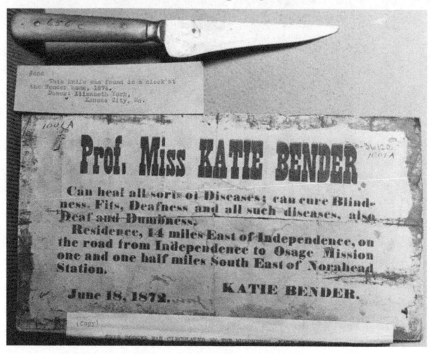

A knife found in a clock at the Bender House in Kansas. The notice
was handed out and posted in public places to publicize
Kate Bender's lectures on Spiritualism.

This is supposed to be a Tintype of Kate Bender,
but there is no absolute proof that it is her.

Another unsubstantiated image of Kate Bender.

KANSAS
HISTORICAL MARKER
THE BLOODY BENDERS

Near here are the Bender Mounds, named for the infamous Bender family -- John, his wife, son, and daughter Kate --who settled here in 1871. Kate soon gained notoriety as a self - proclaimed healer and spiritualist. Secretly, the four made a living through murder and robbery.

Located on a main road, the Benders sold meals and supplies to travelers. Their murders were carried out by use of a canvas curtain that divided the house into two rooms. When a traveler was seated at the table, his head was outlined against the curtain. The victim was then dispatched from behind with a hammer, and the body was dropped into a basement pit, later to be buried in an orchard.

As more and more travelers disappeared, suspicion began to center on the Benders. They disappeared in the spring of 1873, shortly before inquisitive neighbors discovered the victims' bodies. The Benders are believed to have killed about a dozen people, including one child.

Although stories abound, the ultimate fate of the murderous Bender family is uncertain. Some say that they escaped, others that they were executed by a vengeful posse. Their story is unresolved, and remains one of the great unsolved mysteries of the old West.

Erected by Kansas State Historical Society & Kansas Department of Transportation

The Bender Museum in Kansas; it is no longer in business.

THE BENDER HAMMERS

Three hammers found in a clock, along with a knife,
at the Bender House in Kansas.

Governor's Proclamation.

$2,000 REWARD

State of Kansas, Executive Department.

WHEREAS, several atrocious murders have been recently committed in Labette County, Kansas, under circumstances which fasten, beyond doubt, the commissions of these crimes upon a family known as the "Bender family," consisting of

JOHN BENDER, about 60 years of age, five feet eight or nine inches in height, German, speaks but little English, dark complexion, no whiskers, and sparely built;

MRS. BENDER, about 50 years of age, rather heavy set, blue eyes, brown hair, German, speaks broken English;

JOHN BENDER, Jr., alias John Gebardt, five feet eight or nine inches in height, slightly built, gray eyes with brownish tint, brown hair, light moustache, no whiskers, about 27 years of age, speaks English with German accent;

KATE BENDER, about 24 years of age, dark hair and eyes, good looking, well formed, rather bold in appearance, fluent talker, speaks good English with very little German accent:

AND WHEREAS, said persons are at large and fugitives from justice, now therefore, I, Thomas A. Osborn, Governor of the State of Kansas, in pursuance of law, do hereby offer a **REWARD OF FIVE HUNDRED DOLLARS** for the apprehension and delivery to the Sheriff of Labette County, Kansas, of each of the persons above named.

In Testimony Whereof, I have hereunto subscribed my name, and caused the Great Seal of the State to be affixed.

[L. S.]   Done at Topeka, this 17th day of May, 1873.

THOMAS A. OSBORN,
Governor.

By the Governor:

W. H. SMALLWOOD,
Secretary of State.

THE BENDER FAMILY.

Great Excitement Over Increased Unearthings of Crime—A Little Girl Buried Alive.

PARSONS, KS., May 12.—Col. Bondinot, who has just returned from the scene of the Bender murder, reports three more graves discovered yesterday. Over three thousand people were on the ground, and a special train has just arrived, with seven cars, filled with people. There is intense excitement all over the country, and a firm determination to ferret out the parties engaged in the murders. It is understood that a large reward will be offered by the community and the State for the arrest of the assassins. Nearly all the bodies of the dead are indecently mutilated. It is considered certain that a little girl was thrown alive into the grave with her father, as no marks of violence were found on the body.

New York Times, January 12, 1890

KANSAS CITY, MO., Jan. 11.—It is altogether probable that two women alleged to be Mrs. John and Mrs. Kate Bender, who are now confined in the Labette County (Kan.) jail awaiting trial for the murder of Dr. York, will be liberated in a few days. An attorney of this city represented the women at the preliminary trial. Since that time he has been quietly at work collecting proof which will establish the fact that the women are Mrs. Almira Griffith and Mrs. Sarah E. Davis. He now claims to have affidavits showing that from 1870 to 1874 these two women were in Michigan. The crimes with which the Benders are charged were all committed during these years. On being acquainted of this fact the Prosecuting Attorney of Labette County wrote the attorney for the defendants telling him that if he could prove these facts by affidavits he would discharge the prisoners. Mr. James will leave for Oswego next week with his affidavits.

THE BENDER FAMILY.

Arrest of These Notorious Murderers in Arkansas.

LITTLE ROCK, April 5.—The Kansas detectives passed through Fort Smith yesterday, en route for Kansas with the supposed Bender family, arrested in Crawford county, Tuesday. The family went under the name of Keofer. They were arrested by a Mr. Beard of Kansas, a private detective, upon a requisition from the Governor of Kansas upon the Governor of Arkansas. Beard is the man who discovered the bodies of the murdered York and others on Bender's place in Kansas in 1872. He followed the family down the Atlantic & Pacific Road to Pierce City, Mo., thence to Fayetteville in this State. The family separated at Fayetteville, but reunited at the house of a son of the old man Bender on Cedar creek, where they engaged in agricultural pursuits. After satisfying himself as to the identity of the family the detective, Beard, proceeded to Kansas. The Governor offered a reward of $2,500 and a requisition for George Keofer alias John Bender, Lena Keofer alias Kate Bender, Mrs. Keofer alias Mrs. Bender, and Phillip alias John Bender, Jr. The arrests were made quietly by the sheriff, the only resistance being by Kate, who drew a shovel on the detective and attempted to get a pistol, but was prevented from doing anything. The whole party deny that they are the Benders. All the circumstances are so strong that every one in the locality, where the arrests were made, believe they are the real Bender family. Keofer made a good citizen, but has rested under suspicion ever since his residence in Crawford. They came into the county on foot, one at a time, but the old man soon commenced buying farms and agricultural implements, always having plenty of money to pay his way. Since they left Kansas Kate has become the mother of two children.

Examples of "Bender Clippings" from all over the United States. The family was reportedly seen in almost every state in the country.

A sketch of old man Bender.

A sketch of old lady Bender.

THE FIVE FIENDS,

—OR,—

Likeness of Kate Bender, from the Photograph found in
Breakerman's Pocket.

THE BENDER

HOTEL HORROR

IN THE WESTERN PRAIRIES

THE FIVE FIENDS:

OR,

The Bender Hotel Horror in Kansas.

THIS FAMILY OF FIENDS HAVE FOR A NUMBER OF YEARS
BEEN SYSTEMATICALLY MURDERING TRAVELLERS
WHO STOPPED AT THEIR HOTEL OR STORE,

BY A MOST SINGULAR METHOD,

WHICH HAS NEVER BEEN DISCOVERED UNTIL THE KILLING
OF DR. YORK, THE BROTHER OF. SENATOR YORK,
OF KANSAS.

THIS BOOK CONTAINS FULL AND STARTLING DETAILS OF
THEIR LIVES AND AWFUL CRIMES.

*IT IS CERTAIN THAT THEY HAVE MURDERED OVER
ONE HUNDRED PEOPLE!*

PUBLISHED BY

OLD FRANKLIN PUBLISHING HOUSE IN PHILADELPHIA, PA.

Geo. Woods & Co's Parlor Organs.

THEIR COMBINATION SOLO STOPS
are capable of the most beautiful musical effects.

ÆOLINE—A soft or breathing stop.

VOX HUMANA—A baritone solo, not a fan or tremolo.

PIANO—Which will never require tuning.

Few are aware of the perfection the Parlor Organ has reached, the variety of musical effects of which it is capable, and how desirable an addition it is to the parlor. These instruments have created much interest and enthusiasm by reason of their quality of tone, elegance of finish and musical effects.

The Profession and Public generally are earnestly invited to examine these beautiful instruments at our own or agents' warerooms, and compare them with other instruments of their class.

Correspondence with the Trade and Profession solicited.

Agents wanted in every town. Circulars containing music free.

GEO. WOODS & CO., Cambridgeport, Mass.

WAREROOMS, { 66 & 68 Adams St., Chicago.
33 King William St., London.
M. G. Bisbee, 920 Chestnut St.,
Philadelphia, Pa.

IN REPLYING CUT OFF THIS ADDRESS AND ENCLOSE IN YOUR LETTER.

3

THE BENDER HOTEL HORROR

IN KANSAS.

About a year ago not only Kansas, but the whole country, was terribly excited over the discovery of the hideous tragedies that had been perpetrated in their hotel, or rather store, by the Bender family.

These horrible deeds of blood and robbery had been going on between four and five years, and were only brought to light by the following circumstance.

On the ninth day of March, Dr. William H. York, the brother of the York who exposed the attempted bribery of Senator Pomeroy, started to go to his home in Independence, from Fort Scott. He was mounted upon a fine horse. His family were anxiously expecting him, and consequently when he did not arrive they were very much worried, because there was a certain important piece of business for him to settle, and they knew he would hasten home for that express purpose.

Day after day went by, and still he did not come, and the conclusion his family arrived at, was that he had been taken sick. But even then, they argued that he would certainly have sent them a message to say so. The next supposition was, that he had been waylaid and murdered by some of his brother's enemies, who had vowed vengeance against all the York family. So it was determined to institute a search for the missing man, and scouts went out at once to Fort Scott. From the Fort they traced him as far as Cherryvale, in Labette county, Kansas. There all became an insolvable mystery. All traces vanished as completely as smoke wastes away in upper air.

Cherryvale is a small town on the Leavenworth, Lawrence, and Galveston Railroad, in Labette County, about fifty miles from the southern boundary line of the State.

The scouts inquired very closely in Cherryvale and its vicinity for any clue that might lead them onto York's trail, and

4

in the course of their inquiries they came upon a farmer with whom they talked as follows :

"Who might you be looking for ?" asked the farmer.

"Doctor York, who came here from Fort Scott," was the reply.

"Wall, gentlemen," rejoined the farmer cautiously, " I den't know as I oughter to say anything to injure innocent characters, but it does seem to me that there's most too many folks a disappearin' round this region. I've noticed the thing going on for two or three years past."

"Do you suspect any persons in particular?" asked the scouts.

"Yes, I do, gentlemen. But then you know it's a mighty ticklish job to point at certain folks and say things which, after all, may not be so and then get yourself in the devil's own trouble for your pains."

"You just tell us then, like a true man ought to, and we will pass our word of honor as men to you, that we will not say a single syllable about who told us."

"Oh, it isn't that I fear anything like harm to myself about telling, but we may often suspect the wrong parties of doing things, when in reality they are innocent, and I tell you I would feel worse than mean if I happened to be mistaken."

"Well, can't you tell us on the condition that we don't raise any excitement, but that we follow up your information quietly for ourselves?"

"Yes, I guess I could."

"All right, then, we will make you the promise, and stick to it sure."

"Good enough, then," said the farmer. "You all look like straight men, and so I'll tell you. You jest take this road going south from Cherryvale here, till you come to Bender's store, or hotel, as they call it. It's right in a swale of the prairie, as I tell you, about three mile out. When you get there, tell them you are going to put up o'er night. And be mighty careful you don't go to sleep there, but keep your eyes skinned, and see if you don't find out something. I haven't been in that locality for a month or more, but I'm satisfied there's something wrong about that settlement. There's no need for me to say more now, except to say again — Don't go to sleep in the hotel, but keep your eyes skinned all the time."

The scouts thanked the farmer, and bidding him good-day,

rode off toward the mysterious Prairie Hotel kept by the Benders.

They had ridden about a mile, when they met a man galloping toward them and coming in the direction of Cherry Vale. As he got abreast, he suddenly reined up his horse.

"Are you from Cherry?" asked he, pointing toward the town.

"Yes," was the laconic reply.

"Well, there's something wrong out here at the Bender ranch. It is deserted. The stock they left was all tied up and starved to death."

The scouts were instantly in a fever of curiosity, although they said nothing to indicate their own interest in the matter. And they at once, therefore, proposed to the horseman to ride back with him and investigate the mystery. He consented and, all together, the party galloped back to Bender's deserted house. During the short time of the ride the stranger imparted to the scouts his statement as follows :

"I wanted to come up to Cherry for something, and as I chanced to go by Bender's, I seen that it was shut up, as though they had pulled up stakes and lit out. Just as I noticed this, hows'ever, there was something else struck me as mighty queer, which was, that just in the off corner of the lot was a dead calf tied to the rail. And, from the looks of the beast, I made up my mind that it. had been left there, and starved to death. That was so queer that I decided to stop, and take a nearer look at things, for it didn't seem to be the dandy, you know, to leave calves that way. When I reached the house I seen it was deserted, and had been left for some time at least. I didn't go inside; for that ranch has got a devil of a queer reputation. But now that I've got you chaps for company, we'll give it a good ransacking, and see what devil's work they have been at for all these years past."

One of the scouts was Mr. Edward York, a brother of the missing man, and he felt a strange, ominous sensation coming over him as he approached the deserted house, as though the awful fate of his unfortunate relative was already forcing its presence upon him.

Soon the party arrived at the hotel and after dismounting, commenced their search. Neither doors nor windows were fastened, so the scouts had no trouble in gaining ingress to the building and admitting the honest light of heaven. Within the searchers found pieces of furniture and many other evidences that the' flight of the Benders had been sudden as well as concealed.

After the first cursory glances about the place, that object which most struck the attention of the party, was a trap door that was let into the floor about two feet away from the foot of the bedstead.

This trap Mr. York raised, but was obliged immediately to shut down again, by reason of the horrible stench that floated up out of the pit it concealed from view.

"My God, boys!" exclaimed he, turning white with mingled dread and anxiety, "there's some awful wickedness been taking place here."

Indeed, so overcome was he by the fear that in the yawning opening at his feet he would find the corpse of his missing brother, that he asked one of his companions to continue the search. "I haven't the heart to do it myself," groaned he.

One of the others at once raised the trap, and, having lit a long twisted wisp of hay for a rude torch, kneeled on his knees, and, reaching the light as far down as his arm could hold it, he peered to the bottom, which he could by this means easily see at a distance of about six feet.

"There don't seem to be any bodies there at all," exclaimed he, somewhat surprised, as he stood up and looked round into the faces about him.

"But, here! Two of you take hold of my hands, and let -me down into the infernal hole, and I'll soon tell you what's there."

While one took the hay torch, two of the others gave the speaker a hand, and allowed him to slide gradually down till his feet rested on the bottom of the pit, when they released him, and he who held the torch gave it to the bold, determined fellow, who hurried to complete his search while the light should last."

Sure enough, there were no bodies. But what could pause such a horrible smell, thought all. As he stepped around in the pit, the scout remarked how soft and muddy the earth was. As he was speaking, a white-handled pen-knife he had in his vest pocket fell out. As he picked it up, he noticed a peculiarity in the color of the mud which adhered to it, and, on further examination, he found it to be coagulated human blood and gore!

7

"Good God! This is blood!" he exclaimed, in a loathing voice. "What kind of monsters could these devils have been?"

Ejaculations of horror, mingled with rage and detestation, burst from every lip as the scout uttered these words, and held up the torch and the knife together, so that his companions could see that he was correct.

"Where can the bodies be from which this blood was taken?" inquired Mr. York, half-speaking to himself and half to his friends.

"Let's go out and take a look round the plot, and see what we can see," suggested, another.

"Yes," acquiesced he who was in the pit, "let's try that. There's no bodies in here, that's certain."

At this suggestion, therefore, all the party at once adjourned to the garden, as the Benders used to call the patch that surrounded their cabin.

With keen eyes, ready to detect the slightest suspicious circumstance, each man began a systematic inspection of the ground. All at once one of the scouts exclaimed:

"Here's a lump of sub-soil here on top of this hammered place that ought not to be here, that's certain!"

"And there, right across that old furrow," said another, "I can see a straight line. That's a grave, you bet!"

All felt convinced that it was so. A long wagon rod, which was in the shed by the dwelling, was procured, and the party began driving the iron-shod point down into the earth, at short intervals, wherever they imagined that the ground looked as though it had been disturbed, or at all broken.

At the exact spot where the lump of subsoil had been found, the rod was pushed down quite easily a certain distance, when it came in contact with a resisting body of some sort. There were no spades about, but one of the scouts mounting his horse, rode off, and soon returned with half a dozen.

Meantime, the probing with the rod had continued, and resulted in the discovery of fresh graves in all directions.

When the spades arrived, digging was vigorously commenced, and in a very short space of time the first body was exhumed. It was that of a man, stripped of all clothing, except the shirt, and had evidently been thrown into the excavation with the face downward.

"God of mercy!" exclaimed Mr. York, in a suppressed agony

of voice, "that's my poor brother, the doctor!"

And so it was, surely.

While examining the corpse for certain marks by which it could be identified, the nature of the wounds causing death was found to be as follow:

With a heavy hammer, or hatchet butt, the back of his head had been completely crushed in, while on each side of the skull the same deadly weapon had been used to drive in the parietal bones.

Though any one of these wounds was amply sufficient to have caused death, yet, apparently with no other motive than a tiger-like desire to revel in blood, the brutal murderers had cut York's throat so completely as nearly to sever the head from the body!

The next grave discovered contained the bodies of George W. Longcohr and his little daughter. This was the most frightfully fiendish deed, as will be seen further on.

Mr. Longcohr had been killed exactly in the same manner as Mr. York. His body had then been pitched into the freshly dug grave, and, more horrible than all, the little girl, a pretty, innocent child, with long soft brown hair, had been thrown down alive upon the corpse of her father, while the Bender fiends hurriedly shoveled the earth and clods upon her till they had smothered out her life with her last gasping cry for mercy.

We never read a more brutal, awful thing than this; but it is true, as the scouts could tell from the position in which the corpse of the child was found. She was partly on her knees, with her hands clasped in a prayerful attitude, and her face and head inclined upward. Her father, with parental solicitude, had carefully clad his little daughter in warm clothing, and not a particle of this clothing was removed by her fiendish destroyers, thus proving that they had no use for children's clothing.

Her fur cape and hood were still upon her, and even her little red mittens had not been removed from her hands, but were still upon the latter, as the men lifted her up out of the rude coffin-less grave.

By this time large numbers of people arrived upon the scene, who had heard of the dreadful discovery, and curses and execrations could be heard on all sides against the perpetrators of these diabolical acts of bloody murder, and rapacious robbery.

Hardened men were moved to tears as they stood and looked at the bodies of Mr. Longcohr and his child, and could they only have laid hands on the Benders, there cannot be the slightest doubt but that they would have burned them to death with their late abode of sin and blood.

The probing and digging were kept up incessantly all through the night with fresh volunteers taking the rod, and spades, and torches, as fast as the others grew too weary to proceed. Eight bodies altogether were dug up, and recognized by acquaintances, relatives or friends, and all were killed in precisely the same manner.

One peculiarity struck all the spectators. Each corpse had the left arm crossed upon the breast before being buried. Why this should have been done was, of course, a mystery to the scouts, but the reason will be seen further on in the confession of Pauline, the fiendish daughter, who was hung subsequently in Texas.

Among the spectators at this awful scene was a man named Breckerman, and some person remarked that Breckerman was an intimate friend of the Benders, and had often been known to pass a great deal of his time at their store. This was enough to fire the excitement, and, before he knew where he was, the miserable wretch was pulled into the house, a rope slipped round his neck, and he jerked up to a beam in the ceiling, so that he was half stunned with the blow he received by the contact of his head with the beam.

Then he was let down, and the mob, with clenched fists and glaring eyes, yelled and shouted in his ears:

"You know about some of these murders. Tell us all about it, or we'll hang you up for sure."

"I don't! I don't. I — mercy, gentlemen!' gasped Breckerman, more dead than alive. I am innocent. I — I swear before God. I — "

"He's a liar! Up with him!" shouted several furious voices, and again his quivering body was dangling by the neck from the noose.

He was let down again after this second choking.

"Confess! You Dutch hell-hound! Did you help? Where are them other devils gone to?"

Strange as it may appear, this time, although he was so much exhausted that the lynchers were obliged to hold him up, yet Breckerman was now calm and collected, as with the desperation of man who sees certain death before him. And he managed to say:

"If you cowardly fellows are going to hang me without giving me a chance to tell you why I went to the Benders, and so clear myself, why you'll have to do it; but if you are men, and treat me like a man, I can do it to your satisfaction. . If I don't, then you can hang me!"

This exhibition of dogged bravery undoubtedly saved Breckerman's life for. the moderate men of the lynchers admired his grit, and stayed the more furious of .their companions, who were unanimously for running him up and finishing him.

"Hold on! Hold on, men! Let us hear him through first, and see if his story will hold water. Hands off that rope, men, and all be quiet. Now, Breckerman, go ahead with what you have to say. But tell the truth, or you'll hang for sure."

Thus admonished the intended victim said:

"I know I used to come here a good deal to this house, but I swear, before God, that I knew nothing of what was going on. I used to come to see the old man's daughter, Kate. I was soft on that gal, and if all this awful stuff had not turned up, I would have been married to her this Easter coming."

"What proof can you give us that what you say is true?" fiercely and suspiciously inquired one of the lynchers.

"I don't know, unless this'll do."

And he hauled from his pocket a wallet, out of which he took a gold wedding ring, inside of which were engraved the words, "To Kate."

Besides this, he had there another trinket in the shape of a small, cheap locket, wrapped carefully in a scrap of newspaper. In one side of this locket was a half-obliterated, ferrotype of the identical Kate Bender, looking down at and caressing a little dog. On the other side was a bunch of light hair, and it was the grease which had once been upon this hair that had doubtless so nearly spoiled the ferrotype. Or perhaps the stolid, but really affectionate fellow, had kissed the picture a good deal, for that he loved the pretty but fiendish Kate, there was no doubt, as the next incident showed.

"Old Man" Bender

One of the scouts seized the picture rudely, and glancing at it in a contemptuous way, said something about Kate which we cannot print. Breckerman, though in the midst of the crowd who were going to hang him, snatched back the trinket, and exclaimed:

"You're no man to talk that way about any woman, and if nobody here will interfere, just as bad as I'm hurt, I'll take the risk of knocking your head off, and you can have the same chance at me. So, if you're a man, fix yourself."

Breckerman thrust the locket and ring, and wallet back into his pocket, and shaking himself loose from those who held him, made as though he would spring upon the traducer of Kate.

"Stop this! Stop this! Exclaimed the oldest of the crowd," I believe the man is innocent. Let him go. Let him go."

The advice was at once seconded, and Breckerman was at once hustled away by three or four powerful men, one of whom said:

"Don't stop now to make any more bother. Just clear out, or the crowd will hang you any way."

Seeing it was his best plan to take this advice, Breckerman did so, and walked away from the cursed spot at a rapid gait, soon disappearing in the darkness that lay on the prairie like a deathly pall.

All the rest of that night and throughout the entire next day, the search was kept up, while the eager crowd of curious spectators grew in size every hour, many coming from distances of a hundred and fifty miles to satisfy their intense curiosity to see or hear something new of the dreadful tragedies which had startled the land with their enormity.

HOW THE MURDERS WERE ALL COMMITTED.

The peculiarity and evident similarity of the means used to commit the Bender murders struck everybody with surprise, and all were convinced that the fiends had adopted a studied and regular method of perpetrating their bloody crimes.

First, in the selection of their house, they had chosen a spot that, by reason of the natural formation of the ground, enabled them to see in all directions the approach of any person for a distance of two miles at least, while at the same time no one could see either them or what they were about. In this way, even if some traveller were to be seen coming at the exact moment they started to commit one of their butcheries, they would still have time left to finish it and completely conceal every trace by the time the new comer should reach the store.

We have had the following description of the house and the manner in which the murders were committed, most carefully written by an eye-witness. And to complete the understanding of this description, we have had the annexed engraving drawn. The reader must imagine that the roof has been removed, and that he is looking down directly into the house from above, exactly as a bird might view it.

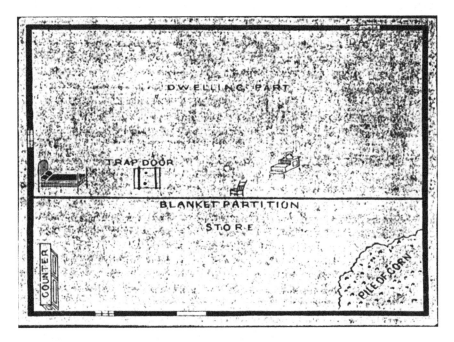

The Bender House was divided into two unequal portions by a partition made of cloth, muslin, and parts of skin robes all sewn together and stretched from floor to ceiling, so as to form quite a neat job for a wall.

On the south side of this partition was the stove. At the west extremity of the south room stood the counter, a rough enough affair; the door and one window being to the east of it. In the southeast corner was a large pile of corn heaped on the floor, while standing about the latter were such articles as are

14

generally found in a store of that description. A few rude shelves here and there clinging to the walls contained various other and lighter things for sale.

The west end of the cloth partition, directly opposite the bed, was loose, to permit easy communication between the dwelling and store, and also for a more deadly purpose, as will be seen further on.

Now then, a traveller entered the store, and, while he was making a purchase, he was eagerly scanned by Old Man Bender. If the latter thought he was worth while killing — that is, if he thought, from his own appearance, or that of his wallet, that he had plenty of money about him, the old scoundrel would give a signal by dropping an old coal bell on the floor.

As soon as Kate heard this, she would run into the store, and, after a short excitement and an exchange of remarks between herself and father, she would succeed in engaging the attention of the stranger. From that moment his fate was sealed, for, besides being quite handsome, Kate was a most charming talker.

Selecting some subject that her quick perception recommended to her as appropriate for her design, she would soon enlist the intended victim in ah animated discussion, and keep him at it till the old woman would thrust her head into the store and call "Supper" or "Dinner" as the case might be.

The old man at once invited the stranger most cordially to have a little, and, in case the latter was backward, or attempted to refuse, Kate's blandishments were brought to bear, and, led by the satanic Siren, he would pass through the opening into the dwelling part of the house, never to come forth again alive.

As soon as the meal was over, Kate would challenge the stranger to a trial of mesmerism, on which subject she had taken care to converse very fully and artfully already. Of Course the challenge was at once accepted.

She placed a chair against the cloth partition, bade the guest be seated, and told him to lean his head back and close his eyes. He did so, and she, placing her hand under his chin, would force his head back, laughing aloud all the while to divert his attention.

In this manner the back of his head was indented, as it were, into the partition, and of course made a bulge on the store, side.

Meantime, the old man, or son, as the case might be, had slipped into the store and stood ready with a hammer swung back. And the instant the bulge was made in the cloth, he would fetch it a blow with all his strength. In this way the victim's skull was crushed in like an eggshell, and he fell dying on the floor at the feet of Kate, the fiendish daughter, who had thus lured him to destruction. But the deed was not yet complete.

With all speed the quivering body was pulled to the pit, the trap door of which had been raised a moment previously, and, with a second hammer a blow was given on each side, just above the ear, which smashed the parietal bones to splinters. Next the clothing, with the exception of the shirt, was stripped from the corpse, all the four fiends assisting. The body was then pushed still further on, so that the head and neck projected over the mouth of the pit. In this position the old man, with a sharp butcher's knife, cut the victim's throat completely from ear to ear. Thus the body would be left to bleed till night. In case any person approached the house, the body was unceremoniously pitched down into the pit, and the trap door closed, thus concealing everything from prying eyes.

At night the father and son went out into the lot, and, measuring off the grave, would deliberately dig it, taking care to set aside the top soil on one side, so that after the burial they could shovel it back into its proper position. The next day they would plough and harrow over the spot, and thus, as they imagined, efface all marks or traces of their frightful crime.

And, as we have already remarked, the actual discovery of the graves by the scouts was due entirely to the fact of a lump of subsoil having carelessly been left by the Benders on the surface of the grave of Doctor York.

THE CHASE OF THE FIENDS.

Of course, immediately after the first excitement consequent on the discovery of the murders had passed away, the next step was to trace and arrest, if possible, the blood-stained fugitives. Couriers, mounted on swift horses, and the telegraph, were at once enlisted into service, and it was thought certain that but a short time would elapse ere the Benders would be in custody.

But, unfortunately, they had a fair start of at least fifteen or

16

twenty days, during which time it was likely they could reach very many places of concealment that would be comparatively secure from the sharpest search that could be instituted against them.

For weeks, it will be remembered, the papers were filled with glowing accounts of the arrest of all, or portions ,of the notorious family. The most positive of these narratives was the following, which, however, turned out not to be the right party at all. And yet the circumstantial evidence appeared most convincing.

From the *Cedar Rapids Republican* (Iowa)

"No little excitement was occasioned on our streets last night by the supposed arrest, and imprisonment in the jail of this place, of no less a personage than the notorious Bender, of Kansas, who was the perpetrator of the late horrible murders that were committed in that State.

On Saturday night, a strange-looking man was hanging around the town of Ely, which is a station on the Burlington, Cedar Rapids, and Minnesota Railway, eight miles south of this place. The actions of this man were very restless, and looking as though he was on the watch for someone, he was suspected at once by J. L. Devault, the railway agent at that place, as a man who had committed some great crime, and who was dodging through the country to avoid his pursuers.

"Mr. Devault, having just read a minute description of each member of the Bender family, soon discovered that this strange man at Ely answered the description in every particular. He at once telegraphed to Mr. Church, the operator in the B. C. & M. office at this place for an officer to come down and arrest the man. Not being able to send word to the sheriff, Mr. Church communicated the information he had received to our city officers acting upon which Marshal Hiel, Hale, Cottle, and Joe secured a livery wagon and started for Ely.

"In the meantime, Mr. Devault and a few of the people of Ely had got the suspected man in a box car, and held him there by means of conversation and other devices until the officers of the law arrived. They were determined at the same time to hold him at all hazards, if he attempted to escape. The officers arriving, at once went to the car, and being satisfied, from a description they had seen of Bender, that this man

17

answered to it fully, they felt it their duty to arrest him, and hold him in custody until his case was finally determined.

"In going from the car to the wagon, he showed that his feet were very sore, occasioned, undoubtedly, by long-continued walking.

"On his way to this place he admitted that he had lived near Independence, Kansas, that he lived on a farm, and that he had an orchard He also spoke several times of his daughter Kate, who, he said, had four thousand dollars in her possession, and that she kept nearly all the money having only given him a small amount of it. He denounced Kate in severe term's for her thievish conduct in keeping the money. He also said his name is Bender.

Suddenly, the sweetly smiling woman whipped out a stilleto, and plunged it into the poor man's heart.

"John Bender, or 'old man Bender,' is fifty or sixty years old; about five-feet, seven-inches in height; rather round shouldered with very dark complexion, and very heavy heard, cut rather short; hair long and dark, mixed with gray; and very heavy eye-lashes; nose sharp and rather long; hands spare, with cords upon the backs prominent; gait slow and sluggish; — seemed rather to stalk around than walk; weight 140 to 150 pounds.

"He had a sleepy, downcast look, and was grim and surly in his deportment. His cheeks are sunken and rather low. He speaks English in a very broken manner; his native tongue., being Low Dutch; his voice seems to come rather from his chest rather than from his mouth. He is slightly bald, and is careless and slovenly in his dress."

The last of these newspaper accounts places the arrest in the Mormon Territory of Utah, near Salt Lake City. We give, it exactly as it appeared It is, about as circumstantial as the others.

"Old man Bender is fifty-five or sixty years old, about five-feet-seven inches in height, round-shouldered, dark-complexioned, has heavy beard, but short; hair long and dark, mixed with gray; heavy eye-lashes, sharp nose, hands spare, with prominent cords on the backs; gait, slow and sluggish; weight 140 to 150 pounds; sleepy, downcast look; grim, and surly in manner. His voice seems to come from the breast instead of his mouth. Speaks English in a very broken manner, his native tongue being Low Dutch."

"The above is the description of the fiend as published by the Kansas authorities, and a man answering it exactly has just been taken here in Salt Lake City, and lies in the jail here awaiting further developments. I have seen him, and with the exception that the prisoner is not dark, and that his beard is not short, the description is perfect."

"A look at the prisoner here is sufficient to stamp him as perfectly capable of all that has been alleged against Bender."

"When taken, all the circumstances were against him. He could not tell where he came from; and when told why he was arrested, he held up his hands in astonishment, and said:

"See, I have lost my right-hand little finger, and my left-hand little finger. I could not have killed all these people. Besides, Bender had all his fingers."

"Soon after his arrest, a strange young man asked to see the prisoner, and the jailor admitting him, the two had a long talk together. After the young man left, it struck the jailor that his manner had been exceedingly intimate with the old man,

19

so much so, indeed, that he concluded he must be the son. So he at once started trailers on the hunt, who, it is reported, have come up with and captured the mysterious young man. As yet, however, there .is.no confirmation of the report."

"To-day Mr. H. L. Crane, who was employed in the office of the county clerk in Pike County. Illinois, in 1866, had a conversation with the prisoner, and says he is satisfied that he is the identical Bender, beyond doubt. To him the prisoner admitted that he had a brother-in-law of the name of Schmidt, who died in Pike County at that time, and that he. had been appointed the administrator of his small estate, at which time and place Mr. Crane, on several occasions, necessarily had business intercourse with him."

Bender also admitted that, he had been farming in Kansas after that, and Mr. E Milhorn. a gentleman who had been in the employment of the Government, and supplied the Indians on the Osage Reservation, stated that he had seen the prisoner every day at Bender's ranch, and that he knew he was one of them. Milhorn had been engaged constructing a road that wend by Bender's place, and had seen him while thus employed. His testimony as to the identity of the prisoner. with the Bender he knew in Kansas is complete and positive."

"The mother and daughter, Kate, are still at large, but it is expected they also will soon be brought in. Late last autumn a woman came out of the mountains into the outer settlements of Provo, which is about forty miles south of this place. She was almost naked and seemed at times mentally deranged. She told the most contradictory stories of her past life. One of her favorite statements was that she had been disappointed in love, and had wandered from Colorado into the mountains in Utah.

"A Mormon woman, touched at the sight of her distress, gave her a home, and also some clothing, telling her she might remain as long with her as she liked. Though thus kindly treated the woman one day bade her benefactress good by, and returned to the mountains from which she had come."

"I obtained from this Mormon lady a full description of the woman, and it agrees exactly with that of Kate Bender; as it was given by the authorities. I have also conversed freely with experienced persons here, and it seems to be their unanimous opinion that the whole Bender family have been hiding in one of the many gulches or canyons of the Wasatch Mountains.

20

How they have maintained their existence in the rigorous, desolate region mystifies all. But I think I can account for it in this way. When they made up their minds to leave their house near Cherryvale, they concluded that they must take with them a sufficient supply of provisions that would not take up much room, and yet that would last them for a long time. In this way they could travel by unused routes, and not being obliged to call on any one along the road to buy anything, why of course no one could possibly say, 'I saw those people at such a time they stopped at our house to buy provisions.' I'm sure this was their plan of action, and in that way they easily reached the mountain recesses, where they have lain securely concealed all winter."

"Senator A. M. York, brother of the murdered doctor, is sure also that this man we have here now, is none other than Bender. He has urged Governor Osborne to issue a requisition to have the prisoner sent back to Kansas. The subjoined letters require no more comment than their own contents."

Executive Department, State of Kansas,
Topeka, March 19, 1874

To:
Andrew Andrew Burt, Chief of Police, Salt Lake City U. T.

Sir:
Governor Osborne directs me to enclose you the letter that you will find herewith from Colonel A. M. York, of Independence, Kansas, brother of one of the victims of the Bender family, in answer to your letter of the 3d inst., enclosing a photograph of the man now under arrest in Utah' Territory, awaiting identification as. the old man Bender. The reward offered is the maximum authorized by law, vis. $500 for the arrest and delivery to the Sheriff of Labette County, Kansas, for each member of the Bender family.

Very respectfully,
C.A. Morris, Private Secretary
Elk Falls, Howard Co., Kansas
March 16, 1974

To:
Governor Osbourne

Sir,

I enclose herewith a statement regarding the opinion of Bender's neighbors of the picture you received from Utah. It is the first instance where any of the pictures sent here for identification have even so much as favored any of the family. In my judgment it is the picture of the old man Bender, and it seems to me that the statements of his former neighbors fully justify sending for him.

Very truly,
A.M. York

FORMER LIVES OF THE BENDERS.

Since public attention has been directed to this now notorious family of murderers, it turns out that they were guilty of the most frightful atrocities in years gone by, and that really they have never been anything else than the most horrible monsters, making a regular trade of murder, for the sake of obtaining money or whatever valuables chance might enable them to get from their miserable victims.

We have received from an esteemed gentleman, now residing in St. Louis, and who was one of the original company that made the celebrated overland journey with Fremont in 1842, the following account. We give it without any alteration whatever, and we have not the slightest doubt that the family referred to is none other than the old stock of the Benders, who then used their correct name, which was Liefen.

St. Louis, April 12, 1874

GENTLEMEN:

"I have your favor of 7th inst., requesting me to give you the details of my adventures while crossing the plain in 1842, with the expedition under General Fremont. I hardly know how long it would take me to put into readable book shape those stirring events, though doubtless they would be quite interesting reading for the present generation, who can, by the Pacific road, run across to San Francisco to Philadelphia in a week! Truly, I can hardly comprehend this myself. Sometimes we would be a week going twenty miles, with no end of accidents and dreadful mishaps. It's wonderful to contemplate. The Pacific road directors ought to send out a party to gather up some of the deserted wagons and other relics of our expedition. I'll guarantee they'd find plenty of them this day lying undisturbed, just where we left them a quarter of a century ago. For I doubt if the foot of a white man, or even a digger Indian, has been over some of those awful spots since we bade them adieu. I do assure you there would be no more attractive curiosities for a cabinet in one of the depots of the company.. Barnum would make a fortune on such a collection.

But when I recall those past scenes and adventures, I am too apt to forget what I am about, and digress from the matter in hand. So, as the Frenchman says, "let us return to our mutton." Now about the narrative for your proposed book, I can give you lots of it, but the only trouble with me is the getting of it into right shape for the reading public. If I only had your editor, Wesley Bradshaw, here for a week, and let him clothe my rough facts in some of those fine word-draperies that he adorns his own productions in, we could, between us, get up a popular book. Persuade him to come out this summer and spend a hot week or two with me here and my word for it, he shall come back to you as full of adventure and early pioneer history, as a bee from a ten-acre lot-of white clover is full of honey.

So much for that. But now then there is another subject, more exciting just now, which is this Bender horror over in Kansas. I've paid a great deal of attention to that affair, because I am satisfied that the Benders are identical with a family I once fell in with, named Liefen, who used to murder and rob, and in the same way as these Benders have been doing. There's no doubt but they are the same exactly, or rather what was left of them. To-night, when I go home, I will write you up an account of what I recollect about these fiends.

> Yours truly,
> Rabe Lukens.

P.S. As I send this off, I wish to say (as I have, perhaps, not made it sufficiently distinct in the enclosed narrative) that the three sisters and Liefen (now known as "old man Bender") were really half-sisters and brother; that is, his father married the mother of the three girls. .Liefen and they of course grew up together, and at the .time of the Nauvoo excitement, he married the whole three, after the Mormon fashion. They started off to the wilderness, to escape the just vengeance of the community which they had thus shocked with their immorality."

THE MYSTERIOUS RANCH

I am well assured that the Benders of Kansas and the Liefens of Texas are one and the same party and if ever there was such a thing as fiends being sent from hell to trouble and curse the earth, they were just these fiends.

After my return from the Fremont expedition across the great plains to the Rocky Mountains, I was knocking around the various towns that had sprung up along the Missouri border, not doing anything much except wasting my time and money. I called it recruiting myself after the awful hardships of that memorable journey.

Not long subsequently my ready money was all gone, and I found myself compelled to get into some sort of employment. This once decided upon, it did not take me more than a week to fall in with a man by the name of Strawn, who was going extensively into cattle and other operations in Texas.

He was glad to come across me, and vice-versa; satisfied to close up our bargain, and the following Monday morning, being splendidly mounted and equipped, he and I, with six men, started for Texas. We could have gone down on the boat, but Strawn, my employer, wished, for the sake of gaining information about certain routes, to travel down across the country. I was exceedingly well pleased with my position, as, beside giving me opportunities of adventure, and seeing more of life, I would have quite a snug sum of money coming to me at the end of our business arrangement. And even then, when this trip was over, I intended to re-engage again with Strawn, for he was a good, open-hearted, liberal fellow, a man among men.

Nothing of any moment occurred until we approached Nagadotches. There, however, we fell in with an adventure that exceeded anything I had ever read or heard of, previously, for weird and horrid details.

In those days travelers were few and far between, in those

south-western countries, except, of course, during certain short seasons, when, along particular stretches, there would every now and then be a few go by. Also, houses were still more scarce than travelers, and, consequently, every traveler was always sure to stop at every house he came to, continuing his stay as long as circumstances permitted. Most especially would the stay be prolonged in case there was a woman in the house, no matter if she were old and ugly. We always liked to get to a house where there were women and children and I have known hunters and trappers to ride twenty miles out of their road, just for the sake of stopping at a house that looked like home, because of the presence of women and children. And I must also add that, although the husbands or sons were often away, and the women folks left thus alone, I never knew the roughest fellows — and there would often be a score of them together — to offer the slightest insult. On the contrary, in those days a female was looked upon as a being equally sacred is an angel, except, of course, she was a lewd creature. But that kind very seldom came out into the wilderness. It was only the brave, honest, virtuous wives and mothers and daughters of the pioneers who would face the hardships of that country, and it was these qualities that rendered them sacred, even in the eyes of the roughest plainsmen.

It was toward sunset that we came in view of a little house built a short distance away from the road, or rather path, for when I say. road, it must be understood that I do not mean any nearer approach to the handy, fenced-in pikes of to-day, than a winding line of beaten down grass, now going through a middling good sized open swath of the forest, and then crooking along the side of a river or stream, of water to the fording place.

We were all surprised to see the habitation, for it came upon us suddenly, just as we, turned a patch of woods.

"Hurrah, lads," exclaimed Martin, reining up his horse. "We're in luck!. I didn't know a ranch was so close as this. We won't go on to the crossing, but we'll stop here till morning."

"'Right glad of it, Captain!" I replied, slipping quickly out of the saddle, while all the rest re-echoed my words and copied my act of dismounting.

"Leading our horses by their bridles, we approached the door, at which stood a youngish looking man, who stepped out as we came up, and said in broken English, "Goot aben,

25

shentlemens. Comes you far away? Glad to see yous. Hopple de horses und comes in mit der hause."

We promptly obeyed the request, which was made with all the clumsy, but ardent, earnestness and pleasant smiles imaginable. Our host led us into what we at once saw was the store, and begged us to be seated and rest ourselves on anything we could find to take the place of chairs. Acceding to this, we made ourselves quite comfortable, though half of the party squatted themselves right down on the floor like Indians.

"Don't see many beeples 'long dis way," remarked the German.

"No, I suppose not," replied Strawn, in German, when he noticed the nationality of the storekeeper. "and," continued he, jokingly, "there's not over many stores or ranches scattered round this region of country, I can tell you."

"Nein," was all Liefen said, and with a manner that indicated he saw no joke about the remark.

"How long have you been here ," asked Strawn.

"Ach! 'bout nine, ten months. So!" answered Liefen,

"Here alone," was the next query.

"Nein," drawled out the German, "nein, nein, mein familie here with me."

"Your wife?"

"Yah, meine frau un szwer sisters."

At once the men assumed a different demeanor from what they had hitherto worn, the instant the presence of females was announced.

"Lena! Lena!" called Liefen.

"And almost immediately quite a pretty woman came tripping from behind one end of the cloth partition next to the counter.. The whole arrangement of this Texas house was exactly a *fac simile* of the Bender House near Cherryvale, Kansas. And that is one of the main reasons why I am satisfied that the Kansas fiends are the same as the Texas murderers.

"The moment we beheld Lena we nodded to her, and were quite in ecstasies when the smiling creature came forward and replied to our recognition in the most cordial manner, just as though she had known us all for years past. She spoke very good English, and said, "Really, gentlemen, it is so seldom that we have any visitors] in this lonely part of the country that it is quite an exciting event to have some travelers stop.

What part do you come from? Somewhere from up toward the States, I suppose?"

"Yes, we have travelled down from Independence, across."

"Why, that's an odd way to do, is it not?" she naively inquired, "Don't they generally take a boat down the river?"

"Yes, that is the general method, Miss Lena."

"Ach! She ist nicht Miss Lena! She is mein frau!" interrupted the German storekeeper with a grin.

"Beg pardon," replied Strawn, "Mrs. Liefen."

"Oh, I'm sure now," laughingly added the wife, "the mistake is complimentary; don't you all think so, gentlemen?"

"To be sure we do, and so ought you r husband," bluntly answered Strawn for the party.

"Well, now, gentlemen," continued the handsome fiend (although at the moment we all thought her an angel) "you must be very much tired, and in want of something to eat. Sisters and I were just going to get supper .for ourselves, so please excuse me, and we shall soon have a little bite ready for you, too."

And, without waiting for our reply, the woman skipped back into the part of the house behind the partition.. In a few moments more, amidst the rattling of pans, and dishes and cups, we heard her singing odd lines of a song, in which something about a tired knight, home from the war had come to the cot of his lady love. She had quite a sweet, musical voice, so we listened intently, and with the keenest appreciation, to the melody, the chorus of which I may say, became perfectly ravishing in our imagination, as, at the same instant it fell on our ears, the delicious odor of fried onions assailed our noses.

"Now, no doubt, this will make nearly everybody who reads it laugh outright; but I solemnly assert the truth, for, to a trapper, or hunter, or traveler, accustomed to the awfully hard and monotonous fare he gets on the prairie, the smell of civilized cooking, especially of anything with onions in it, is perfectly enrapturing. And this was a fact well known to fiends in whose den we were thus entrapped. It makes me tremble even now when I think of it.

Shortly afterward, two other female voices were heard, singing in unison with Lena, and, what with the sweet strains, the rattling dishes, and the savory smells of the preparing supper, we were all in a fever of expectancy and pleasure, and could hardly talk with or give straight replies to Liefen, who, however, did not give us much trouble on that score, as he was quite taciturn; though of this we did not think much, as we supposed it was owing to the fact of his not being able to converse fluently in our own language.

Our suspense was finally ended by Lena frisking through into the store again, and saying, with the sweetest smiles imaginable, "Now, then, gentlemen, supper is all ready, if you will come in."

Of course, none of us backed out, you may depend, but with eager steps and watering mouths we followed Lena into the dwelling part of the house.

This was not a large room, and when we all assembled there, we completely filled it up. But for all that we did not postpone our attack on the savory meal the Liefen women had cooked for us. That these sharp creatures also fully understood the appetites of men under our circumstances, was shown by the fact that they had cooked enough, and plenty more, too, to satisfy the hungriest of us. When the meal was over, we topped off with a draught from our "generals" as we called the whisky flasks we always carried in our side pockets, and then, adjourning to the store, we fired our pipes, and enjoyed ourselves by lounging round and smoking till camping time, when we pitched our shelter tents close by the house, and turned in.

Until bed-time the four Liefens mixed round among us in an exceedingly sociable manner, and we all had what the young folks of to-day would call a "splendid time."

One thing I noticed particularly was, that during the course of the evening Pauline, who was the youngest of the sisters, twice called Strawn into the dwelling part of the house; and we cracked several jokes, on the second occasion, as we heard him laughing most uproariously at something. But when he turned in with us for the night, I could not help observing that he was thinking quite seriously about something or other. Still, this did not come to my mind till subsequent events forced it on my attention.

The following morning we were all up at sunrise, and prepared to resume our journey — not before the Liefens had made us ready a splendid breakfast, the best part of which was the coffee.

Of course, the first thing we did, after getting our breakfast, was to hold a conversation as to how we should show our

gratitude to the kind people who had entertained us so boun-
tifully. The result was that we made up quite a handsome
purse of money, and give it to the old man who took it and
thanked us, and wished us all a safe and prosperous journey.

Strawn lingered at the side door till the rest of us had gone
into line and, as I looked back, I saw him leaning down from
his saddle, and, while he shook hands with Pauline, say something to her. She was listening intently, a smile spreading over
her features, and, as the two parted, she nodded her head and
waved her hand to him.

We had traveled about an hour and a half, when, all of a
sudden, Strawn said, "Boys, you go on slowly, and if you reach
the town before I overtake you, stay there till I come. I want to
go back to the store for something."

Without any other explanation or orders, he turned his
horse and rode back. To be sure, we all had our ideas about
why he really returned, and we got off some tall jokes at his
expense. But as we were in his pay, we did not care, and
.thought we would have a good time till he overtook us.

"Strawn is struck, boys, sure, and he has gone back to
court the Dutch girl, and next thing you'll see him jogging
back with a wife," I remarked after we had been running on a
good while about him, and shortly the subject was changed.

We thought no more till night came, and we were just going into Nagadotches. No signs were there yet of his appearance. But still we thought he'd came before bedtime, and, as
two of the men had been here before with him, they knew just
what hotel to go to. We rode hither, and soon made ourselves
quite at home.

Strawn was still absent the next morning, and this non-
plussed and surprised us greatly.

We held a consultation as to what course to pursue, and
concluded to send back two of our number to the store to inquire about him, — still under the hope, however, that they
would meet him on his way to join us as he had promised.

Night came again, but no Strawn with it, and, still more
mysterious, neither one of the messengers. This was a dreadful event, for it could not be possible for all three to be staying
at the store of the Liefens, or to be stopping anywhere on the
road between that and Nagadotches. We began, therefore, to
think very queer of the affair, and resolved that if none of
them made their appearance by the next morning, to des-

patch two more men on the search, with explicit instructions to halt for nothing, but to return to us the very moment they obtained any clue whatever to the absentees.

Accordingly, very early on the morrow the next two started back on their mission of inquiry. Thoughts of foul play came constantly into our minds — that is, into the minds of what remained of us, which was one man besides myself.

The day wore on and still no tidings came back, nor a single one of the four we had sent to inquire. And when I say that we two remnants did not sleep much the ensuing night, I tell the simple truth.

Morning came again, and still we had heard nothing. What to be done now we hardly knew. But finally, after a good deal of talk, we both made up our minds to go back ourselves, and solve the awful mystery which enshrouded the fate of our friends. For we felt convinced that something had happened to them, be it what it might. The journey back being decided in the affirmative, the next thing was to settle how we should accomplish our object, and yet avoid whatever ill had met our comrades. We settled as follows: Lots were to be drawn between us as to who was to go in advance. Whichever one it might be, was to go on cautiously, while the other was to follow at a distance of a quarter of a mile or so, according to circumstances, and, in case of any attack, he in the rear was to hurry up and help the one so assaulted.

My comrade drew the lot that ordained him to the advance, and, according to our arrangement, we at one started off on our terrible journey; for we both felt a dread of that mysterious something to happen to us. We took the precaution, however, to arm ourselves thoroughly, and we pledged our sacred honors mutually to stand by each other to death.

THE MYSTERY SOLVED

Nothing whatever occurred to disturb our quiet ride, and I saw my friend enter the house of the Liefens, and I was within an ace of giving my horse the rein and dashing up after him when something, I could not tell what, caused me to halt in my design. It seemed to tell me not to do it, but to stay back and watch what became of my companion. At first I felt mean like, as though I was not keeping my promise to him ; but the feeling was irresistible, to wait and see what happened. I dismounted, and concealed myself where I could be secure from discovery, while, at the same time I could see all that might transpire around the house.

All that day I waited, anxiously watching and eagerly expecting every moment to see my comrade emerge from the store. But he did not do so, though several times I saw one of the Leifens come out and re-enter. I never moved from my hiding-place till sundown, by which time I felt convinced that every one of the six men was within that cursed place and also that all were dead! Then flashed to my remembrance the odd looks and words which had been given or said by the Germans, during our stay in their hellish abode. Then did all the tales I had ever read about Sauney Bean, the Land Pirates, and such characters come trooping into my mind, like horrible pictures. At first, as I left the spot where I had been concealed, I thought I would ride directly to the house and arrest the wretches, or blow their brains out. But, on sober second consideration l saw that perhaps this might not only fail, but also that I myself might quite likely fall a fresh victim to the murderers. There might be several men there and the house might be the rendezvous of a large, organized band of robbers.

So, in view of these contingencies, I made up my mind to ride back to Nagadotches and summon help to extirpate the whole infernal crew.

Upon arriving at the hotel in the town, I told the landlord — his name was Stevens — and he at once called together n party of determined friends, who, under my leadership, rode back to the house of the Liefens.

We did not know exactly how to complete our work, so as to make sure of obtaining proof positive of the crimes of which I knew in my own mind the Germans were guilty. Besides, among my companions, there was a sort of mysterious dread of the magic power of the mysterious Liefens. In the first place, the three women resembled each other so closely in size and general appearance, that a stranger could scarcely tell them apart. And, no doubt, to increase this, all three dressed exactly alike, even wearing their hair in one and the same fashion.

During the time the Liefens had lived at the store, several of the men forming our party had chanced to call there once or twice, and they remembered this peculiarity. One of these fellows, although as brave as a lion in facing any known

31

danger, was quite nervous, and half regretted joining our expedition.

"You see," said he, "I don't mind fighting wildcats or bears, or Indians; but, scalp me, if I ain't afraid of witches like them three Dutch girls are.."

I noticed that his remarks had a great effect on the rest of the party, and said, "I see you chaps scaring, so we better give up and go back, with our fingers in our mouths."

This rallied them somewhat, and each voted to put the job through without flinching — even should Satan himself appear. But I did not have much confidence in their bravado, and therefore I proposed the following plan :

Just as it was coming dark, I was to ride up alone to the store, and go in and see about the missing men. Meantime, the rest were to approach the house, and when I gave the signal — which I was to do by discharging a pistol through the window — they were to rush in and make the capture.

This being settled, we started at an hour that would, bring us to the Liefens' house at dusk. The plan worked well, and just as the sun went down, and the shadows of night wrapped the face of the country in gloom, I boldly, and with quite an unconcerned manner, strode into the store.

Liefen was sitting by the counter, smoking his pipe, and when be saw me, he leaped up with every exhibition of extraordinary joy, and, reaching forth his hand, grasped my left hand, for I took the precaution to keep my right in close proximity to the butt of my pistol, ready for instant use on the defensive. I did this thing, however, in such a careless way, that he did not notice what I was really about.

"Ach! vot for you cooms pack, sir! Bot shtill I glad for to see you. Vere all you frients? Vot for you cooms back all alone. Or may pe you has your frients outside, eh! Haf yous enny vons mit yous?"

"I saw the point of this shrewd questioning instantly ; and, accordingly, replied: "No, I'm entirely alone. And that's the reason, because I don't know What you've done with all my friends."

I laughed jokingly as I said this, and slapped him on the shoulder. "First," I continued, "Strawn came back, telling us he would overtake us soon. But he did not, and then we sent two men to look after him. They did not come back. Then we sent two more to look after them. They did not return and then we sent one man to look after all that had gone before. And I'm the last of the party, and I've come to see where my friends have all got to."

"Mein Gott! vos you vas tell me das! No vun cooms pack to see me. Dere moost pe roppers mit der road, vot kills all dese mens. I haf not see von mit ems since you alls vent avay togetter."

My blood chilled with horror as I looked into that fiendish face with its well-pretended sorrow and surprise painted on it, and glanced at the upraised, bony, powerful hands, on which in imagination at least, I could fancy I saw the blood of my friends. I was almost confused, but instantly I remembered that I was playing a part, and a very desperate one, so I collected my thoughts, and answered after a pause: "That's startling news, Leifen, I must say."

At this moment Lena entered the store, and her husband repeated to her the substance of what had passed between him and myself. She was terrified quite nicely. Indeed, the whole group — for the other two now came in — would have made their fortune at acting. Their exclamations were well done, and their attitudes well taken, though I took the greatest care to let none of them slip near enough to me to give me, as I thought they might wish to, a deadly stab or a crushing blow on my head.

"Oh, Mr. Lukens,," exclaimed Lena, at last, "you must not think of leaving, at least till daylight. We have heard very strange reports latterly about this region, and I am afraid there are bad characters abroad. No, no, you must not go back to-night. You must stay till morning, and then you ought to go directly to Nagadotches, and raise the men there, and scour the whole country round. There must have been some foul play with your friends."

"I think so, myself," I replied.

"I did not know what course to take now. I wanted to have everything complete before I gave the signal to my friends outside, and not thinking the right moment had arrived as yet, I was in quite a quandary. But I soon made up my mind what to do, and with many thanks I accepted the kind invitation of my intended murderers for I felt certain that when I went to sleep they would kill me. Pleading extra fatigue, I retired quite early, my friends insisting that I should occupy the only bedstead there was.

33

"Now if I should not wake at daylight, will you rouse me, so that I can go to Nagadotches early," I asked of Leifen, as I went to bed.

"Yah, yah, I vill," he said.

Now the perilous position of my plan really commenced, but as I thought, the easiest, for I had made up my mind to only pretend to sleep, and in reality to keep wide-awake till the man should come to the bedside with his club or knife to. finish me, when I would quickly shoot him dead and take the women prisoners. That was how I thought the attempt would be made on my life, because in the tales I had read of such affairs in Europe that was always the way it had been done.

"But the sequel proved the fallacy of my ideas.

Quite unobserved, as I thought, I slipped my pistol into bed with me, and I lay there wide awake ready for the emergency. Meanwhile Lena and her sisters went round in the store, singing in low soft tones some ditty or other. Presently I heard Liefen softly call out : "Lena! Lena! the mosquitoes coming in — schmoke dem off."

A few minutes later I became aware of the presence in the atmosphere of an aromatic smell, caused by the burning of some kind of herbs. I little thought that the old wretch alluded to me when he said mosquitoes. But I found it out in a little while after, as I felt myself growing drowsy in spite of my strongest efforts to keep awake. And this was how I ascertained it all.

Just as I began to lose myself, I heard Liefen say: "Ach! Lena, he's all right now. We've got him sure. He was playing a good part."

"'Yes! Yes! I know it. I saw him take the pistol to bed with him, laughed the she-fiend. And he intended to shoot you when you went to finish him."

"Ha! Ha! He's the seventh — that's all of them, and he's the dumbest goose of the whole flock!"

"This remark, which was made by Pauline, enraged me, and summoning all my energies, I endeavored to spring from the bed and level my pistol at the window. But I could only move the slightest bit, and, just as I sank away into utter unconsciousness, I hoard some one of them say, in taunting tones: "Lay still, little goose, you will soon have your neck slit, and go down with your six other friends. Lay still, little goose!"

Oblivion followed, and when I next opened my eyes and

saw Stevens and my rescuers bending over me, I was utterly astounded to find myself living, and could not resist the temptation to feel my throat where I though the cut ought to be.

"I tell you, old fellow, you was pretty near a goner that time. Them sweet gals just had their shiny little stickers ready to slit your weasand for you as we bursted in on 'em."

These words brought me at once to my full senses, and I exclaimed: "'What happened, Stevens? Tell me how I was saved."

"'All right, Lukens; but first, here, take another nip of this whisky to keep back What we've already poured down your throat."

I gulped a good drink of the liquor, and then, with the assistance of one of the men, sat up and listened to Stevens' recital of the previous events as they happened from the moment of my insensibility. Said he: "We had waited, as we thought, most too long for your signal, when I got quite uneasy, and proposed to the boys to rush in anyhow, and see what had become of you. So we crept up quietly, till we could peep in at the window there. Just as we got up close, I seen the gal lighting some herbs on a plate, and the man sprinkle some powder over the flames, which then made a dense smoke. I thought that meant some devilment, and also that it was quite time for us to mix in. So I whispered to the boys to be ready, and when I clapped my hands and jumped for the door, to rush right after me. I waited a minute or two till I heard the fiends laughing, and saying something about a goose, and then I clapped my hands and jumped for the door. We were just in time, for them pretty-looking devil-cats of women were just going to stab you, when we lit in on 'em. We knocked the man down and tied him, and then we tied up all three of the gals; and just as soon as you're ready, and feel well enough, we'll take 'em back to Nagadotches."

"But what about poor Strawn, and the others? Have you found out where their bodies are?"

"No, we thought we'd take in the devils that done the mischief first, get them secure, and then come back and search the house."

"Well, don't do it," I said, "Let us make the search at once. We can take the murderers in afterward."

"You can take me only, gentlemen."

It was a woman's voice that spoke; and as we all turned, we saw Pauline standing behind us, contemplating us with quiet, smiling features.

Stevens sprang to his feet, exclaiming: "Hallo, gal! How'd you get undone? I tied you myself."

"And I untied myself, and the others, too," she replied.

The three fiends were in the very act of killing their drugged victim when the rescuers burst in upon them.

Stevens stared at her in mute wonder, as did also the rest of the party. "You did! Then you must be the Devil's daughter that's all, for I tied you so there was no chance for you to get loose."

"No human being can do that," said the girl.

Several of our party edged away from the speaker, as though they feared she was possessed of an evil spirit.

"Well, if you could untie yourself, why didn't you run away with the rest of your infernal friends?' asked Stevens, who was not at all superstitious.

36

"Because, if I had, we should all have been captured, whereas now the rest will make good their escape, and all you can do, you can't find them."

"She's right!" exclaimed a third one, "here's the thongs, Stevens. They're not cut, either.." And the speaker held up the raw-hide cords with which the murderers had been tied.

"Well, you sha'n't get away, anyhow, you infernal hell-cat," exclaimed Stevens, seizing the woman roughly.

"I don't intend to try," said she, with a most provoking manner.

"And more than that, when daylight comes, we'll track the rest of your band, and see if we can't prove you in another lie."

To this Pauline said nothing.

Acting on my suggestion, my rescuers set themselves about searching the house to find the bodies of the murdered men, but did not succeed in making any discoveries, till I thought of asking the woman, plainly: "Show us where your folks put those men after you killed them. It won't make your situation any worse than what it is."

"To be sure, I will," said she, just as cool as a cucumber: "Why didn't you ask me to do so before?

I could not make any reply to this cold-hearted, monstrous woman except, "Well, show us."

She did so, and we found that the victims had all been buried in graves that were dug on the opposite side of the house from Nagadotches, each one, in a grave by itself; and we noticed that each one had the left arm crossed over the breast. After we had exhumed our six comrades, we thought we would take a further look at the ground, and ascertain if there were any other victims. We got more bloody proof of the Liefens' hellish wickedness.

"Close together were two graves. In one we found a man, killed just in the same way as the others. The next grave contained what I think was the most sickening, pitiable sight I ever looked at. There was a youngish looking woman who had once been quite handsome. She had very long hair, and it was all twisted in disorder about her head and face, as though, whoever had buried her, had dragged her to the grave by taking hold of her hair; lying upon her stomach was the corpse of an infant, apparently thirteen or fourteen months of age, for between the little lip we could see the white edges of two teeth just coming through the gum.

We could see no marks of violence upon the child's body, so we concluded that it had been pitched, while alive, in upon the mother, after she was thrown into the grave.

I thought the men would have gone most wild when they saw all this and more than one of them, with oaths that it wouldn't do to print in a book, proposed to knock Pauline's brains out on the spot, and pitch her right into the hole from which the dead mother and child had just been taken. But this was disagreed to.

"No, that would be too merciful for her," said Stevens, "let's take her into town and have her hanged like a dog," only he did not say the last word in that way.

"That's all there is," remarked Pauline, in a cool way, after these three bodies had been taken out. "They were a man and his wife and child that we thought would be better off in the other."

"For God's sake, hold your demon tongue, will you?" I exclaimed, becoming myself quite enraged at the devilish creature.

She said no more and shortly afterward, we started back to Nagadotches, taking care to keep our captive safe. There we obtained the services of several old plainsmen, who at once started back with the purpose of tracking the rest of the Liefens who had escaped.

Like wild-fire the news of our horrible discoveries spread through the town, and the whole population turned out en masse to see the prisoner we had brought in with us. Wagons were hitched up speedily and sent up to the Liefen store to fetch away the corpses we had found, and when the mournful procession returned, I never beheld people so bitterly enraged against a culprit as were the citizens — especially the women — against Pauline. Had we not, with the assistance of the Sheriff and his officers, hidden her, she would no doubt have been torn limb from limb.

"Finally, we promised the incensed populace that she should be hanged in their presence the next afternoon at five o'clock, if they would promise not to interfere, but allow the law to take its course.

I wish the reader to understand, that, during the early days in Texas there were no silly quibbles in law about insanity or anything of that sort like there is now-a-days in the refined and flimsy practice of our modern courts. Now had this fiendish woman been in St. Louis, or New York, she would have had all sorts of sympathy, and perhaps would have been made a martyr of. But we made up our minds that such a hideous wretch should be put out of the world as speedily as possible. So the next morning, at nine o'clock, court was called, a jury picked out, and we witnesses told just what we knew, and what we had done. The prisoner was condemned to be hung at five o'clock in the afternoon, and she wasn't asked either what she had to say or why the sentence should not be carried out.

The minister in Nagadotches then, who was an Episcopalian, was allowed to remain with the wretch during the few hours that intervened between her conviction and execution, as he requested, to see if he could not pray her into some sort of repentance. And in justice lo that estimable man, I must say that he performed his Christian duty in the most zealous way. But, Pauline was too deep for him. She played her part most deftly; for playing a part she was, undoubtedly; and this she did apparently from some previously determined motive, the object of which with her was the insuring of the final escape of the other three members of the family in some mysterious way. I do not pretend to be a believer in magic or occult lore; neither do I wish to say that I do not believe in any such science, for I have seen some very singular and unaccountable things, in the course of my life, that I do not know how to give reasons for or against. And this very affair of Pauline Liefen was one of them. She laughed at the idea of our tracking the fugitives. And it is a fact that we despatched four of the sharpest and best plainsmen that ever put eyes on a trail, men who would unerringly trace Indians for hundreds of miles through the driest parts of the wilderness, no matter how carefully the redskins tried to cover up their tracks.

I say these men went out, and were particularly cautioned to use more than ordinary sharpness, as the people they were after would be likely to thrown them off the scent.

"Don't you bother, boys," laughed the oldest of these scouts, as they were setting out. "If you'll only put off hanging that she-devil for forty-eight hours, we'll bring in the other three as sure as shooting."

"That we can't do," was our reply, "for if we attempt it, they will hang us, too. We'll make sure of her, and you see that you make as sure of your three, and that will give us another satisfactory job day after to-morrow."

The scouts started in the perfect assurance that they would soon return with the captives. We did not expect them back under the third day. Instead of that, they returned the next day, and very much chapfallen, with this report, exactly in their own words:

"Why we had no trail to follow. We went straight to the house from here, and worked round it in a regular ring for a mile or more, not missing a single spot where even a coyote could get through, and yet not a sign of a trail could we find. Them people must be related to the Devil, sure, for they got away without making a track. They must have flew off up through the air, or gone down through the earth."

I never saw a set of frontiersmen looking or feeling so mean as these scouts did, to be thus, all of them, so utterly "whipped out" as they called it.

But, meantime, we had executed the wicked wretch whom we had secured.

I shall never forget that scene. It was a bright, splendid day, the sun shining with extraordinary brilliancy, and the air being soft, balmy, and filled with that delicious dreaminess which is a characteristic of the far South. From daylight, the minister I have referred to never left Pauline till he shook her hand just before we hung her. Indeed, he considered that, in spite of all her awful crimes, we were little less than murderers ourselves, for visiting thus her offenses with the punishment of death. He said that we ought to have sent her to an asylum somewhere in which she might be kept during the rest of her life. And he quoted the text to us, Vengeance is mine; I will repay, saith the Lord."

But we had our own notions about things, and so far from being sorry for our act of stern justice, we only grieved that we had not caught every one of the other wretches, so as to hang all four in a bunch.

Long before the hour of execution, the spot selected for the gallows was packed with human beings, eager with curiosity to see the untoward sight of the hanging of a woman. But I only write the truth when I say that, in all that multitude, there was not a solitary expression of sympathy or sorrow for Pauline Liefen's fate — not one. And even the minister's objections to the execution were not prompted from any personal good feeling he had for the woman, but because he could not conscientiously approve of society taking any human being's life, even for the crime of murder.

Promptly at four o'clock the sheriff led forth the doomed woman from the front door of Stevens' hotel. The gallows was but a short distance away, and Pauline, supporting herself on the arm of the minister, walked to the fatal spot without a tremor. She was wonderfully composed. Only once did she show the slightest sign of trepidation, and that was when she first came out of the hotel, for, just as she did so, the crowd burst forth into a storm of yells, hisses, groans and imprecations. Yet in a moment more she had herself under complete control, and surveyed her enemies in the coolest manner imaginable.

It was an ugly job to hang a woman, and we wanted to be clear of it as soon as possible. Therefore, the moment we got her under the gallows, which we had constructed hurriedly of rough timber, the minister asked her if she desired to say anything.

"No," she replied. All that I wished to say you have already written down. I desire to say nothing more."

"Shall I not pray for you once more?" inquired he.

"Oh, yes, if you want to do so," she answered, with a smile passing over her features, that implied a very firm disbelief in the efficacy of the proposed prayer.

Nothing daunted, the clergyman at once made an exceedingly fervid supplication to the Throne of Grace for mercy and forgiveness.

As soon as he had concluded, the execution proceeded. Pauline stepped forward, and, with her own hands turned down the collar of her dress to facilitate the putting of the noose around her neck, after which her arms were pinioned with a raw-hide lariat, while, with a second one, we bound her skirts round her ankles.

"And now, All Merciful Father," said the minister, "have mercy, oh, have mercy and receive this poor sinful soul, cleansed of all wickedness and sin, through the merits of our Blessed Redeemer!"

The next instant, a dull whirring kind of a thud disturbed the stillness, and the form of Pauline Liefen was whirling and twisting round, limp and lifeless. Her neck was broken and all was over instantly.

Speedily a grave was excavated and the body buried. And

41

so ended that part of the tragedy.

MURDERERS BY PROFESSION

Having a great curiosity to know something more of the previous history of these Liefens, I waited till a favorable opportunity occurred, and then I had an interview with Mr. Kolman — the clergyman. That gentleman, with great courtesy, handed me the following narrative, or Confession, that he had written out in conversational language which had passed between him and Pauline. At first he did not wish it made public: but afterwards he, in a measure, relaxed this condition. I made a copy, intending at the time to send it to the Philadelphia Sun. But after I had finished the manuscript. I did not just have postage stamps handy, so I laid it away, and the whole matter passed out of my recollection completely, until here I have lately read in the papers about the Benders and their dreadful, bloody deeds. The remarkable similitude between the two families struck me with great force, and after thinking the whole matter carefully over, I am convinced that the Liefens were no other than the Benders, and that Bender is their proper name.

THE CLERGYMAN'S NARRATIVE

"Well, my unfortunate young woman," said I, as I entered the room in which Pauline Liefen was kept a prisoner, awaiting her execution, "I am deeply grieved to find a human being, and most especially a female in such a dreadful situation as this."

"Yes," replied she, "it's not very pleasant, but every one has her fate, you know, in this world."

"I am a minister of the gospel," I continued, after waiting a few minutes for her to say something else, "and I have come here to offer you such religious consolation as is in my power."

"Yes, sir, you look like a clergyman, but as to your consolation, I scarcely believe it will be of any account to me."

"There was such a peculiar look upon the woman's face as she made this remark, that I was astonished at her. I thought at the time she must have a heart of steel or adamant. However, I was not discouraged, but resumed: "Your name, I have been told, is Pauline Liefen."

"That's my name, sir."

"And that you are condemned to death for criminal participation in several murders, which were committed at various times in your brother-in-law's hotel or store."

"Oh, Lord keep you sir — my husband's."

"Oh, then I was misinformed. I understood it was your brother-in-law."

"Well, yes, he was my brother-in-law, too, I suppose; but, at the same time he was also my husband."

"In what way?"

"Oh, quite easy. There were three sisters of us; Lena, Sophie, and Pauline — that's me. We all liked Liefen, and we could not agree to divide him into three parts, so we all three married him."

"Why — are you Mormons?"

"Oh, I don't know; if that's being Mormon, then we are Mormons."

"Who was the clergyman who married you thus?"

"We married ourselves, that's all."

The hardened woman smiled as she made this reply, and noticing my unmistakable horror at her statement, she laughed outright and heartily.

"I don't suppose that would suit your civilized notions of piety," said she, after a fresh ebullition of mirth.

"No, indeed, it would not," I replied, with some sternness in my manner, "and if you could really comprehend what a terrible sin you have committed, you would be on your knees crying for mercy and forgiveness. And that is what I am here for, to try to point you, as a poor, lost soul, out of the fold, to seek again the right and narrow path."

"But, my sweet sir," she retorted, "according to your belief and creed, I am past redemption, just like the pitcher broken at the well."

"Oh, no, you are not. The worst sinner that ever lived may obtain mercy and redemption, if he thoroughly and earnestly repents of sin and casts himself on the power and love of God."

"Mr. Kolman," said she, "I've no doubt you are a gentleman of the best intentions, but if you could really read human nature, and the general plan of creation as you call it, you would not worry your good soul about anything that happened. Horses and sheep can't live on meat. Whales can't

43

walk through the woods. Birds can't swim in the ocean. Tigers will always be tigers, lions, lions, and panthers won't be lambs, even though you feed them on grass. Now you belong to the lamb order, while I am a human tiger, and I never could be anything else but a tiger. So it is useless for you to attempt to change me into a being like yourself. Don't you see clearly that you are wasting time? Now your friends are going to hang me for what I have done. I do not object to this. I have not injured any of them personally. Yet, they are going to kill me. To be sure, this is, as I have said, the workings of nature, just as a pack of hounds tear a wild or savage animal to pieces. I have my instincts, they have theirs, and, in the course of nature, or rather nature's arrangement, the time has come that I should be destroyed by them. They, in turn, will be destroyed by some other antagonistic power, whether it be one that is seen, or one that is not seen."

"I was perfectly astounded at the subtlety of this singular woman's powerful sophism. She had entrenched herself in an armor, as it were, of impenetrable steel, from which, in her belief at least, all my arguments fell as harmless as wooden lances would have glanced from the mailed breast of one of the ancient crusaders.

"How long have you indulged in this doctrine of yours?", I asked.

"Well, I hardly know. It grew up with me, I guess. Would you ask a lion why he was not born a jackal"

"I would give a great deal to know your previous history, and to trace back your habits of life to your early childhood."

"Ah, I see, you are after a life and confession. Yes, yes, there's nothing so powerful as human curiosity. Well, now, my dear sir, if you will sit down at that table there, and take your pen, and write what I tell you, you will have a famous confession. It shall be every whit true, you may depend on that. Now don't object," she continued, as I made an impatient motion with my hand, "your doxologies and hymns, and pious preaching, will all be thrown away on me; for nothing you may say will turn me from my convictions."

I could not help saying, "It is fortunate all people are not like you, Pauline."

"That may be," she laughed. "It would not do, you know, to have the world filled with no other species of animals than tigers. But pray sit down and listen to me."

44

"I did so, and taking up the pen, I wrote out her narrative as fast as she rehearsed it to me. While doing so, she often reached over the table, and picked up the manuscript, which she would read it through and point out corrections and alterations she desired made here and there. She appeared to read readily and fluently, but she said she could not write. At least she refused to touch the pen."

"I was completely astonished at here. I never, in all my experience, came across such a woman."

"I was born in a little village, a few miles from Nauvoo, Illinois," so she began her account, "and when I was four years of age, I displayed a great precocity of intellect. In this, however, I was not a bit in advance of my sisters, one of whom was older, this was Lena, and the other younger, which was Sophie. We were all born exactly fourteen months apart. That is, Lena was fourteen months older that I, and Sophie was fourteen months younger than myself, which among us made the occult numbers of "three sevens" and "one seven.""

"This, however was not the only peculiarity about us. There was another, still more singular. We looked so much alike that even our parents sometimes made mistakes; now calling me Sophie or Lena, and then calling either of them by my name."

"When we were between the ages of sixteen and nineteen, we were well-grown girls, and father, having a good business opportunity, moved into the town of Nauvoo. While we had been living in the village near by, we had early learned all we could from the occasional books and papers that father got for us; and when we took up our abode in Nauvoo, we had a great increase of these facilities by reason of the many new acquaintances that we made."

"It was about this period that Anton Liefen came to the town of Nauvoo, and between us a strong friendship sprang up. We all liked him very much, and, as soon as we began to understand the habits and doctrines of the Smith religion, we thought it would be a splendid thing for us. But now, to tell you the truth, we did not accept it at all as a religion. We three girls loved each other very much, and if we all married separate men we knew that we should be parted from each other, which we could not bear to think of. So we all three agreed that if Liefen was willing, we would let him marry us all; or if not, then we would remain single. Liefen had no objection

45

after we told him why, and also told him that we would all work, so that we would not be any burden upon him."

"All these preliminaries being settled, we were married. We never told anybody; but it leaked out, or was suspected, for in a short time, our pious, good neighbors made a frightful commotion about what they called our wickedness and immorality; and threatened to tar-and-feather us, ride us out on rails, and then hang us, if the first part of the program would not drive us out."

"We tried to dissuade them from their wild projects. I remember distinctly saying to the most ferocious woman, that our malady was not contagious, except to those who wished to imitate us; and really we could not see why they should interfere with our peace and happiness, when we did them no harm. This seemed only to enrage our foes the more. There were plenty of really bad people among them, and I noticed these were the most clamorous of any, as though by their eager demonstrations against us they would lead the community in general to deem themselves the purest of the pure."

"There was, however, no use to combat such overwhelming odds as these against us, so we quietly left the town, and set out to find a spot where we might live, and thrive, and have our being, independent of our neighbors. Yet it seemed as though this, too, were impossible. Everybody seemed to deem it his or her special duty to persecute us, and in the course of time this began to impoverish us. We found we could not make our living honestly, by the ordinary means of intercourse, of business, or labor; so we at once made up our minds to do so by force; and to make our force equal, or superior, to the great majority against us. We saw that we must resort to cunning and duplicity. This we decided to do. We must take from others what was necessary for our wants. If we did this without preventing the result of the revenge natural under such circumstances, we would soon be killed. That we did not intend should occur; so we concluded that the only save method we could adopt was to kill all the people we robbed."

"This was quite a risky business, and we were obliged to use all sorts of devices to insure ourselves against discovery. But, as you see, we have been tripped up at last, as everything human must always be when its course is run."

"The first spot we selected in which to operate was on the trail to Santa Fe. We set up a house of entertainment for men crossing the plains."

"Our first customer was a Frenchman. He had been to the diggings and was well loaded with dust. He stopped at our house, and, seeing that he would be a rich prize, we quickly made up our minds to put him out of the way, and take whatever we found on him."

"But, I tell you, he was a shrewd, cute fellow, and came very near slipping through our fingers. He never moved about except with his pistol and Bowie-knife sticking in his belt, ready for instant use. And he was as suspicious as a buffalo bull. Twice we were just on the point of completing the work which would give us his wealth, when he spoiled the plan by his malapropos movements. But the third effort was successful."

"He was a great gambler, you must know, but, at the same time, he was a cautious one, and never would bet any amount of money. We all sat down one afternoon to play a game of "Vingt-Une" of which he was exceedingly fond, and at which he was always, as a general thing, successful."

"Liefen was away on a little hunt, and therefore we three women were alone with Quantréle — that was the Frenchman's name. He had drunk considerably just after dinner — quite an unusual trick, and in consequence he was exceedingly boisterous and good-natured."

"After winning several pieces of money from us, We told him we could not afford to lose any more."

"I tell you vat," exclaimed he, "I'll play un dollar against un kiss wis each of you. Now if I vin, zen vun I names musht kiss me, and if I lose, zen I pay to her un dollar."

"We accepted this challenge, promptly. But still luck was on the side of the Frenchman, and he kept us kissing him till we got tired of it, for he was an ugly looking wretch. So we made an excuse to talk in a corner by ourselves about a move we were to make in the game. And while making the Frenchman believe we were doing so, we were in reality making up a plan of attack upon him."

"It did not take us long to agree upon one, which we immediately put into practice."

"Now, see here," Quantréle," said Lena, "We want to win our money back before supper, and we are surely going to do it."

"Eh! Bien, my pretty dove," laughed the Frenchman, "vat

you say? I vill make you von pet vat you all tree vant to kiss me at ze same time."

"Well, yes, but you must bet three dollars at a time then, instead of one."

"Zat is goot. I makes ze pet tree dollars by vun. Ha! Ha! Ha! And I vill makes you leetle gals kiss me all ze time. Now zen, zere is my play."

"He then drew a card — the seven of spades- — and I covered it with the ace of hearts. He laughed loudly at this. I pretended to be very angry, and rose up from my chair, thus drawing his attention to myself. This was the preconcerted signal. As I turned, I tilted his chair suddenly backwards, and the next moment the other two stabbed him and he fell dying on the floor. He still made a desperate fight, however, trying to pull out his own weapons, but we all jumped on him, and he was soon quiet enough.

"We Quickly took from him all that he had hidden about him, and dragging his body back to a place we hid fixed as a corn-crib, we pushed him in there, and covered him up, in case any person should chance to come in."

"As soon as we had put the body out of sight, we got hot water and commenced scrubbing up the floor. While we were doing this, Liefen came in, and informed us that a party was approaching. This scared us, and made us quite nervous. But we soon overcame this, and, by the time the strangers arrived, everything was in complete order. To insure that there would be no possibility of discovery, we nailed up the corn-crib in which the Frenchman's body was lying. But all the while that the travelers were there, we were in constant dread for fear that perhaps Quantréle was not quite dead, and might recover sufficiently to make a struggle and thereby attract attention, in which case we should all have been shot or hung on the spot, Had that taken place, you see, my dear Mr. Kolman, that you would never have had the pleasure of waiting on me on this interesting occasion."

"I looked at the woman in more horror and astonishment than ever but she only smiled sardonically and requested me to go ahead, as time was growing short. My natural inclination was to throw down my pen and tear up what I had already written. At the same time my curiosity was so thoroughly excited that it conquered my aversion, and I wrote on.

She continued: "The Frenchman was certainly dead, and

so we had all our anxiety and dread for nothing. There were too many of the new party, and they kept too much together for us to get the advantage of any of them. Besides at that time we had not got the boldness and skill that we afterward possessed."

Lena gave the signal, and the other two stabbed the Frenchman, killing him instantly.

"As soon as our guests had left the house for certain, Liefen and we un-nailed the corn-crib and hauled the Frenchman out, so as to bury him. This last we did by digging a grave near the back end of the house, and planted potatoes over the place so as to disarm any chance suspicion of searching friends who might come along."

THE FATE OF MR. CORNING

"Our next patient was an Englishman, who was traveling in the far West for the benefit of his 'ealth, as he termed it. We managed this case in a different manner from the Frenchman's."

"Sophie pretended to be much smitten with the man, and took pains, as well as the rest of us did, to let him know it. Of course, had he been a strictly virtuous man, this would not have worked, but he was not, and so he fell quite easily into the trap."

"Mr. Corning vowed a great deal of love and all that sort of thing for Sophie, and she let on that she reciprocated, which quite made the old fool forget himself and his family at home. Finally he made some insulting proposition to her, when she instantly set up a great screaming, and whipping out her dagger, she settled the matter just in the way we had previously arranged it should be settled. That is, she drove the weapon into his heart, and that ended his love speeches and his life together."

"Had this man no servants nor friends traveling with him?" I asked her.

"Yes, to be sure he had," answered she, "but, like the drover, he told them to go ahead, and he would follow on after them to the next camping place, which he mentioned to them."

"Well, if they had all proceeded, and he was alone in your house, why did Sophie scream?"

"Only in case some stranger might happen to be around, who of course could be a witness to hearing a woman scream for help. She, to save herself, must kill the wicked man, and so she would be clear, and receive much praise beside, for her bravery. Don't you see?:

"Go on," said I, "without replying to this query, for I could not."

"After the man was dead, we took what he had, and buried him at night, taking great care to conceal the grave thoroughly. In order also to disarm suspicion further, the next morning at day-break, Liefen saddled a horse and rode off after the party, taking with him the Englishman's wallet containing all his papers and some bank-notes. The object of this, you will notice, was as follows. He knew when the servants found that their master did not come to camp, as he had promised, that night, they would send some of their number back the next morning to look after him."

"It was this deputation that Liefen went out to meet. And, as soon as he saw them he said: 'Mr. Huskins, when he left yesterday afternoon, forgot his wallet, and I rode after him so as to restore it to him, as it has money and papers in.' "

"Why we have not Seen Mr. Haskins," they exclaimed, "he has not been to camp yet; when did you say he started?"

"Yesterday about four o'clock, he started on after you. He paid me, and then went into the other room for something. When he came out, he bid us all good by and rode off at a quick trot. I did not go to bed till about nine o'clock, and when I did, I found this lying on the bed he had slept in. So I determined to ride after you this morning, and give it to him."

"He must have got astray, then," said they, "for we have seen nothing of him, that's certain."

"Then he must be found, or he'll starve to death mighty quick!" replied Liefen. "Let's hunt him up right away. But better we had go on to the camp first, perhaps we'll find him there. He may have lost himself in the darkness but found his way all right this morning. For, from the way in which he talked, he must have been a hard man to lose in the wilderness."

"Yes, he was; for a green one, I never fell across any one so sharp and quick at picking up a plainsman's business," observed one of the party, addressing Liefen.

All hands rode back to the camp of the travelers, but there was no sign of Haskins, and Liefen was obliged to repeat to them all the tale of the latter's departure from the house, the finding of the wallet, &c. There might have been some suspicion against Liefen, had not the good device of returning the wallet with money in it turned it completely aside.

"A search was at once set afoot for the missing man, and no one was more earnest apparently than Liefen himself. But of course Haskins was not found, and finally his followers set off to return to the States, being careful, however, to retain all his things, and especially the wallet with the money it contained, all to remember him by of course. We did not care though, as we had secured the big share of the booty."

"Did you never experience any dread," Inquired I, "that the spirits of these victims would haunt you?"

"Oh, yes, for a while we did," laughed the doomed woman in a careless way. "The truth is, I believe they did bother us sometimes, but we got used to it, you know, at last, and they got tired of haunting us, because they couldn't scare us any more."

"Thinking we could make more money by changing our

location, we concluded to pull up the stakes and settle down somewhere else, nearer a city where there wold be a good deal of travel. Our idea was this. After a while it would come to be noticed that travelers disappeared about the time they came to our house, or just after they left it. And, these plainsmen were so used to tracking any one by their trails, that they would soon find there was no trail, except to our house. None from it. I Then they would begin to dig and delve around, and the next thing we knew we'd get caught. We wanted to avoid that, of course."

"As soon as we concluded to alter our scene of operation, we studied up the subject of where we should locate, and presently we decided that the best spot for us would be close by Santa Fe. Nor did it consume much of our precious time, after we had concluded to move, to get ourselves in motion. So, in a very short period, we were almost within sight of the venerable city of Santa Fe."

"We lived in the city itself for a few months, until we could prospect around and select a proper spot outside in which to commence business. It was not an easy matter to do this. However, in the course of that time we succeeded in getting just the identical kind of a position from which to operate. And we had not been in it a week before we came across a lucky pigeon to pluck. He was a rich and misanthropical kind of fellow, a Mexican, who had amassed much wealth, but had no relatives that we knew of. He had lived for a number of years in Santa Fe."

"One day, he came out to see us, and we concluded that he would be a good prize for us. But we were at a loss for a plan to get rid of people without noise, and without having blood about the house; so we were obliged to study some good method that would answer our purpose. After a monstrous amount of effort and trial, we finally settled on the following as the safest and best:"

The horrible creature here described the cloth partition, the chair, the pit, and the grave, as the reader has already read of. And she did it with such a fiendish delight as to quite appall the minister.

"Finally," resumed she, "after we had decided on the details of our plan, we put it into execution on the Santa Fe merchant, and found that it worked splendidly — so well, in fact, that we have never used any other since that time."

"There was now only one difficulty in the road, and that was that the merchant always had with him a companion in the shape of a vaquero or herder. Lopez — that was his name — was one of those suspicious, ill-turned, little, dried-up runts of men that are always in the road when anything is to be done that you do not want them to know of or meddle with."

"We saw from this that Lopez must be got away with first, but it was very seldom the two were separate. They were invariably close together. Perhaps the reason of this was that Lopez suspected something, and, being thus on his guard, was determined to prevent any harm coming to his master."

"One day Sophie got round Lopez quite nicely. The vaquero had his weak spot, the same as every other individual, and this weak spot was on the subject of horses. Sophie resolved to make a point on him about horses. It took three visits to consummate her plans finally. On the day I refer to she had an old book describing several celebrated race-horses, such as Peytona, Flying Dutchman, Eclipse, &c. This book contained pictures of these horses. But the trouble with Lopez was that he could not read .English. He could not converse even, except in a quite a broken way. So, she got him quite excited over the volume — so much so, that he begged of her to translate it for him, and promised her if she would only do so, to do anything for her that she would ask him."

"Well, now, I'll tell you what I will do, Lopez," said she to him,: "I'll read this for you with pleasure, if you will only help me to perform a trick in magic that I used to play when my brother was alive. And do you know, by the by, that you closely resemble my brother?"

The Mexican vaquero grinned at this, and promptly replied, "Yes, I will, only read me to the horse book."

"Sophie complied immediately, and the fellow's eyes actually jumped with delight. I never saw anybody enjoy anything like he did that reading. But Sophie knew the Mexican character too well to finish her job before she got her part of the bargain. And, therefore, when she had read half-way through the book she complained of feeling wearied, and added, "Lopez, I am awful tired; now, before I finish, let me rest a little. And, while I am doing so, you can help me to perform the little trick of magic I was talking about. I will teach you that too, and you can make a good deal of money by performing it in public."

"Ah, vat it called?" asked Lopez.

"It is called, the Barber's Pet. Sometimes it is called mesmerism. It is quite laughable when it is done correctly and quickly. First, now, you sit down in this chair, cross your arms thus, and lean your head back against the wall. You need not shut your eyes till I tell you to. Now then, lean back a little further. Now! now! now I shut your eyes, and go to — "

"This was the signal agreed on between Liefen and Sophie. When she said that to Lopez, she was to push his head back against the partition, and Liefen was to strike it with a heavy hammer he held ready in his hand. So, as she uttered the word "to" she seized the Mexican's chin and forced his head back."

"The next instant Liefen sent the hammer crushing into the vaquero's skull, and Lopez, without a groan, lay dead at Sophie's feet. This was the first triumphant step toward the accomplishment of our general plan in regard to the old merchant. Lopez had nothing much, so we buried him, after taking out of his pockets a little silver and gold coin — all he had, for we thought there was no use in letting it be buried with him and wasted."

"The old merchant himself was to come out to see us the next morning and we felt quite sure of him now, as we had thus secured his faithful servant from interfering with us."

"Everything was ready for him when he did come. The first remark he made when he came in was: 'Has Lopez been here? He never disappoints me. It is very strange, indeed.' "

"No, sir, he has not," replied Liefen, "was he to come here? Did you send him here on an errand?"

"No, I did not, but he was talking yesterday about visiting you sometime soon, to get something you had promised to give him — a book about horses, or something of that sort."

"Oh, yes, Sophie was to do it. He was to be here next time you came, which we expected would be to-day, you know."

"I am greatly afraid an ill-wind of some kind has overtaken Lopez. He must be sick, I am sure, or perhaps dead. He had, I believe, one or two enemies over in Santa Fe."

"The subject was presently changed that of building secure houses, that is, houses in which treasure could be concealed safely. We all took part in this conversation, as our object was to find out how the old merchant's house was built, as we ascertained that he had it put up with this special object in view. He never traveled with money about him, but we

54

had no doubt that he had his keys on him, and once in possession of these, we could easily find out the way of getting into his strong boxes or money chests."

"During the conversation we managed among all of us to get the full particulars of everything we wanted to know."

"This done, our next job was to send the old man were we had despatched Lopez, which we accomplished in the following manner:"

"Do you believe in mesmerism?" asked Lena.

"Well, I hardly know that I do," replied he, "I never had much opportunity to examine the matter. I believe you have faith in the ."

"Yes, sir, we do," said I, "we believe in it thoroughly."

"Well, how do you perform it? I mean, how do you get at the peculiar manifestations that occur?"

"We don't know how, we only know that they take place, that is all."

"Well, can you show it to me?"

"Certainly, and we will do so here now, right on the spot. You sit down on this chair, lean your head hard back, and close your eyes for a few moments. Do this first, and then tell me how you feel."

"Oh, no," protested the old man, "I don't want to be put to sleep!"

"We don't want you to go to sleep."

"But, if I shut my eyes, I certainly will go asleep."

"Very well, then, don't shut your eyes. You can soon tell how you feel without that, I guess."

"Then I'll try it; so, now here, I sit down."

"And he did so."

"Now what must I do?"

"You must sit perfectly still, and gradually bend your head back. There, that's it, — no, just a little further back. Now then!"

"The same instant Liefen struck at the bulge in the cloth partition made by the head of the old man, who the following moment fell dead before us without a groan."

"We soon stripped him in order to find what else he had about him beside the keys. But we found nothing of much account of anything else. That same night we buried the old man just as the moon was setting and Liefen went the same night over to Santa Fe to the house. He did not come out of it

55

till the next night, when he returned with a lot of gold and jewels of great value. As the old man had been very retiring, and had no friends and acquaintances, the fact of his house being shut up thus did not attract any special attention. This was quite lucky for us, as Liefen could go and come without being observed. He did so for four nights, each night taking care to thoroughly alter and conceal his tracks; because he knew that when the discovery took place there'd be a great excitement about it."

"During these four visits he managed to bring away nearly all the treasure that was in the house, and we took good care to conceal it in the woods, away from our house, so that there'd be no accident of its being discovered with us."

"As we expected, toward the end of the next week the people in Santa Fe, who lived near the old merchant's house, began to notice that the latter was not opened as usual, and that he must therefore be away. Then it was mentioned that no one had seen him for several days, an unusual thing; and then it was concluded to enter his dwelling and see if anything had happened to him. Sure enough, something had happened, for not only was he not there, but it was evident that all his valuables had also disappeared."

"You have heard the old saying, that Satan takes care of his .own and it proved true in this ease, as you will see. All the neighbors knew that the old man had a body-servant, a Mexican, named Lopez. It was noticed that this villain Lopez had suddenly disappeared, and that ho was nowhere to be found. The treasure had disappeared also, and therefore, the wise heads turned all suspicion away from us by asserting, with great positiveness, that no doubt Lopez had murdered his master, and, after concealing his body somewhere, had taken all the money, and left for unknown parts."

"After a day or two of searching in the immediate neighborhood, the whole matter dropped out of mind as well as sight, and, in a month, people hardly remembered it at all. So you see how nicely al that fitted in together for us."

"About six months after, that two miners came to the house, who had been out to the diggings for a long time, and were loaded with dust. We resolved to kill them, and as is too often the case under such circumstances, we had become too careless, and so we nearly paid very dearly for our want of caution. These men were wild, jolly fellows, but at the same time sharp and cunning. I suppose their way of living at the mines had caused them to be so. We thought to kill them both at once, and, while Sophie and I ˆengaged the two in conversation, Liefen and Lena took the hammers into the other room to strike the heads at the same instant. But unfortunately the man Sophie was talking to did not hold his head far enough back, or rather perhaps Lena was a little too much excited to do her part properly.

Whichever it was, the hammer merely wounded him by cutting his scalp. At the same instant he saw his companion fall dead at his side he felt the blow on his own. The next moment Sophie and I, knowing what would be the result, sprang on him, at the same time calling Liefen and Lena to come quickly and help us. They did so, and we four struggled desperately to conquer the fellow, but he was as strong as a horse, and as active as a panther and though we succeeded several times in knocking him down, he finally got away from us, and ran from the house, hallooing for assistance as he went."

"Liefen caught up his pistol, and pursued him, while we hurriedly put the body of his companion out of sight, and straightened things up so as to be ready, for the sudden appearance of any unfriendly visitor. Soon afterwards, Liefen returned and told us that he had caught the fugitive, and shot him dead."

"It was evident, however, that, this was the ninth victim, our good luck was at an end, and that we must go to some new locality. We did so, and, sure enough, we had not been a gone a week before there was a hue and cry raised. The miner's body had been found, and, of course, it was not long ere those who found him traced their way to our deserted house, and then the whole affair was out. But meantime we had not been idle, you may be sure. We disguised ourselves, and took up our abode — where do you suppose? — not in the woods, nor in caves, but right over in Santa Fe. The reason we did this was because we felt certain that all those who would start off to hunt us, would never dream that we were in Santa Fe, but suppose that we had run off across the country. We rather enjoyed the excitement for awhile, but, in a short time thereafter, our joy was almost turned to sorrow. It happened in this way. There was a circus in the town, and Lena and Liefen went to see the performance. While they were looking on, there was a man watching them closely. This fellow had been twice to our house some months before, and evidently he recognized them, for, watching his opportunity, he slipped out of the tent, and raising a crowd of rough men, he re-entered, and giving the others a signal, Lena and Liefen were captured."

The capture of Liefen (alias Bender) and his wife.

"Of course there was immediately a great commotion, and when the mob heard who they were, they wanted to hang both of them. But, finally, somebody persuaded them out of that notion, and advised that the prisoners be locked up till morning, when they could be tried and hung. This little delay was their salvation, for during the night we two managed to release them and in the morning we were all missing. We made ourselves scarce, and covered up all trails so that no one could possibly find us."

"How did you manage that?" asked the clergyman.

"Oh, I couldn't tell you that, because if I did, you would be able to find out where the others were now, and that would never do, don't you see? We have our little secret about such matters that we never can divulge. When they have done for three more nines, then one of the other two women, Sophie or Lena, must die just as I am dying now."

"At this moment the sheriff entered the room, and informed the culprit that her time was nearly up, and therefore that she must hurry her devotions."

"Without the slightest change in her demeanor, she heard the officer through, and then replied: 'Ah, my dear sir, as to the devotions, I should not trouble you to wait another second of your valuable time for them. But I would like you to grant me ten minutes or less, till I have narrated a little incident to the clergyman here, with which he can finish up my confession, as he will call it.' "

"All right," said the sheriff as he left the room, looking at his watch.

She then resumed: "What I referred to was an affair which took place some four years later. It was this: We had selected a man for a patient who came in our way, but as the sequel proved, he was really a stool-pigeon. That was about the only time we were. ever sold."

"At the time he made his appearance he let on that he was a traveling agent for a mill company in the East, and that he had come West for the purpose of purchasing a suitable site of land on which to put up a mill. He displayed quite a considerable quantity of bank notes and checks. Had we only given this display the second thought, we would have suspected him immediately."

"Playing his part, he let us draw him on until he had his part of the plan all ready, and then he sprung his trap on us. There was one mistake we had made ourselves, which was this: In this house we unfortunately had not made a pit, nor used the cloth partition. Had we only done so, this fellow would have been killed sure."

"Our play was to wait till he got asleep, and then stab him. He pretended to be asleep, and then, just as we were about to dispatch him, he signaled and at once a posse of men rushed in, and there we were trapped ourselves."

"However, we escaped the same night after they captured us, and gave them the slip for new fields of operation."

"I might tell you some more things, but really time is too short, my reverend friend, and so you must excuse me — that is all. Call back the sheriff."

59

"The hardened, wretched creature smiled at the clergyman, who, almost bewildered with her frigid audacity, folded up the manuscript, and placing it in his pocket, stepped to the door and summoned the sheriff. That officer at once re-entered the room, and led the prisoner forth to the scaffold, accompanied by the minister, who, true to bis holy calling, never ceased his exertions to turn the wicked woman's attention to the salvation of her blood-stained, guilty soul."

The execution of Pauline for her horrible crimes.

"Some of the assembled crowd hissed and hooted as Pauline made her appearance, but presently ceased their demonstrations, and the execution proceeded with all celerity, as we have before stated. The culprit died cold, firm, and unrelentingly wicked and, though a woman, there was not, in all the mob, one single expression of sympathy or pity uttered for her."

"Time passed on, and the Liefens disappeared from public notice — at least nothing of their depredations have ever been heard of until these late horrible murders in Kansas have been unearthed. And the fact that nine bodies were found buried away in the garden, and the further fact that the Benders had moved away before any alarm was given, first struck me with the idea that they and the Liefens were the same. Sophie, the other sister, has evidently died or been killed, while the young woman they call Kate is either her or Lena's daughter."

"There is no doubt in my mind that 'Old Bender' now, of course, far advanced in years, is the Liefen I knew of in Texas, and near Santa Fe."

"Not only this, but, from what I know of the fiends, I have my doubts whether, even yet, they will not succeed in escaping from the meshes of the law, except, of course, their hitherto good fortune should forsake them."

"Since the foregoing was in press, a despatch has been received that the old woman, who is, no doubt, Lena Liefen, has been taken prisoner in the mountains. If that is really true, then the whole band is captive, and we hope, for — the sake of humanity — that they will not be allowed to escape by any means, but adequately punished for their awful crimes. Such human wild beasts should be put surely out of the road.

End

Lena, Pauline, and Sophie (Bender). The three sisters
who resembled each other so closely that a stranger
could not tell them apart.

The daughter, Kate, taken from a ferrotype
found in Breckerman's pocket.

The Benders in Kansas

From A Report Concerning:

The trial of the
"Bender Woman" at Oswego,
Labette County, in
1889-1890

The Complete Story;
Facts, not Fiction

INTRODUCTION

The story of the *Benders in Kansas* and the dreadful murders committed by that family, has often been written, and in many different forms. The horrible details are familiar to the people who lived in Kansas and the West during 1873, and for many years thereafter.

Of their "deeds most terrible," it is said that the first news given to the world, was published May 10, 1873, and that the story of the "devilish" crimes of the Benders was obtained from a passenger conductor on a Southern Kansas railroad, three days after the flight of the criminals. This was quite rapid in those days of limited telegraph facilities.

The story itself, seems like the recital of some dream, in which nightmare mirrors upon the disordered brain, a countless number of monstrous and unusual things. Yet, the story is as true as the sun. Fiction tells of no more horrid, atrocious crimes, than those committed by the Benders. The memory of the offenses of those murderers stands yet, as a crimson blot upon the pages of the history of that part of the West.

Whether the Benders were overtaken and exterminated by a posse, have been mooted questions ever since their flight was discovered. Over and over again, has the statement been printed, that the Benders were all shot to death. Another story is told, that they were over taken in the Indian Territory and speedily lynched. Others just as positively, declare that the Benders escaped and were not captured.

One the day that the discoveries were made at the Bender House and the bodies of the victims were exhumed, a number of well-armed, determined men organized a posse, prepared to follow the fleeing family of murderers, and at once started in pursuit.

Shortly after the discovery of these Bender murders, in 1873, the *New York Ledger* published the very gratifying narrative that all of the Benders were shot to death. That story so pleased the people, and it seemed such a fitting and just retribution for these crimes, that nearly everybody accepted that statement without questioning its correctness. Papers all over the country published the *Ledger* report of the case, and it was accepted as news, believed by most people. For many years following that report, the Benders were permitted to slumber in silent oblivion, in the minds of the people, along with many victims.

Sixteen years later, in 1889, that repose was disturbed by a clew furnished through a woman, at McPherson, Kansas, which led to the identification of two women, then living in Michigan, as Old Mrs. Bender and her daughter, Kate Bender. These two women were arrested in Michigan and with requisition papers, an officer took them to Oswego, Kansas, charged with the murder of Dr. William H. York.

From testimony given in court by many former neighbors of the Benders, when that family lived in Kansas, as witnesses at Oswego; from statements of fact made by persons who claimed to have positive knowledge; from Governor Osborn's Proclamation issued at the time of the flight of the Benders; from Court records, official certificates, affidavits, and numerous letters; from manifold articles published in different newspapers at various times, in different localities, and by personal interviews with several members of the posses which pursued the fleeing criminals, has been obtained the facts which are written here, and it is not fiction.

All the story of the Benders of Kansas is presented in this book.

The unreliability of human testimony, the tendency and case of mistaken identity, the difficulty of establishing an alibi and the abnormal desire for criminal notoriety in some human minds, are lessons to be learned by the perusal of this book.

The general reader will enjoy this story with avidity of fiction; the active lawyer will gather many thoughts of use in trial cases, while the law student may glean much beneficial knowledge; all will read this book with interest and be glad of its perusal.

The evidence is here presented and the case submitted, upon which the reader many render verdict, as should each juror in a case, from the preponderance of the testimony.

That verdict should answer the question: "Whether the Benders were overtaken and exterminated."

THE BENDERS IN KANSAS

CHAPTER I
The New Arrivals

In the latter part of the year 1870, there came into the north-west part of Labette County, Kansas, four persons constituting one family — an old man, an old woman, a young man, and a young woman, who lived together and were known by the name Bender. Each of the men was called John, and each woman was called Kate. The old couple lived together as husband and wife, and the young man and woman were reputed to be the son and daughter of the older people.

The old man, John Bender, Sr., was a Hollander by birth. He had lived in Germany near the French line, where he conducted a bakery. He said he had lived in America for several years prior to 1870. He was about sixty years old, five-feet-nine or ten inches in height, square-shouldered, just a little stooped, of spare build, dark complexion, very rough in manner, had no whiskers, spoke very little English, and what he did say was very broken, with a strong German accent.

The wife, Kate Bender, Sr., was about fifty years of age, rather heavy set, had blue eyes set close together — unpleasantly so — and brown hair slightly tinged with grey. Her countenance was uninviting. She was decidedly German and talked the German language. When she attempted to use the English language, it was very broken, so much so that most persons could not understand what she said at all.

The younger man, John Bender, Jr., was also known as John Gebhardt. It is a mooted question whether he was the son of the old people. He was five-feet-eight or nine inches tall, of slight build, had grey eyes with a brownish tint, brown hair, light mustache, no whiskers, was about twenty-seven years of age and spoke the English language with a German accent. He may have been born in the United States.

The young woman, Kate Bender, Jr., was between eighteen and twenty-four years of age. Her hair was a dark, rich auburn. She had deep, grayish-blue eyes. She was over medium height, some five-feet-six or seven inches tall, slender, well-formed, voluptuous mold, fair skin, white as milk, rose complexion. She was good-looking, a remarkably handsome woman, rather bold and striking in appearance, with a tigerish

69

grace and animal attraction, which but few men cold resist. She was a fluent talker, gifted with fine conversational powers, but she did not display any educational advantages of a high order. She used good English with very little, if any, German accent. She was a Spiritualist, occasionally giving seances and lecturing on that subject. Here success in the lecture field was not sufficient to encourage her to continue that work. She claimed to be a Medium. She would go into a trance and call up the spirits of departed loved ones for the neighbors. In her lectures she boldly advocated "free love" and pleaded justification for murder.

Some people believed that she was a paramour of John, Jr., and that she was not his sister, as was generally supposed by the neighbors. She was a good horseback rider and she danced well. She attended Sunday-school and "meetin's" at the Carpenter school-house often. She served as dining room girl at the Cherryvale Hotel in 1871.

Some of the neighbors called Kate a "she-devil." The light which at times flashed from her hard, steel-grayish blue or dark-grey eyes was sinister and forbidding. Her rather tall form seemed to lift up, when the spiritualistic influence took possession of her, and to become gigantic in its proportions, while she appeared supernatural. She dealt with incantations, boiling herbs and root, which she claimed had charms and spells about them for cures.

Her will was indomitable and all of the family feared her, dreaded her, obeyed her, and did the "devilish" work that she required of each of them. She was the ruler of the household and directed the actions of each one, whether that was for good or for evil — most usually for evil. She was qualified for deeds of any nature, even to the taking of human life. She had the disposition to use any means, to go to any extremes of action to accomplish her desires and secure the end of her purpose as she willed.

She had a great desire for notoriety, longed to become a great lecturer, and she possessed an insatiable craving to gain wealth, money, and position. With her, any means justified the end to acquire money.

It was believed by many, after the discovery of the awful crimes which were committed by the Benders, that Kate had struck blows with the hammer to crush the victim's skull, of which act she was clearly capable.

It is very probably that John, Jr., was the son of Old Mrs. Bender by a former husband, whose name was Gebhardt. Hence the name John Gebhardt by which John, Jr., was also known. If that be true, John, Jr., and Kate, Jr., were only half brother and sister, if they were at all related.

CHAPTER II
Location.

During the first ten days after the arrival of the Benders in Labette County, they lived on the claim of Rudolph Brockmann, a German. Within that time, they built a small log house on the quarter-section to the south-west of Brockmann.

The log house was built on the north-east quarter of Section Twenty-Three, in Township Thirty-One, South, Range Seventeen, East, which was the claim of Maurice Sparks, who was at that time absent, and had been for nearly a year. This claim cornered with that of Brockmann on the south-west. The Benders moved into that log house when completed, and lived in it through the winter of 1870-71.

Learning that Sparks had not relinquished his claim, but would return soon to live on it, the Benders made a location. John Bender, Sr., filed on the north-east quarter of Section Thirteen, Township Thirty-One South, Range Seventeen, East, in Labette County, Kansas.

The Brockmann claim was the south-west quarter of Section Thirteen. The Brockmann claim and John Bender, Sr., claim touched at the corners. That made them near neighbors.

John Bender, Jr., alias John Gebhardt, filed on the south-east quarter of Section Twelve, in the same Township and Range, adjoining the claim of John Bender, Sr., on the north.

Upon the claim of John Bender, Sr., while they were living in the log house, the Benders built a frame house. When it was completed they moved into it, and all lived together there. John Bender, Jr., did not live on his claim nor make any improvement upon it. He made his home with the Bender family in the new frame house.

These claims were situated upon high, rolling prairie. The new house was built in a slight depression at the foot of a

71

long vale in the prairie. This vale led towards a small stream near the house, along which a heavy growth of wild plums and cottonwood trees, with underbrush, was standing and bordered the stream for some distance.

This new Bender house was about twelve miles west of Parsons, seven miles north-east of Cherryvale, and ten miles south of Thayer. The Neosho County line was two miles north, and the Montgomery County line was four miles west. Osage Township was the northwest Township of Labette County. Oswego, the county seat, is about twenty-five miles from the Benders. Moorehead station on the Santa Fe railroad is about two miles northwest.

At the time, the Benders lived in this house, a well traveled road crossed the prairie and ran almost east to west past this house. This was the main road from Parsons to Cherryvale. It was also the road principally used by travelers going from Fort Scott and Osage Mission to Independence, and the Indian Territory to the southwest.

Bender House.

The Benders moved into the new house in the Spring of 1871 and lived in it until their sudden departure in the Spring of 1873. This house was a frame, sixteen-by-twenty feet in size, and it had a shingle root. A row of studding was set across near the center to divide the house into two rooms. The front room was smaller than the rear room. This front room was used as the living, cooking, and dining room and also as a small store.

To the right of the door in the front room, entering from the road were rows of shelves upon which was kept the small stock of canned and other goods for sale. To the left of this door, a table always stood. Along the side of this table next to the partition was placed a bench, on which persons sat when eating meals at that table.]

The rear room was used as a sleeping room and was scantily furnished. The only partition between the two rooms was the row of studding upon which a curtain or wagon cover about eight feet long was fastened at the top and hung loose to the bottom. At the end of this curtain, near the center of the row of studding, one of the studding was left out or removed to make a doorway through the partition between the two rooms. At the right of this doorway, but close to it, in the floor of the rear room, was a trap door through the floor by which communication was had with the cellar under the house, from the inside. This was a circular cellar about six feet in depth and a little more than six feet in diameter. From this cellar a narrow passage, just wide enough to admit the body of a man along it, led under the rear room floor to the outside at the rear of the house.

A garden and orchard of small trees was located a short distance back from the rear of the house.

The only other building upon the place was a sod stable large enough to accommodate several head of horses. In it were places to hang harness, saddles, and other usual article belonging to a team when used, or to a horse under saddle.

Ready for business.

The Bender House, located as it was upon the main traveled road, at the point where the traveler would stop about noon for dinner, or those reaching there late at evening would stop for night, taking supper, bed, and breakfast, began business as soon as the Bender family had moved into it. The store was a very convenient place for the traveling public, as well as for neighbors, to buy such goods as were kept there for sale.

CHAPTER III
Life in a New Country.

For daily life, the settler, or claim holder, was occupied in the various ways necessary to make a home in that newly settled country. They plowed, harrowed, sowed, planted, cultivated, reaped, harvested, and gathered, or "shucked" the corn. They cut the prairie grass, cured it, and stacked it for hay. They made gardens, set out fruit trees, took care of stock by herding upon the prairie, and, sometimes, feeding hay and grain.

Often they were away from home for days and weeks at a time, to do work by which to earn money to enable them to live until the claim became a farm to afford means of support and require all of their time.

Neighbors.

All who held claims and lived within ten miles of each other were neighbors, taking friendly interest, very social and often visiting with each other, and especially in case of sickness were they ready and only too willing to lend neighborly aid and help.

Life of the Benders.

The Bender family led the usual life of the new settler, adding to it the entertainment of travelers for compensation, and they kept a small stock of goods to sell to those who came to buy, whether it were the traveler or a neighbor.

The old man Bender and his wife were always about the place. John Bender, Jr., was frequently away for days at a time, but that attracted no particular attention as that was usual and a part of the settler life in the new country. Kate was often away, going to nearby towns to give seances, to lecture, and — at one time — to work as a dining room girl in Cherryvale. Sometimes, John, Jr., and Kate were seen in the neighborhood together but most often Kate was seen going about alone, to the neighbors' houses, attending Sunday-school and meetings. She also went to dances.

In 1871, Kate worked as a waitress in the dining room of a hotel in Cherryvale for about six weeks. C. W. Booth was cook at that hotel at that time and he became well acquainted with Kate. He went with her to a dance at Big Hill in 1872 and danced with her. She was reported to be a good dancer.

Travelers Entertained.

During the two years the Benders lived in that house, many stopped and had dinner, while many others were there during the night, sleeping in a bed in that rear room.

Some of those went there never to go away, but to mysteriously disappear and not be seen again.

John Bender, Sr.

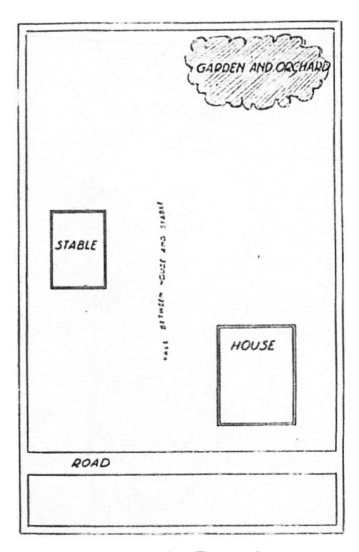

The Bender Property

Old Mrs. Bender

Kate Bender

John Bender, Jr.

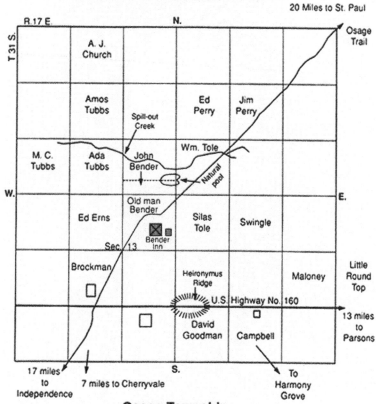

Location of Bender Claim

20 Miles to St. Paul

R.17 E. N. Osage Trail

T 31 S.

A. J. Church

Amos Tubbs

Spill-out Creek

Ed Perry

Jim Perry

M. C. Tubbs

Ada Tubbs

John Bender

Wm. Tole

Natural pool

W.

E.

Old man Bender

Ed Erns

Silas Tole

Swingle

Sec. 13

Bender Inn

Brockman

Heironymus Ridge

Maloney

Little Round Top

U.S. Highway No. 160

David Goodman

Campbell

13 miles to Parsons

17 miles to Independence

7 miles to Cherryvale

S.

To Harmony Grove

**Osage Township
Labette County Kansas
1873**

The Bender House; Scene of the Grisly Murders.

CHAPTER IV.
The Bender Neighbors.

Rudolph Brockmann, a German, lived about a half-mile southwest of the Bender house. He was often at that house, saw all of them, and conversed with them in the German language.

Silas Toles lived about half a mile west. He bought goods from the Benders during the two years they lived there, saw John and Kate often, and in 1872 he walked from camp-meeting with Kate and had a long talk.

George Frye lived a half mile south, and frequently bought goods at the store during the two years the Benders lived there.

Thomas Jeans lived a mile southwest, saw them building the new frame house, was often at the Bender house, and sold them wood up to the time they left.

Maurice Sparks lived a mile southwest, adjoining Mr. Brockmann, on the claim where the Benders built the log house. He was at the Bender store several times during the two years they lived there, and he knew John, Jr., quite well. Mrs. Bender was always at the store and he saw Kate at home at work, plainly but cheaply dressed. He met Kate along the road and saw her at meetings. There she was well dressed. He said Kate was a sprightly, active girl.

Michael Hill, a near neighbor to the west, often saw them at home.

David Monahan, Mr. Lindsay, and Mr. Linn lived near, southeast, and each had seen the Benders a number of times.

Mrs. Dientz, Mrs. Delia Keck, and Mr. Boyd were each near neighbors and often saw the different members of the Bender family.

Dr. G. B. Smith lived two and one-half miles southeast. He met both Mrs. Bender and Kate several times at the houses of neighbors helping to care for the sick when he called to treat patients.

William Dick was a Pennsylvania Dutchman, who, with his son, T. C. Dick, lived three miles southeast of the Benders. Both often saw the Benders.

Sunday-School Girl.

Mrs. Delia Keck met Kate in a class at Sunday-school during 1872 in the Carpenter school-house, several different times. Kate was very attentive. She also saw Kate at meetings in the same place, and met Kate twice at Mrs. Dientz's on Sunday afternoOns when Kate called there.

Medium.

Kate Claimed to be a Spiritualist Medium and was ready to call up the spirit of Mrs. Keck's husband, but Mrs. Keck would not consent. Mrs. Dientz saw Kate twice at her house and once in the wagon with John, Jr., during 1872. Kate told Mrs. Dientz she was willing to call up the spirit of Mrs. Dientz's son, but made no further attempt when told to let all of the Dientz relatives alone, whether dead or alive.

Visitor to the Sick.

Dr. G. W. Gabriel met both Mrs. Bender and Kate at neighbor's houses during 1872 and 1873 when he was called there to treat patients. Both were at the bedside of the sick aiding in caring for the patient. He met Kate at Parsons, also, when she was there on one of her lecture tours.

William Dick herded cattle on the prairie near the Bender place during the years 1872-1873. He was a Lancaster County, Pennsylvania, Dutchman and had learned to speak German while working for a well educated German. He frequently bought goods at the Bender store and the old man Bender waited on him every time. He saw all of the Benders. Mrs. Bender talked German and could not talk English. Dick talked German to old man Bender and Mrs. Bender understood all that was said. She told Dick — in German — that she did not think that they could keep or run the place. The old couple were at the story every time Dick was there.

John, Jr., and Kate were often absent when Dick was there. Dick saw Kate riding on horseback, met her at Sunday-school, and observed her doing the house work at the Bender house. He never talked to her. They simply nodded their heads to each other when they met.

John Bender, Sr., talked very broken English. He told Dick

that he was a Hollander, had lived in Germany on the French line, and there kept a bakery. John Bender, Jr., told Dick that he was born in the United States.

Township Trustee

Leroy F. Dick was at that time a newly married man and was also Township Trustee. He lived four miles southeast of the Bender place. He met both John Bender, Sr., and John Bender, Jr., at the elections in 1872 and 1873. He met both of them in the timber and tried to trade horses with them. Mr. Dick saw Kate at Sunday-school and at a singing which he conducted, several times. He saw both Mrs. Bender and Kate at meetings in the Carpenter school-house. He saw all of the members of the Bender family at their house several times and knew them well.

Freighter

J. A. Handley was hauling freight from Fort Scott to Independence during the years 1871, 1872, and 1873. He passed the Bender house about once each month during that time. He stopped there to buy goods and get water. He saw all of the Benders quite often and knew them well.

"Kranky Kate."

Handley stopped at the Bender house in April, 1873, to get water. Kate was sitting in the doorway. Handley asked her for a bucket to get water. She replied in a very insolent manner, "You ought to have it." Kate sat still. Handley jumped over her lap into the room and asked Mrs. Bender for a bucket and she, at once, gave it to him.

These neighbors were at the Bender house on different occasions and for different purposes during the years 1871, 1872, and the Spring of 1873. Frequently they met and talked with members of the family. Often they went there to get water and to buy goods at the store. They met John, Jr., or Kate, sometimes both of them, on the road. They saw Kate at Sunday-school, singing, and meetings. Nothing suspicious was seen by any of these neighbors. They not only had no knowledge of any criminal acts on the part of any of the Bend-

84

ers, but no suspicions were aroused during the entire time and they did not suspect them of any deeds, or other conduct of sufficiently bad character to require any investigation.

CHAPTER V.
Incidents at Bender House.

A man by the name of Corlew, who lived at Independence, in passing the Bender house stopped in to buy a can of oysters for his noon-day lunch. He heard a peculiar struggling and moaning under the house. He asked Kate Bender what it was. She told him that a hog had gotten into the cellar. He offered to help get it out. Old man Bender fiercely informed Corlew that it was none of his business, and that if he did not like that noise, he should "move on." Kate sold the oysters to Corlew. She then asked him to sit on the bench at the table and eat his lunch. Corlew wanted to go a short distance farther on his way where there was some good grass for his horses to graze while he ate his lunch. He declined her invitation and did "move on." Probably Corlew thereby preserved his life and escaped becoming one of the Bender victims.

"Happy Jack" Reed, as he was familiarly known, of Cherryvale, in passing the Bender house, caught a glimpse of Kate *en déshabillé* and was charmed with her appearance. He at once entered the house. Kate engaged him in entertaining conversation and gave him a seat on the bench at the table. He sat but a few minutes when he heard a shrill, peculiar cough, from the door step, as two travelers rode up close to the door and dismounted. He felt a peculiar motion as of something lightly and swiftly swishing past him behind the curtain. That was probably the fatal hammer started on its murderous mission when arrested by that signal which was given by old Mrs. Bender. Reed went away with those two horsemen, having first promised Kate that he would stop by as he returned and spend the night.

The next evening he arrived and Kate greeted him gladly and warmly. Soon after his arrival two of his friends came to the door on their way to Independence. Reed said he would send a message home by them. Kate tried every way that she could devise to keep him from sending that message but Reed sent it.

Kate immediately became very sullen and acted cold and distant toward Reed. She did not talk with him as she had done before he sent the message. Things became very monotonous for Reed and he retired to a bed in the rear room to sleep.

Near midnight, he heard a wagon drive up to the front door and old man Bender went out to conduct the driver and horses to the stable. In a few minutes, Reed heard a heavy blow followed by a scream. Then there was a rain of blows in rapid succession. Kate Bender arose from her bed and walked to the side of the bed in which Reed lay and she stood there. Reed feigned sleep.

At breakfast the next morning, Kate asked Reed if he slept well. Reed said that he had not awakened once during the whole night. As he made this reply to Kate, old man Bender came from behind the curtain and joined them at the breakfast table, and he sat silently and sullenly through the meal.

At Independence, Reed told this story. He was laughed at so much by his friends for his cowardice, as they termed it, that he dropped the matter and it was forgotten until after the flight of the Benders, and the discovery of the bodies of their victims, when its revival was convincing that Reed had told a real incident at the Bender house and was not believed.

German Guests.

About the last week in February, 1873, an old German woman, just over from the Old Country, stopped with the Benders for a few days, while her son-in-law was looking for a location. She put in the care of the Benders fifteen hundred dollars in gold coin, two thousand dollars in jewelry, and two drafts on bank, each for a large sum of money. When she left, they did not return any of her property but made some excuse about having sent it to a bank for safe keeping. The money and jewelry were never returned. Payment was stopped on the drafts and after some time she received the money for them.

The Woman Canvasser.

Early in March, 1873, a woman was canvassing through the County selling goods and went to the Bender house late one afternoon. She sold Kate Bender some of the goods and was invited to spend the evening there, which she did. After supper the family all insisted that she remain for the night, which she consented to do. Kate was washing the dishes and John, Jr., began to sharpen a very ugly looking knife. She was certain that she saw sinister glances and evil looks exchanged between members of the Bender family. These things made the woman very nervous and terrified her extremely.

The woman made some excuse to step outside the house and as soon as she was outside of the door, she fled to the timber along the creek and hid herself. Some of the Benders soon followed and hunted for her but did not find her. She made her way to Independence and there told her story to a lawyer. On his demand, the Benders promptly returned the goods which the woman had left behind in her flight. That lawyer concluded that there was nothing in his client's story, but that she had an unnecessary fright.

CHAPTER VI.
Mysterious Disappearances.

Sometime during the latter part of the year 1872, people began to mysteriously disappear when they were guests at the Bender house.

First Victim.

A man arrived at the Bender house early in the Fall of 1872 and said that he wanted to stop there a few days while he looked for a location. The Benders consented for him to stop with them. He had with him over fifteen hundred dollars in cash, was well dressed, and talked to Kate about his money and plans. He was never seen about the place nor elsewhere again. No one knew when he went away nor anything about him. He disappeared from sight absolutely.

This man was the first victim of the Benders. Fifteen hundred dollars cash was secured from him and the old man Bender offered to sell some "good clothes" in Cherryvale.

The "good luck" attending this first victim, together with the fiendish craving to gain money, no doubt seared the consciences of the Benders and steeled their hearts for the commission of the "hellish" deeds of crime which followed this first one in quick succession.

More Victims.

Shortly after this first one came the second. H. F. McKinzie was a guest at the Bender house. He was looking for a claim and had a sum of money with him. He suddenly disappeared and was seen no more alive.

Following, came George Brown and M. R. Boyle, both of whom stopped at the Bender house and they suddenly disappeared and were never again seen alive.

John Greary went to the Bender house while a very sick man. The Benders believed that he had a large sum of money. His death occurred very suddenly. After his death, it was found that he had only forty cents.

William F. McCrotty and Benjamin M. Brown became guests at the Bender house. Both were looking for locations. McCrotty had with him over two thousand dollars and Brown carried more than one thousand dollars. All was in cash. Both suddenly disappeared from there.

G. W. Longcohr lost his wife. A little daughter was left to his care. He decided to take the little daughter back to Iowa to live. They stopped at the Bender house for the night. Both disappeared and were no more seen alive.

A very handsome young woman between twenty and twenty-two years of age was a guest at the Bender house. Where she came from, who she was, and what she was doing at that place were mysteries which were never solved. She suddenly and mysteriously disappeared.

The Last Victim

Dr. William H. York resided at Independence, Kansas. His brother Col. A. M. York, lived at Fort Scott, Kansas. Doctor York had been visiting with his brother at Fort Scott for some days from the first week in March, 1873.

On the 9th of March, Doctor York left his brother's home on horse-back intending to go directly to his home in Independence. He rode a good horse, had a fine saddle, nice blanket, and splendid bridle. He carried a large sum of money on his person, had a fine watch, and he wore good clothes. The first night he stopped at Osage Mission. After breakfast, the next morning, March 10th, he continued his journey on horseback. Some acquaintances met the doctor riding alone, along the road near the Bender house and talked with him. He told them that he would stop at the Bender house for his dinner and have his horse fed.

That was the last ever seen of Doctor York alive by any of his friends or acquaintances. He reached the Bender house about mid-day on March 10th, 1873. He did stop there for dinner but never left. Doctor York, the horse, saddle, blanket, bridle, clothes, watch, and money all suddenly and entirely disappeared. Neither he nor any of the other things were ever again seen except the remains of Doctor York. Those remains were afterwards exhumed at the Bender place.

CHAPTER VII.
A Dinner at the Bender House.

Within one month after Doctor York had stopped at the Bender house for his dinner, L. T. Stephenson, Treasurer of Montgomery County, with Judge H. G. Webb of the District Court, who lived at Parsons, were going together from Independence to Parsons along that road past the Bender house and they stopped for dinner.

Mr. Stephenson had a splendid team of horses, silver-mounted harness, and a good two-horse buggy in which they were riding. The team was in find condition, high strung, and good lookers. He gave explicit instructions to the old man Bender to feed the horses without unhitching them from the buggy, because, as he explained to Bender, he and the Judge were in a great hurry and very anxious to get to Par5sons early that afternoon.

Kate Bender took their order for the dinner. While waiting for her to prepare the meal, Mr. Stephenson went out to the stable to see if the horses had been fed as he had directed Bender to do. The horses had been unhitched,, put into the stable, and the door was locked. He returned to the house and told the Judge what had been done.

Their suspicions were at once aroused and they began

looking about the room. They discovered that the partition was a curtain which was fastened on the studding at the top. They saw that the table and bench were placed near that curtain.

Kate came in and placed the dinner on that table and said to them, "Draw up." She at once left the room. Mr. Stephenson and the Judge quietly lifted the table and placed it at the other side of the room, took chairs, sat down facing the curtain and began eating their dinners. The bench was left in its former position near the curtain.

While they were eating, suddenly a quick, vigorous blow struck the other side of the curtain and glanced down toward the floor. At once they both arose from the table, drew their revolvers, and walked rapidly to the stable. Mr. Stephenson broke the lock on the door, led out his horses, and hitched them to the buggy, while the Judge stood watching, with revolver in hand, expecting an attack from the house. When Mr. Stephenson finished hitching the team to the buggy, both jumped into it and drove rapidly away towards Parsons. As they drove from the Bender place, several shots were fired about the place, but both escaped without being harmed.

Upon their arrival at Parsons, Mr. Stephenson left the Judge there and drove alone to Oswego, attended to his business, and from there he went directly to Independence, not passing the Bender house on the return trip. When he arrived at Independence, he learned of the disappearance of Doctor York. He then told of their dinner at the Bender house.

The Search for Doctor York Begins.

Several days elapsed. Doctor York did not arrive at home, and nothing had been heard from him. Colonel York started out from Fort Scott in a search for him. He followed the trail of Doctor York from that place with the tenacity and skill of an Indian scout. He learned that the doctor had remained all night at Osage Mission, left there in early morning on his journey, had been seen on the road some miles west of Parsons only a few miles east of the Bender house, had there talked with acquaintances, and told them that he would stop at the Bender house for dinner.

Colonel York made a most careful inquiry as he went along the road. He looked in every direction and manner possible to discover if he could learn something of Doctor York or get some trace of the horse, saddle, blanket, bridle, and other property which the Doctor had with him. Spots fit for ambush were searched and streams dragged. Not a vestige of anything was discovered and not a shadow of evidence was found to show the fate of the doctor. Thus, Colonel York went through to Independence where he first heard the rumors about the Bender incidents.

At once he made plans for a thorough return search and was joined by some men from Independence. At Cherryvale, C. W. Booth and others joined the party, making in all about twelve men. The rumors of the events which had taken place at the Bender house were fully discussed by these men, including the adventure of Mr. Stephenson and Judge Webb. The party decided to go straight to the Bender place and institute a search. As they neared the Bender house, they saw a man sitting by the roadside reading a Bible. One of the party recognized that man as John Bender, Jr. Someone in the party made inquiries about Doctor York, in answer to which John Jr., informed that he had been attacked by bandits along the creek and he believed the doctor had fallen a victim to those same outlaws. The party, led by Colonel York, rode on to the Bender house, which was the last place that Doctor York was known to have been alive.

As the party rode up to the door, in front of the house, old Mrs. Bender came and stood in the doorway, saying in German, that it was "too bad a peaceable family man must be disturbed by such a crowd of men." Kate was standing just inside the house, near the old lady, and the old man Bender stood not far from Kate. John, Jr., had walked along past the stable and came up near the door, and stood outside close to old Mrs. Bender.

In answer to Colonel York's inquiries about Doctor York having been there, Kate said that she served him with dinner and that he had gone on his way after dinner. John Bender, Jr., again said that he believed that Doctor York had been foully dealt with on Drum Creek, where he had been attacked.

One of the men in Colonel York's party was inclined to Spiritualism and knew that Kate claimed to be a medium. He requested Kate to make in inquiry and ascertain the whereabouts of Doctor York. Kate at once went into a trance, but soon revived, and said that the spirits refused to answer her, because there were several unbelievers present. Kate told this man that if he would come alone in five days, she would tell him personally where the doctor could be found. He replied to her that he would be there.

Drum Creek Searched.

Old man Bender and John, Jr., proposed to accompany the party to Drum Creek and to help them search for Doctor York, and this proposition was acceded to by Colonel York and the searching party. Both of the Bender men went with the party and remained all day, helped drag the creek, and make a search for the body of Doctor York. John, Jr., pointed to a supposed human grave, but when it was opened the remains of a hog were found. Again, he said that he had been shot at several times along there, and pointed to many bullet holes in the trees to verify his statement. This was on Thursday, April 24, 1873.

Suspicion Allayed.

The answer given by Kate Bender when questioned at the house, the readiness with which both of the Benders went along and aided in the search on Drum Creek, together with the arrangement between Kate and the Spiritualist of the party for him to go back to the Bender house and she would tell him where Doctor York could be found, allayed all suspicion at that time, and Colonel York, with this first searching party, leaving Drum Creek and old man Bender and John Bender, Jr., returned to Cherryvale and Independence, going away from the scene of the Bender crimes with suspicion allayed and knowledge deferred, to return again in eleven days, only with a much larger party of searchers, to then reveal what had transpired there and arouse the people to investigation and discovery, the horridness of which has never been equalled in a civilized community.

CHAPTER VIII.
No Suspicion, No Knowledge of Crimes Committed.

The four members of the Bender family had made their home in that house for two years. Many neighbors were going to and from that house, others passing and stopping to get water, and buy goods, and many travelers took meals and lodging who did go away.

During most of that time, if not all of it, crimes were committed by the Benders. The neighbors not only had no knowledge of the deeds committed, but did not even suspect the Benders of the foul crimes, until Colonel York and the party came as searchers for absent ones, and made the inquiries which Kate and John, Jr., met in such a manner that it allayed all suspicion, even of the party of searchers.

Another Searching Party Organized

Colonel York was determined to find his brother or secure evidence as to what had become of him. But, what should be done?

Everybody was now aroused by the disappearance of Doctor York. The discussion of the rumors afloat about the suspicious incidents and events which had occurred at the Bender house were rife.

Between twenty-five and thirty determined men from Independence, Cherryvale, and the country around, joined Colonel York, all well armed and ready to go with him for a thorough search. Among the men who joined that party were C. W. Booth, of Cherryvale; Colonel Frank Triplett and his brother, who was then living on a claim in Montgomery County, and they both joined the searching party with Colonel York; Jake Herberger, George Evans Downer, and L. T. Stephenson. Both of the last named men were members of the Vigilance Committee, and they lived at Independence. In the party were several Civil War veterans, who were settlers on claims in that new country.

After a full discussion of the many rumors about the Bender house, it was decided to go directly to that place and make a thorough investigation. Just eleven days after he had been there with the first party, Colonel York returned to the Bender house accompanied by these men. It was Monday, May 5,

1873, when this party reached the Bender house, where they found several of the neighbors of the Benders engaged in searching the house, and later several other neighbors joined them. Among the neighbors present when Colonel York and party arrived, were Silas Toles, Rudolph Brockmann, J. J. Johns, and Leroy F. Dick.

CHAPTER IX.
The Bender Flight Discovered.

Silas Toles, one of the neighbors of the Benders, with his younger brother, were the first to discover that the Benders had left.

On Sunday morning, May 4, 1873, about eight o'clock, they were passing the Bender place, when they heard the plaintive bawl of a hungry calf in its pen, while just outside stood its mother, with swollen and distended udder, lowing piteously in answer to the calf. Evidently she was in great agony from want of attention. Thinking that the family must be ill, Silas Toles went to the house to offer their services in caring for things about the place. He rapped on the door but received no answer. He peered in at a window and beheld a scene of confusion, the evidence of a hurried departure. They at once turned the cow and calf together and hurried away to inform other neighbors and secure assistance to make an investigation.

On Monday morning, May 5, Toles induced two other neighbors to go along with him, and together they went to the Bender house and broke open the door. They found things in a chaotic condition. Clothing of all kinds belonging to both sexes, with babies' garments and expensive articles of wearing apparel for both women and men were scattered about the rooms. Household utensils littered the floor. Lying about was a considerable quantity of manuscript containing Kate Bender's lectures.

Bender Place Searched.

While these neighbors were examining the Bender house and its contents, Colonel York with the second searching party came and joined in the examination of what remained after the Benders had taken flight. All movable things were taken out of the house and piled on the ground some distance away. The house was then carefully scrutinized, including the partition of studding with the curtain fastened on them.

The trap door was most carefully examined, and when it was lifted the men looked through the opening beneath and saw the cellar. They saw its gloomy, forbidding outlines, cavernous and uninviting. A light was brought and men descended into that abyss, shaped like a well, more than six feet in diameter and fully six feet deep. They found damp looking spots in the bottom, which upon examination were pronounced to be human blood. From this cellar they followed a narrow passage, just wide enough to permit a man to go along it under the rear room of the house and come to the outside towards the garden and little orchard.

These men moved about cautiously, carefully looking over things, yet entertaining no suspicion of the true state of affairs. The search was continued in and about the house and cellar for more than an hour, but nothing was discovered which was evidence of the commission of any crime.

The Garden and Orchard.

Back of the house, running parallel with the road, were several rows of corn fringed with high weeds. Beyond these rows of corn was a small garden and little orchard of young trees. The ground was freshly plowed and nicely burrowed, making it look fresh and clean.

It will be readily observed that this whole arrangement, including the trap door, cellar, and narrow passage from under the house towards the garden was carefully planned to facilitate and conceal crime. It was also afterwards discovered that every particle of subsoil that was removed from the garden and orchard to make the holes in which the victims were laid had been taken to the stable lot and carefully covered with manure.

Colonel York and several of the men were outside of the house and in full view of the garden and orchard. Suddenly, the Colonel exclaimed, "Boys, I see graves yonder in the orchard." The men laughingly answered him that he had "graves on the brain." But, he insisted that he saw graved and pointed

95

to what he thought was a grave. Finally, after some looking about them, other men could see a number of depressions shaped like graves in the freshly plowed and harrowed ground.

Discovery.

Drawing the ramrod from his musket, Colonel York thrust it into the first depression and drew it out. It showed human hair on the end. He pushed the ramrod into the second depression, drew it out, and held it up to their view displaying a fragment of clothing on the end. The wildest excitement prevailed among the men gathered about him, and all thought of the escape of the murderers was for the moment entirely forgotten.

Spades and Shovels

Men wildly rushed about looking for spades or shovels. Finding them, they worked in turns with feverish energy and anxiety to uncover that first depression and discover if it were, in fact, a grave. They dug to the depth of five feet and discovered the body of a man practically nude. It was lying face down and they gently dug around it, tenderly lifted it out with trembling hands, and laid it on the ground with the face up that it might be seen by all present.

One single glance into that ghostly face and men cried out with expressions of horror.

"It Is Doctor York!"

All of the depressions were then rapidly opened by those excited men and each proved to be the grave of a human being. When all were opened and the work finished, there were eleven human bodies laid out upon the place. Nine of those bodies were of men, one was that of a young woman, and the other was that of a little girl with its long locks of golden hair. Men wept aloud when the body of that little girl was, by gentle hands, tenderly lifted up from its grave and laid before the view of that crowd of strong men, all of whom instinctively uncovered their heads, realizing that it was an innocent little girl that they beheld.

Vows of Vengeance.

With hands uplifted towards Heaven, terrible vows of vengeance were taken by those men against the murderers.

The body of the young woman was that of a very handsome girl between twenty and twenty-two years of age. Who she was, or where she came from, was a mystery to all of those present at that time, and it remains a mystery unsolved to this day. Her description was widely published at that time and every means used to make known the fact of finding her remains, but her body was never identified and no one has ever been found who could give any information about her.

Each body removed from those holes was practically nude. Doctor York's right temple had been crushed by a blow from some blunt instrument. Each of those bodies, except that of the little girl, had the skull crushed in one or more places by a blow from some blunt instrument.

In the rear room of the house was found three hammers of different sizes. Upon examination of these hammers, the men present concluded that all of the blows had been struck with these hammers.

Little Girl Smothered.

Every indication about the remains of the little girl was that she had been smothered. Her body was found in the same hole with that of her father and was lying under his body, so it was the opinion of those present that it must have been put in there first.

Buried Alive.

From the horribly distorted appearance of the features, limbs, and body of that little girl, many of those present insisted that it was clearly evident that she had been put into that hole while she was yet alive.

House Pulled Down.

Every corner and thing about that place was thoroughly searched and it was completely torn up. The house was pulled from its foundation. Afterwards it was torn into pieces and carried away as souvenirs by the curious who visited the place.

CHAPTER X.
German Neighbor.

Rudolph Brockmann lived on the claim which cornered on the southwest with the Bender claim. He was a German. When the Benders first came to make a location, they stopped on his claim for ten days. Brockmann frequently went to the Bender store to buy goods while they lived there. The Benders had been seen to visit Brockmann's place, too. Brockmann talked with the Benders in German. Brockmann came to the Bender house that Monday morning, as did other neighbors, to make an investigation. He aided Colonel York and party to search the Bender house and premises. He worked as hard and earnestly with spade and shovel as did any of the party in opening those holes containing bodies.

Someone in that party intimated that Brockmann knew about the commission of the crimes by the Benders. He was questioned very closely but denied all knowledge of their crimes. He admitted that he had been at the Bender store, had bought good there, that they did stop on his claim at first, and that some of the Benders had visited at his house since, and that he always talked in German language with them.

Many of the men in that party were much excited by the day's events and were justly aroused and indignant. They had vowed vengeance on the murderers and they thirsted to avenge the foul murders that had just been discovered.

Someone cried out, "Get a rope!" Excitement was intense. A rope was brought, a noose made on one end of it, and that was put around the neck of Brockmann. The other end was put over a support and several men caught hold of the rope and pulled Brockmann up into the air. He was held there a while and then let down to confess his guilt. He still protested that he was innocent and knew nothing to tell. He was drawn up and let down several times to make him tell of his supposed complicity in the Bender crimes. To the end, he denied all knowledge and vigorously protested that he was innocent. That "hanging" was repeated several times until Brockmann

98

was more dead than alive, when cooler heads prevailed, and he was set free and permitted to go to his home.

Leroy F. Dick went to the Bender place that Monday while the search was in progress, but he did not remain all day. He made a hasty disposal of the property left behind by the Benders, retaining three hammers and a clock as evidence. The hammers were a six-pound Collier, an Alsatian shoe hammer, and a common small hammer.

Bodies of Eleven Victims.

The bodies of those victims which were exhumed and identified were: Dr. William H. York; Benjamin M. Brown; John Greary; William F. McCrotty; H. T. McKinzie; George Brown; M. R. Boyle; and G. W. Longcohr and his little daughter.

Those which were not identified were the bodies on one man and that of the unknown young woman.

Other bodies and some skeletons were afterwards found along the bottom, in the timber, and one some distance from the Bender house, near Cherryvale, in a creek or pond. All of these were very probably victims of the Benders, and from these facts it is known that they did not put all of their victims in the depressions discovered by the party with Colonel York, back of the Bender house in the garden and orchard.

CHAPTER XI.
How the Benders Did It.

When the meal was ready, the guest was given a seat on that bench between the table and the curtain. When seated on the bench, the back of the person would be toward the partition close to the curtain.

Behind this curtain, the "she-devil" Kate, or one of the other members of the family dominated by the evil mind of Kate, would steal quietly and take a standing position, hammer in hand, close to the curtain, and with the foot push the curtain along the floor towards the bench until the outlines of the form of the person seated on the bench were clearly shown. The hammer was held in the hands uplifted, ready to strike the blow at the proper moment. As soon as the outlines of the head were seen, the blow was struck. This blow crushed the skull and the stunned victim fell on the floor.

The trap door was very near, just to the right, inside the opening between the studding of the partition for a doorway. The body was at once dragged to this trap door, it was quickly raised, the head of the victim was placed so as to hang into the opening over the cellar beneath. The throat was cut with a large knife, the body was dropped onto the cellar, and the trap door quickly closed. In a moment, nothing remained visible to tell the tale of the horrible deed which had thus been committed. All evidence of what had been done had disappeared into the cellar and with the trap door closed, things moved along as though nothing had transpired in that room and the Benders were ready to receive and entertain the next guest.

At night, the body was robbed of money, clothing, and valuables. Under cover of darkness, the body was taken from the cellar along that narrow passage to the outside and buried in the garden and orchard.

When Mr. Corlew was informed that a hog had fallen into that cellar, it was probably another of the Bender victims, a human being and not a hog that had just been thrown through that trap door into the cellar. What he heard was the dying moans and struggles of a fellow being. It is not to be wondered that old man Bender so fiercely said it was none of Mr. Corlew's business, and for him to "move on."

The Date The Benders Fled.

Colonel York was at the Bender house with the first party on the 24th day of April, 1873. In answer to the request of the Spiritualist of the party, Kate promised that if he would come alone in five days, she would tell him where Doctor York could be found. That would be the 29th of April.

Kate expected to answer that inquiry to that inquirer alone, and she waited expectantly for that opportunity. She looked for him to come, and to come alone. The Benders all waited for his coming undoubtedly certain of another victim. He did not return and none of the party came again. When he did not come for that answer, and none of that party returned to make any further inquiry, it was ominous. The Benders then took alarm and they hastily prepared for flight. The condition of the house disclosed the fact of the hasty departure.

It was on Sunday morning, the 4th of May, that Silas Toles and his brother discovered that the Benders had gone. From the condition of the cow and calf, it was evident that they had been gone some three or four days, but not more than that.

The Benders did not leave before the 29th of April, the day that they expected that Spiritualist to come alone to get the answer from Kate to his inquiry as to the whereabouts of Doctor York. It is evident that they had been gone three or four days only when Mr. Toles found the condition of the cow and calf to be so pitiful, and relieved it, and went to get neighbors to investigate.

The Benders fled the night of the 29th of April, 1873.

The Direction the Benders Fled.

The Benders knew that country well. They also knew that Colonel York had been at Parsons making inquiries in his search for Doctor York; they knew that at Cherryvale and Independence there were many people who would recognize some of the Benders if they saw them; they would expect that Colonel York had reported the result of the visit to the Bender house and the search on Drum Creek. To go towards Parsons, Cherryvale, or Independence, certain recognition awaited them.

To the South lay the high rolling prairie and mounds about Mound Valley from which a long view could be had, so that would not be a safe direction to travel. To the North, the timber bordered the streams as far as Thayer, Kansas. The country in that direction was sparsely settled and the roads were but little traveled. In that direction, the Benders could travel at night and could easily disappear in the friendly growth of underbrush. They would meet but few persons, if any. That was the best course for their flight.

How the Benders Went Away.

The Benders drove a team attached to a two-horse farm wagon, which they left in the timber about one mile from Thayer. This is evidence of the fact that they left Bender house by driving a team away. The horses had been taken from the wagon and tied with ropes about their necks to the sides of the wagon bed. When found, the horses had eaten large

101

notches in the sides of the wagon-bed and were almost famished with hunger and thirst.

Where the Benders Went.

The Benders bought railroad tickets from Thayer to Humboldt, Kansas, a small town about twenty-five miles north on the M. K. & T. railway. That road runs south from Humboldt to Vinita, Indian Territory, and on through to Denison, Texas. The Benders traveled from Humboldt on that railroad to the South and have never been seen since.

CHAPTER XII.
Band of Desperadoes.

Colonel Frank Triplett and several others who were present at the Bender house with Colonel York, after careful investigation, were of the opinion that the Benders were members of a large and well organized gang of desperadoes, who were at that time operating extensively along the Southern Kansas border, throughout the Indian Territory, and away to the West into the Texas Panhandle and No-Man's-Land.

There was not one of the victims of the Benders but what went there with either a team and wagon, a horse and saddle, and other personal property and effects, besides having money with them. None of the horses, wagons, harness, saddles, or any of their equipment, nor any of the personal property, was ever disposed of by any of the Benders in that locality, nor was any of it ever heard of afterwards. No one knew of any member of the Bender family being away from the Bender house for any great length of time.

Confederates.

This was conclusive evidence to many that confederates of the Benders ran off all of the stock at once and disposed of it in some place safe from discovery. It was doubtless some of these confederates who made possible the escape of the Benders.

102

Another Abandoned Team.

About the time of the flight of the Benders from Bender house, the people at New Chicago, now Chanute, Kansas, then a little town, discovered a team of horses attached to a wagon which had been tied in one of the streets for two days without food or attention. That team and wagon was never claimed by anyone. It was at once supposed that this was the team by which the Benders made their escape. This fact was never established, however, though believed by some, but flatly contradicted by the fact of the abandoned team near Thayer some miles south. The shrewdest heads throughout that part of the country believed that the team was driven to Chanute by confederates and left there merely as a blind to throw pursuers off the real trail of the Benders and to let them escape.

Posse Organized.

Colonel York took charge of the remains of Doctor York and gave them proper care and interment, while others looked after the remains of the other victims which had been exhumed from the Bender graveyard.

Many of the others in that party at the Bender place who were brave, determined men, lost to time that day, but organized a posse to pursue and, if possible, capture the fleeing Benders. This posse, after it was organized, was divided into four parties, each of which at once started in a different direction in pursuit. Among the members were old veterans who had only a few years before been seasoned by service in the Union army. Naturally the "fall in" and unite for service when duty calls to courageous and hard work of the character required to pursue violators of the law, especially of the class to which the Benders most clearly belonged. Seven of those old veterans, good and brave men, tried and true, formed one of the four divisions of that posse and they chose for the leader a former Captain of a Company in one of the best Regiments and most serviceable, of a leading Western State.

The Pursuit of the Benders.

The division of the posse led by the Captain started in a Southerly direction, headed for the Indian Territory line, as they believed that was the most probable course the Benders would take to get where they would be safe and find shelter among other outlaws. Within forty-eight hours, that posse was "hot on the trail" of the Benders. A second division of the posse went towards Thayer, Kansas. A third division went towards Cherryvale and Independence, a fourth division went toward Parsons, and from there to Oswego. The pursuit of the Benders was begun in that manner from the Bender place that day.

The Captain and his men followed the trail into the Indian Territory for some distance and returned in a few days from pursuit. They said they had given up the hunt, and they at once dropped the subject of the Benders or their pursuit. After their return, the whereabouts of the Benders never seemed of any interest nor did it seem to bother any of that group of men.

It was a surprise to their friends and acquaintances how quickly they dropped the whole matter and would not talk about it.

When they returned, it was generally understood somehow that they had attended — while gone — a "lynching bee" somewhere in the Territory. That they disposed of the entire Bender family has always been suspected by many and fully believed by some.

Not one single member of the Captain's men has ever peached.

Each of the other divisions of the posse skirmished around all over that part of the country in the direction they first started and the members returned to their homes believing that the Benders escaped.

Since that time, there have been numerous Benders located in various parts of the country, but none of them have been fully and satisfactorily identified as members of that notorious family.

Governor's Proclamation.

Under date of May 17, 1873, Governor Osborn of Kansas, issued a proclamation, which read, in part, as follows:

Whereas: Several atrocious murders have been recently committed in Labette County, Kansas, under circumstances which fastens beyond doubt the commission of these crimes upon a family known as the Bender family.

The reward was offered of Five Hundred Dollars for the capture and delivery of either of the parties to the Sheriff of Labette County, and it also contained the following:

Description of the Benders.

John Bender, about sixty years of age, five-feet, eight or nine inches in height, German, speaks but little English, dark complexion, no whiskers and sparely built.

Mrs. Bender, about fifty years of age, rather heavy set, blue eyes, brown hair, German, speaks broken English.

John Bender, Jr., alias John Gebhardt, five-feet, eight or nine inches in height, slightly built, grey eyes, with brownish tint, brown hair, light mustache, no whiskers, about twenty-seven years of age, speaks English with a German accent.

Kate Bender, about twenty-four years of age, dark hair and eyes, good looking, well formed, rather bold in appearance, fluent talker, speaks English with very little German accent.

All trace of the Benders was lost. The entire family had disappeared. Many believed that they were all exterminated. Others denied that they were dead. What had become of them was an unanswered question.

More than twelve years passed and the question whether the Benders were yet living was not answered. Finally, a supposed clew was given by a woman, who had obtained her information, from a statement made to her by another woman, at this time washing for the informant. This led to the positive declaration that the Benders were alive and then living in the State of Michigan.

CHAPTER XIII.
The Washerwoman.

A woman, who had lost her husband a short time before, lived at McPherson, Kansas, in the year 1886. She was compelled to do washing, to earn the living for herself and two little girls. She washed for many people at their homes. She had formerly lived in Michigan and came from that State to

105

McPherson in the year 1884. The name of this washerwoman was Sarah Eliza Davis.

A Dream Interpreted.

Among those for whom this woman did washing at their homes was Mrs. Frances McCann, the wife of a hardware merchant of McPherson.

Mrs. McCann had a strange dream during the time that Mrs. Davis was doing washing at her house. That dream revealed to Mrs. McCann the murder of an old man by and old woman and her daughter. Mrs. McCann told that dream to Mrs. Davis and informed her that she was very much troubled over it. Mrs. Davis interpreted it for her:

There was a murder of an old man. The murdered man was John W. Sanford. It was committed at Windsor, Canada. It was committed by the mother of Mrs. Davis and an elder daughter who was the wife of the murdered man. It was done when Mrs. Davis was a little girl. Mrs. McCann was the little daughter of that murdered man.

This was the interpretation of that dream by Mrs. Davis, and she told Mrs. McCann that the wife of the murdered Sanford afterwards married Stoked, of New York, who killed Fisk. This was the story told to Mrs. McCann by her washerwoman.

Parent Discovered.

Mrs. McCann did not know her own parentage. She was so impressed with the interpretation of her dream by Mrs. Davis that she made the journey to Kentucky, where she visited the orphan asylum in which she was reared. There she discovered that she had been received at that institution as Frances Sanford.

Her next journey was to Windsor, Canada, where she learned that a man by the name of John W. Sanford had been murdered there many years before.

The Woman Detective.

Mrs. McCann returned to McPherson determined to prosecute her search for the murderer of her father and bring that murderer to a conviction and punishment. She at once began her work as a detective by shadowing Sarah Eliza Davis, her own washerwoman.

Mrs. Davis, at the time, was confined at home by sickness. Mrs. McCann went to the home of Mrs. Davis to see her and sympathize with her. Mrs. Davis was an ignorant, superstitions woman and believed that Mrs. McCann was a Spiritualist having supernatural powers. Mrs. McCann expressed great sympathy for Mrs. Davis and for several weeks during her sickness made daily visits to see Mrs. Davis, saying that she was doing so, "For sweet charity's sake."

She first placed a magnet in Mrs. Davis' hand. The effect was mesmeric and she had Mrs. Davis mesmerized. Then she showed Mrs. Davis an instrument which she said would write the maiden name and birth-place of Mrs. Davis, if she would just hold her hand upon it. Mrs. Davis placed her hand upon it and the instrument wrote: "Sarah Eliza Mark, Cattaraugus County, New York," the maiden name and place of birth of Mrs. Davis. What it meant, Mrs. Davis did not know. It was a deep mystery to her.

From that moment, Mrs. McCann could do anything she wished to do with Mrs. Davis. She was absolutely under her control. She would ask a question and Mrs. Davis would answer it just as Mrs. McCann desired her to answer it.

Bender Idea.

Mrs. McCann said that there was one thing Mrs. Davis had declared that she would never tell to Mrs. McCann. That one thing Mrs. McCann was determined to make Mrs. Davis tell her. She kept thinking about that matter and how to get Mrs. Davis to tell it to her. Suddenly, like a flash of bright light, it came to her mind that Mrs. Davis and her mother, without any doubt were Bender women.

The Bender Women.

Mrs. McCann asked Mrs. Davis the point blank question, "Is your mother Mrs. Bender?" Mrs. Davis became very indignant and told Mrs. McCann to never again refer to that subject. On another occasion, while Mrs. Davis was busy over the washtub, Mrs. McCann in a careless, off-handed manner, asked Mrs. Davis how many there were in the Bender family.

Mrs. Davis replied, "Well let me see. There was Mother — ," She stopped for an instant, and then throwing up her hands, exclaiming, "Now you have my secret! I have told you all." She then warned Mrs. McCann to never mention that matter again, either to her or to anyone else.

In many other conversations after that, Mrs. Davis told of murders committed by her mother and family, and left the impression stronger each time that they were indeed the Benders. Mrs. McCann believed that the rehearsing of the murders was for the sole purpose of convincing her that she was in danger from that family.

That dream, its interpretation and the conversations with Mrs. Davis, as well as the confession which had followed in consecutive order, formed the groundwork of all subsequent investigations, and the result of the whole was the arrest of Mrs. Davis and her mother in Michigan as the Bender women.

CHAPTER XIV.
Intuition – Guided.

Mrs. McCann claimed that she was guided in all of her work solely by intuition, or impressions made upon her mind by some mysterious influence. She was convinced that Mrs. Davis' statement that her mother had murdered the father of Mrs. McCann was true, and she was determined to establish that fact by evidence and convict and punish the murderer.

The State Would Prosecute.

After getting the confession from Mrs. Davis that her mother was old Mrs. Bender, it was clear to Mrs. McCann that the State of Kansas would prosecute the Benders if located and identified.

If she located and identified these as the Bender women, she would secure the reward which she had been informed was outstanding for them, and she would also obtain a world-wide reputation as a woman detective. Perchance, she would also punish the murders of her own father, which she so much desired to do.

Mrs. Davis Leaves Kansas.

A short time after the disclosure to Mrs. McCann than her mother was old Mrs. Bender, the washerwoman left McPherson and with her little children moved back to Michigan.

Mrs. McCann Goes to Michigan.

Soon after Mrs. Davis left, Mrs. McCann followed her to Michigan and there constantly shadowed her. Upon her arrival in Michigan, she located the mother of Mrs. Davis who was living at Niles and was known there as Mrs. Elmira Griffith. She also learned that these women bore a bad reputation and were said among officers to belong to the criminal classes. To keep a close watch on every movement by Mrs. Davis and her mother, Mrs. McCann would often spend the whole night in the outbuildings upon the premises where they were living.

Mrs. McCann induced the officers at Niles, Michigan, during the summer of 1889, to advise Mr. John H. Morrison, the Prosecuting Attorney of Labette County, Kansas, living at Oswego, that the two women, Mrs. Davis and Mrs. Griffith, were known to be bad criminals, and that the authorities believed that these women were old Mrs. Bender and her daughter, Kate, members of that notorious family, and formerly of Labette County. After quite a correspondence with the Michigan officers, Mr. Morrison decided to submit the correspondence on the subject to the County Commissioners of Labette County, which he did.

Leroy F. Dick Goes to Michigan

The County Commissioners carefully considered the matter when it was submitted to them by Mr. Morrison, and decided to send Leroy F. Dick, a former neighbor of the Benders — well acquainted with them when they were living in Labette County, and who took charge and disposed of the property left behind by the Benders — to Michigan to investigate. Mr. Dick had retained the hammers and clock, left by the Benders, as evidence. He had been Sheriff of Labette County and was at this time living in Parsons.

The County Commissioners instructed Mr. Dick to go to

109

Niles, Michigan, and carefully investigate the whole matter, to identify the Benders if they were found, and to ascertain if these suspected women were really the Bender women. Mr. Dick had often met both Mrs. Bender and Kate when they lived on the Bender place and would know them if he met them anywhere. He was instructed to go wherever necessary, to get all the facts possible, and to locate the Benders if they could be found.

Mr. Dick, so authorized by the County Commissioners, made the trip. Afterwards, he reported that in making this investigation, he traveled all over the State of Michigan, then went to Indiana, Ohio, Pennsylvania, New York, and Canada. He said that in making investigation he traveled more than eleven hundred miles.

The Benders Found.

Mr. Dick found the old woman Bender, Kate Bender, and two other daughters of old Mrs. Bender, but of the old man Bender and John, Jr., he could not get any trace at all.

He saw and talked with Mrs. Griffith and Mrs. Davis while in Michigan, and he was convinced that these women were the old woman Bender and Kate Bender, whom he knew so well in Labette County, when the Bender family were keeping the Bender house. He conferred with Mrs. McCann and the officials, and he was in daily conference with Mrs. McCann, to determine what was best to be done to prevent these noted criminals, the Bender women, from making their escape, before he could return to Kansas, make his report, secure requisitions necessary to take them to Kansas as the Benders, and again get to Michigan to take charge of these women.

To prevent escape, it was decided that Mrs. Griffith and Mrs. Davis must be held by some court process until requisition papers arrived. One or both of them must be arrested and either placed in jail, or be put under bond and the case must be held along until Mr. Dick could go to Kansas and get back with the necessary papers.

Mrs. Griffith and one of her daughters were very much incensed and angry towards Mrs. Davis for having told Mrs. McCann that Mrs. Griffith was old Mrs. Bender. That made it easy for the officials at Niles to induce Mrs. Griffith to file a charge of larceny against her daughter, Mrs. Davis.

110

Mrs. Davis had lately moved to Lansing where she had secured work. The larceny charge was filed at Niles, a warrant was issued, and the Sheriff of Berrien County went to Lansing with that warrant, arrested Mrs. Davis, and brought her back to Niles as a prisoner where she was arraigned in Court and charged with larceny.

CHAPTER XV.
Mrs. McCann Keeps Watch.

To be certain that Mrs. Davis and her mother, Mrs. Griffith, did not escape until the papers arrived to take them to Kansas, Mrs. McCann remained in Michigan, watching every move they made and waiting for Mr. Dick to come from Kansas with the requisition papers.

Dick Returns to Kansas

In the meantime, Mr. Dick went to Oswego and made his report. In his opinion, they were, beyond doubt, the guilty parties. Mrs. Griffith was old Mrs. Bender and Mrs. Davis was Kate Bender. He knew them when they lived in the Bender house in Labette County, he knew them now, and he was sure they were the parties.

Upon the strength of Mr. Dick's positive identification, the papers for requisition were prepared, they were submitted to the Governor of Kansas, The Governor approved and signed the papers. He appointed Leroy F. Dick as the agent of the State of Kansas to receive the prisoners from the officials of the State of Michigan and bring them to Kansas as the Bender women. With these papers, Mr. Dick again traveled to Michigan, where he presented them to the Governor of that state, and they were approved. He went to Niles where the officials delivered to him Mrs. Griffith as old Mrs. Bender and Mrs. Davis as Kate Bender.

While Mr. Dick was gone to Kansas to get the papers, the officials in Michigan had played the usual game of delay in court proceedings to hold Mrs. Davis and Mrs. Griffith thereby preventing their escape.

The case against Mrs. Davis on the larceny charge was pending in Justice Court and had been continued from time to time with no effort really made to complete the hearing, until the people were wearied with the talk about the case, completely disgusted and were censuring the officials for so much delay.

On the 22nd day of October, 1889, the preliminary in that case was presented before a Justice in Niles, Michigan. Mr. Dick had returned from Kansas and both he and Mrs. McCann were present and heard the testimony in the case.

Mrs. Davis — in her testimony on her own behalf — stated that she had been threatened by the son-in-law of Mrs. Griffith, and by the Prosecuting Attorney Bridgman with the penitentiary. She stated her unwillingness to give her testimony, as it would be against her mother, Mrs. Griffith, and would, "Send her to the pen."

She proceeded to tell a story of much length in which she said that she saw her mother murder an infant, the illegitimate child of another daughter, when Mrs. Davis was a little girl in 1859; also that her mother killed an old woman with an ax-helve and disposed of the body by weighting it and sinking it into a slough, taking the witness, then a little girl, with her at night; and that her mother had been arrested, tried, convicted, sentenced, and committed to the Detroit House of Correction, and had served a term there for manslaughter.

As witness, she stated that she had received letters from her mother which were written from Kansas, Colorado, and Texas from 1872 to 1874; that those letters had lately been stolen from witness; that Elizabeth, an older daughter of Mrs. Griffith, married a Mr. Sanford; that he was murdered by that daughter and her mother, Mrs. Griffith, at Windsor, Canada, when witness was a little girl, eight or nine years old.

Witness described the killing and her running away; that the same daughter, Elizabeth, married Stokes, the man who killed Fisk in New York; that her mother told her of the killing of her husband, Griffith, and that his body was thrown into a well.

Thus was the uncorroborated story of Mrs. Davis.

After Mrs. Davis gave that testimony — which shows how unreliable were statements made by her — and the uncertain evidence of identity by persons who had not seen old Mrs. Bender for more than sixteen years, it was decided that Mrs. Elmira Griffith really was old Mrs. Bender and she must be taken to Kansas to be tried for the murder of Dr. William H. York and other victims of the notorious Bender family.

But more strange than this — and without any evidence except the fact that she was the daughter of Mrs. Griffith — it was determined that Sarah Eliza Davis — who had resided in Kansas several years of late, and who had told Mrs. McCann the story upon which the Bender Idea had developed — was the veritable Kate Bender, Jr.; that she must be taken to Kansas with her mother, and also be charged with the murder of Dr. York and the other Bender victims.

Leroy F. Dick was present and heard all the testimony in that larceny case as given by Mrs. Griffith, Mrs. Davis, and others. He saw and talked with both of these women in Michigan, heard their numerous stories, talked with two other daughters of Mrs. Griffith, and with other people who had known both of these women since the early sixties. He was there as the representative of Labette County, Kansas, with authority to fully investigate and determine whether they were, in fact, the Bender women. He knew the Benders when he lived near them, and he should have known them when he was them in Michigan.

The court's decision was to take these two women to Oswego, Kansas as "the Bender women."

Doing so, would thereby separate Mrs. Davis from her three little children, all of whom were dependent on her labor for support. They would be thrown into "public charge" as subjects of charity which they had never been while living with their mother. But more sad than all of this, Mrs. Davis' youngest child was nursing, and if the mother went to jail, so must that child; and so it did, with its mother, to Oswego, Kansas, remaining there until its mother was discharged.

The Bender Women in Jail.

Leroy F. Dick, accompanied by Mrs. McCann, took those women from Niles, Michigan, to Oswego where they were charged with the murder of Dr. William H. York, at the Bender house, in Labette County, Kansas.

With its mother, he took the nursing child along to a pris-

113

on. He delivered them to the Sheriff at Oswego, W.P. Wilson, on the 1st day of November, 1889, thereby performing his part in that sad drama, as fully and successfully as he possibly could.

News of the apprehension of such noted criminals was widely published in the newspapers all over the State of Kansas and in the large cities of the West.

The two women, Mrs. Elmira Griffith and Mrs. Sarah Eliza Davis, and the little two-year-old girl languished in *Durance Vile.*

CHAPTER XVI.
The Defendant's Attorneys.

On the second day of November, 1889, Judge H. G. Webb of Parsons, and J. T. James, lately from Minneapolis, Minnesota, became the attorneys for the defense of these two women. The women were far from home, friends and acquaintances; they were without money or ready means to make their defense and they cold not pay counsel fees. These two attorneys undertook the defense, well knowing that they would have a long, hard fight and they gave their time, money, and legal ability to the service of these defendants.

As lawyers, they were ready and willing to do this work, and thus perform their duty in the defense of the poor, as under the oath taken upon admission to practice, all lawyers are required to do. They trusted in that reward of the future, which will always come to the worthy lawyer, who gains a reputation honorably in the defense of those charged with some great crime, as was that of the Benders.

The Trial of the Alleged Benders.

Under the laws of Kansas, at that time, a preliminary hearing must be given persons charged with the commission of a crime. The hearing of the charge for murder, against these women, as the Benders, was set for Monday, the 18th day of November, 1889, at the hour of 10 o'clock in the forenoon.

The specific charge was the murder of Dr. William H. York, on the 5th day of May, 1873, at and within Labette County,

Kansas. The Justice record recited that the warrant was returned and filed November 2, 1889, with Kate Bender, Sr., and Kate Bender, Jr., in court. The hearing was had in the District Court room, in the Court House at Oswego.

For the hearing of the case, Justice of the Peace E. D. Kiersey associated with Justices C. T. Bridgman and D. Doyle, under a provision of the Statute of the State of Kansas, which authorized such association to be made, if the Justice considered the case of sufficient importance to require it.

The State was represented by Prosecuting Attorney John H. Morrison and Judge Frank H. Atchinson. The defense was represented by Judge H. G. Webb and J. T. James.

At 10 o'clock in the forenoon of Monday, the 18th day of November, 1889, the hour set for this hearing, the Court room was crowded with an eager audience, a fair proportion of those present being ladies.

The defendants, Mrs. Griffith and Mrs. Davis — with the little girl — were brought into court by Sheriff Wilson and his son, D. H. Wilson, under-sheriff. The defendants took seats as cooly as the most disinterested spectator. After a while, Mrs. Davis, about whom the little daughter was playing, seemed to become impressed with the seriousness of the charge against her and she shed tears freely. Mrs. Griffith, on the contrary, bore the ordeal with stoic indifference.

That hearing lasted through sessions of two days and evenings. Upon the calling of the case, a recess was taken until 1 o'clock in the afternoon.

To accommodate the Attorneys for the State and save the time it would take and the trouble to call witnesses to make the proof of the facts, Judge Webb, of counsel for defense, on behalf of the defendants, admitted that the body of a man identified as that of Dr. William H. York, was found buried on the Bender Place, in Labette County, State of Kansas, on the fifth day of May, 1873, thus waiving the necessity for the State to prove the life and death of Doctor York. With these admissions of record, the only question for the Court to pass upon was the identification of these defendants, Mrs. Elmira Griffith as Kate Bender, Sr., and Mrs. Sarah Eliza Davis as Kate Bender, Jr.

Upon request made by Judge Webb, witnesses for the State were called, sworn, and excluded from the Court Room. Upon a like request by Prosecuting Attorney, witnesses for the

115

defendants were called, sworn, and excluded from the Court Room. The reading of the charge against the defendants was waived by Judge Webb, for the defense, and the case proceeded with the introduction of testimony.

The State called as the first witness, C. W. Booth of Cherryvale, Kansas:

Knew the Benders . . . was best acquainted with Kate . . . she worked several weeks as a dining room girl at hotel in Cherryvale during 1871 . . . witness was cook there . . . took Kate to dance at Big Hill in 1872 . . . saw her last time when with Colonel York and party at Bender house in 1873 . . . sufficiently acquainted with Kate to identify her.

Witness' attention was called to Mrs. Davis by Prosecuting Attorney Morrison. He scrutinized her closely, then said, "She bears an awful striking resemblance to Kate Bender." The witness was not able to identify old Mrs. Bender.

The second witness was T. C. Dick of Arcadia, Indiana, about thirty-five miles north of Indianapolis:

Witness lived with his father William Dick, in Labette County during time Benders lived at Bender house . . . personally acquainted with Bender family . . . frequently at Bender house . . . met Kate at church and Sunday-school . . . knew John, Jr., and Kate well . . . familiar with general form and features of Kate . . . could identify her . . . Leroy F. Dick brother of witness . . . on telegram from met defendants with him at Indianapolis . . . saw Mrs. Davis step from train at depot . . . said, "She will fill the bill as Kate Bender." . . . from best recollection said, "She is Kate Bender." . . . can't identify old Mrs. Bender.

The third witness was John A. Handley of Greenwood County, Kansas:

Freighted from Fort Scott to Independence from 1869 to 1874 . . . knew all of the Benders . . . saw Kate and John, Jr., often . . . was at Bender house once a month during those years . . . stopped to get water and buy goods . . . remember distinctly how each looked . . . able to identify them.

When asked to look at the two defendants, he pointed to Mrs. Davis and said:

"That is Kate." . . . pointing to Mrs. Griffith, said: "That is old lady Bender." . . . Witness, with his wife and Mr. and Mrs. William Littler, stopped at Bender house in April 1873 to get water . . . asked Kate for a bucket . . . she said "You ought to have it" in a very insolent manner . . . from her actions then and the actions of Mrs. Davis at the trial, witness was able to say that Mrs. Davis was Kate Bender.

The fourth witness was Mrs. Delia Keck:

Lived close to Benders . . . knew old man, John, and Kate . . . knew Kate best . . . met her at Sabbath-school and at home of father-in-law of witness . . . saw her often enough to get good impression of her . . . Mrs. Davis' eyes and hair, and hight cheek bones resemble strongly those of Kate Bender . . . in witness' judgment she is Kate Bender.

Fifth witness was T. B. Smith:

Mrs. Davis' nose and hair resemble Kate Bender . . . unable to identify Mrs. Bender.

Sixth witness was Rudolph Brockmann of Osage Township, Labette County:

Lived there since 1870 . . . knew Bender family well . . . four members . . . two men and two women . . . old man Bender was six-feet high . black hair . . . straight broad shoulders . . . about fifty-five years old . . . the old woman had dark hair . . . five feet, six or eight inches tall . . . pretty tall woman . . . medium shouldered . . . walk lively . . . forty to forty-five years old . . . broad head . . . fleshy face . . . Kate had dark hair . . . broad shoulders, a little stooped . . . slight mark or scar under left eye . . . five-feet, three or four inches high . . . slower than old lady . . . about eighteen years old when they left . . . not a full girl when they came . . . she talked about supernatural power . . . spiritualism . . . a great deal of talk in neighborhood . . . hair dark as witness' hair . . . very dark . full face . . . high cheek bones . . . chin bowed a little over . . . not much . . . big mouth . . . old Mrs. Bender never talked English . . . Benders came first to witness' place . . . Benders settled on claim northeast . . . were nearest neighbors northeast . . . Hill lived north

117

*and Frye lived east of witness' place . . . Benders came in Fall of
1870 . . . left Spring 1873 . . . lived as a family on their claim,
all together . . . first went southwest of witness' place . . . built
log house . . . lived in that one winter . . . in Spring moved to
the Bender house . . . John and Kate were talked of as brother
and sister . . . Benders lived on witness' place ten days when
they first came . . . could all talk German language . . . Mrs.
Bender was not a Yankee woman.*

Judge Webb requested both of the defendants to stand up.
He asked the witness, "Are either of these women the Benders?" Witness said:

*"They may be, but I will never believe it." Old Mrs. Bender
was a bigger woman than this old lady . . . think Benders came
from old country . . . John, Jr., might have been born in this
country . . . old man Bender said he had lived on the French line
and ran a bakery . . . they were not Americans . . . Mrs. Bender
was a taller woman than this old lady . . . Mrs. Bender was not
so fleshy . . . had higher cheek bones . . . longer face . . . might
be mistaken.*

The court took a recess until seven o'clock in the evening.
During that recess, those who were so very sure that Mrs. Griffith and Mrs Davis were the Bender women, were particularly
interested in discussing the testimony of Rudolph Brockmann.

With a sneer and an assumed wide look, they attempted to
recall those suspicions aroused against Mr. Brockmann by the
searching party with Colonel York, at the Bender place, when
Mr. Brockmann was repeatedly hanged to make him tell of
his supposed complicity in the Bender crimes. By insinuating
that he was an accomplice and by numerous innuendoes, it
was attempted to revive those suspicions, give them new life,
and thereby discredit his testimony. Through more than sixteen years, which had elapsed since that eventful day, those
suspicions had slumbered.

As a witness in Court, under oath, Mr. Brockmann had told
what he knew about the Benders and their doings, just as he
did in reply to the inquiries made by the members of that
searching party at the Bender place. He testified that he did
not believe that the two women under arrest and on trial were
the Bender woman. Mr. Brockmann had lived on his farm dur-

118

ing all these years and nothing had developed to establish any complicity on his part with the Bender crimes, nor to show that he was not a law abiding citizen. He had been called as a witness by the State, which was sufficient to guarantee that he was a truthful man and to be believed.

The evening session of the court was commenced promptly at 7 o'clock.

The Seventh witness was Dr. G. W. Gabriel of Oswego, Kansas:

Forty-seven years of age . . . resided in Labette County since 1871 . . . knew Bender place . . . Bender family composed of old man, old lady, John, Jr., and Kate . . . met all . . . met Mrs. Bender frequently when visiting family that lived near Benders, to treat patients . . . saw Kate at same place a time or two . . . would know them if had met them in this County . . . have seen these defendants in this court room . . . old lady resembles Mrs. Bender . . . she is fleshier and older . . . haven't met Bender women since 1872 or 1873 . . . say there is some resemblance . . . more in old lady than in younger . . . had conversation with Mrs. Bender and Kate . . . heard both talk . . . Mrs. Bender had German accent . . . she was German descent . . . nothing of German accent in voice of Kate . . . heard this old lady defendant talk here to-night . . . she didn't talk as broken as Mrs. Bender . . . only resemblance is in general appearance . . . Mrs. Bender was larger . . . Kate's hair was auburn, neither light nor dark . . . never saw Mrs. Bender except at two houses . . . saw Kate at Boyd's and think at Parsons . . . will not swear positively that the defendants are the Bender women . . . do say, there is a wonderful resemblance . . . never saw these women, only to-day, in the court room . . . Kate Bender claimed she could call up spirits and commune with them.

The eighth witness was Mrs. Dientz who had lived in Osage Township since 1871:

Remember Bender family . . . not acquainted . . . have seen the two younger members, John and Kate . . . she had auburn hair . . . very nice . . . done up in roll once and braided next time . . . girl of pretty good size . . . weight about one hundred and thirty pounds . . . about nineteen or twenty years old . . . light eyes . . . high cheek bones . . . common-sized nose, bent a little, not much . . . saw her three times . . . twice in house and once

119

with John, Jr., in wagon . . . younger defendant in countenance resembles Kate some, but her features are not like Kate . . . Kate had a mark on one of her cheeks up close to the eye . . . not a mole or wart . . . looked like it had been a burn . . . not large . . . Kate claimed she could call up spirits . . . wanted to call up spirit of my son . . . told her to let my folks alone, dead or alive.

The ninth witness was William Dick, who had resided in Labette County since 1870 and was seventy-two years old:

Lived in Oswego Township 1870 to 1873 . . . knew Benders well . . . lived three miles from the Bender place . . . been there frequently . . . met two man and two women . . . not much acquainted with women . . . herded cattle on prairie near Bender place . . . would recognize women if met them out from home . . . have seen these defendants . . . older one resembles Mrs. Bender . . . younger one resembles Kate some . . . could not describe Kate so well . . . it is my judgment that this old lady resembles Mrs. Bender some . . . could not swear positively that it is here . . . as to Kate cannot be positive . . . met Kate on horseback . . . saw her in Sunday-school at school house . . . old man Bender talked very broken English . . . we talked German . . . old lady said in German, she did not think they could run the place . . . did not think old lady could talk English."

Cross-examination by Judge Webb:

Lived three miles southeast of Benders . . . Monahan, Lindsay, and Linn lived near neighbors to Benders . . . nearer than witness . . . John, Jr., held claim north of old man Bender . . . no one lived on John's claim . . . west of Bender's Linn claimed the land . . . knew the men of Bender family . . . better than women . . . knew old Mrs. Bender better than Kate . . . never conversed with Kate . . . we nodded heads as we passed . . . men were there all the time but once, John, Jr., was away . . . traded a little at Benders . . . was waited on by old man Bender every time . . . saw Mrs. Bender but one time . . . am a Lancaster County, Pennsylvania Dutchman . . . learned German when at work for a German . . . couldn't decide whether old lady was a foreigner or not . . . old man Bender tole me he was a Hollander . . . John, Jr., tole me he was born in this country . . . this old lady defendant to-day when she had side view made me think of Mrs. Bender as I saw her stand in the door oat Bender place . . . should say

Mrs. Bender at that time weighed one hundred and thirty pounds . . . this old lady might not weigh quite so much . . . not much difference . . . Kate was fair complexioned . . . fine features . . . saw her once at home going about household duties . . . same girl I saw at Sunday-school . . . noticed no particular things about her . . . Kate was five-feet, two inches or thereabouts . . . weighed one hundred and twenty to one hundred and twenty-five pounds . . . sprightly, good looking lady . . . nicely, well proportioned . . . stood erect and walked lady like, sprightly.

On re-direct examination, at the request of the Prosecuting Attorney, the defendant, Mrs. Davis, stood up. Witness said her height was just the same as Kate Bender.

The State recalled C. W. Booth to the stand and he said that the last he saw Kate Bender was at the party at Big Hill:

First saw these defendants since dinner to-day . . . was in Oswego last time before to-day at June term of Court . . . have not been here for thirty days.

The Tenth witness was Maurice Sparks, who lived in Osage Township at the time of the discovery and exhuming of the bodies on the Bender place:

Not much acquainted with Benders . . . especially women . . . saw women about place . . . remember general appearance . . . old lady Bender seemed to be fifty years old . . . some grey . . . slender of build . . . rather broad across the shoulders . . . hair had been dark . . . some grey . . . medium height . . . Kate was not very tall . . . medium size . . . square, blocky girl . . . stout build . . . round face . . . auburn hair . . . never spoke to her . . . observed these defendants here in court room to-day . . . resemble some parties I have seen . . . don't think Mrs. Bender was so full in face as the older defendant . . . can't form an opinion at to Kate . . . if there is any resemblance, younger defendant looks like Mrs. Bender . . . older defendant's hair is as I remember Mrs. Bender's hair . . . Kate at home was dressed cheap and plain . . . at church she was well dressed . . . don't remember any particular mark or feature by which I could recognize her . . . was sprightly, active girl . . . hair kind of auburn . . . between light and dark . . . am not positive about hair . . . observation of Kate was general . . . have seen her at Bender house . . . pass along road . . . at church in schoolhouse . . . she was about twenty years of age . . . there was a mark on Kate's face on the cheek . . . a kind of mole . . . cannot locate it . . . was not sunken . . . if anything, projected a little . . . think it was on the left cheek . . . could not say that seeing scar on this defendant's eye does enable me to say more definitely where Kate's scar was . . . Benders were there something over a year after my return . . . I lived about one mile southwest from them . . . Brockmann lived between my place and Benders . . . I had been away about a year . . . returned in Spring . . . they were living there when I returned . . . they left in April 1873, or about that time . . . may be I lived by them for two years . . . know young John better than the others . . . have seen Mrs. Bender at home twice or three times.

It was nearing midnight when the testimony of Sparks was completed, and the Court took recess until Tuesday, the 19th of November, 1889, at eight o'clock in the morning. Promptly at that hour, the Court convened, ready to proceed with hearing witnesses offered by the State.

The second day of this hearing attracted a great deal of attention. The Court room was packed with ladies and gentlemen as an audience. Mrs. Griffith retained her serenity, but would wince a trifle and her mouth would twist, when witnesses pointed at her and were positive in their statements that she was old Mrs. Bender. Mrs. Davis frequently gave vent to her feelings in a flood of tears. Her baby, bright-eyed and flaxen-haired, was at her side and about her knees constantly, and nursed the mother's breast at regular intervals during the proceedings in full view of the audience.

Mrs. McCann occupied a seat within the bar, close to the Prosecuting Attorney and took careful notes of the proceedings for future use in the prosecution of her search for the murderers of her father. She was a slightly built woman, not weighing over ninety-five pounds, had large, penetrating grey eyes, prominent chin, which showed her to be a woman of determination. During the progress of the hearing, her features remained passive, no matter what turn the evidence would take.

The first witness called for the State on Tuesday morning, and the eleventh that the State offered in the hearing, was Leroy F. Dick:

122

Reside now in Parsons, Kansas . . . resided in Labette County township twenty-one years . . . lived in center of Osage Township 1871 to 1874 . . . was a married man at that time and Township Trustee . . . knew Bender place . . . lived four miles from it . . . knew Bender family well . . . better acquainted with men folks . . . met them at elections . . . tried to "swap" horses with them one time in the timber . . . met Kate at Sunday-school . . . old lady Bender came to meeting . . . have seen all of them at home . . . my acquaintance was such that I would recognize them any time . . . remember them now as they were then . . . country was sparsely settled and new . . . all who lived within ten miles of each other were neighbors . . . several things about Kate would attract attention . . . form . . . looks . . . fact that she was a spiritualist . . . have seen both women at home, twice . . . nothing particular to attract attention . . . was present when bodies at Bender place were exhumed . . . Bender's absence was discovered on Sabbath . . . went there myself Monday morning . . . did not remain all day . . . made a hasty disposition of the stock.

Witness here prepared a pencil diagram of the Bender premises:

Had conversation with Benders . . . not with women . . . have heard them talk to each other . . . old lady talked German and English . . . she had German accent . . . have talked with this old lady defendant in German . . . said to her, "Kann ich nicht verkaufen?" . . . she replied, "Das kann du nicht " . . . interpreted it means, "Can I sell you?" . . . "That you cannot do." . . . Have seen these defendants often . . . saw them at Berrien Springs, Michigan . . . they did not know what I was there for . . . later I asked them to tell me where they lived during 1871 to 1875 . . . they told me many places . . . younger defendant, in her testimony in Michigan, said this old lady is not her mother . . . that she was the veritable old Mrs. Bender . . . I would recognize the Benders were I to see them . . . defendants are old Mrs. Bender and Kate . . . in private conversation younger defendant she told me old lady was old Mrs. Mark . . . that younger defendant was her step-daughter . . . told me history of old lady . . . said she is old Mrs. Bender . . . told me that in Michigan and on way here . . . Kate Bender had small wart or mole under her eye . . . my recollection is it was under left eye . . . saw it at a singing of mine . . . witness described finding of mutilated bod-

123

ies of Bender victims and their appearance . . . gave detailed description of Bender house, cellar, and garden, and orchard where victims were buried . . . heads of all, except little girl, were badly crushed by blows from hammers of different sizes . . . found three hammers . . . a Collier weighing six pounds . . . an Alsatian shoe-hammer and common small hammer . . . have all these hammers and a clock.

Cross-examination by Judge Webb:

Kate Bender had auburn hair . . . between light and dark . . . eyes between hazel and blue . . . was between nineteen and twenty-one years of age . . . shoulders square and thrown back . . . step, quick and sprightly . . . talked freely . . . large mouth . . . heavy lips, slightly pouting . . . perfect teeth . . . very bright . . . height five-feet, two to five inches . . . old lady Bender I saw as she and Kate were standing in door . . . saw her twice in 1871 . . . think I saw her at meeting in Spring, 1872 . . . twice after that at the Bender house . . . she had German accent . . . have now in my mind how Bender woman looked them.

Witness was asked to look at defendants, which he did, and said:

They are Mrs. Bender and Kate Bender, I have no doubt as to them . . . Mrs. Davis told me in Michigan that she is step-daughter of Mrs. Monroe . . . Mrs. Davis told me this is the veritable old lady Bender and that she would always so testify, when permitted to do so . . . Kate had no mark or mole under her left eye . . . see Mrs. Davis has one under her left eye . . . Went to Michigan to see the women alleged to be Bender women . . . picture of women saw on Bender farm that I knew resembled closely women here now . . . from features and countenance would say they were one and same . . . In Michigan old lady defendant said she thought she had seen me somewhere . . . Eliza said she had, too . . . old lady gave me a wink and wished to know if I would talk with her privately . . . she said, "Before God, if there was a Kate Bender, Mrs. Davis certainly was." . . . Had been married several times . . . first to Van Alstein . . . afterwards to Mark McCann . . . she had read of Bender outrages . . . how they buried dead in orchard . . . that I occurred near Cherryvale in southern Kansas . . . afterwards had long conversation with Mrs. Davis . . . she told me Mrs. Monroe

124

was old Mrs. Bender.

The Prosecuting Attorney, Mr. Morrison, here announced, "State rests."

The testimony of Leroy F. Dick was the most important presented by the State, and was the most damaging to the defendants.

Mrs. Griffith had the keenest realization of this fact. Several times she rose to her feet, muttered in a low tone her denunciation of what she termed the false statements Dick was making in his testimony. Especially did she give indignant expression when Dick gave the conversation between himself and her in German. She did not understand German and could not speak it. Dick had clearly sworn false about her in that matter and she was furious. To the audience her mutterings were unintelligible, and the uninformed were certain that it was evidence of her guilt.

Once only, and that was when Maurice Sparks gave evidence of the mark under the left eye, did Mrs. Davis show the awful effect the identification had on her. She winced, the color mounted to her cheeks, and her eyes filled with tears repeatedly. Many were sure that this was evidence that she really was Kate Bender.

The little child played around as if nothing was being done. It knew not, fortunately for it, that identification of the mother as Kate Bender, meant prison for life, possibly death on the gallows for the mother, and for this little one a home in an alms-house, where two of the children of Mrs. Davis had been placed in Michigan since she had been arrested and brought to Kansas and placed in jail. Or that, perchance, it meant a life in an orphanage somewhere, and being brought up as had been Mrs. McCann, the cause of all of the trouble for these defendants since the Bender Idea hatched.

The testimony of Leroy F. Dick, as given in this case will not bear analysis by the trained legal mind. It satisfied the minds of the majority of the people who wee in Court and heard it and it was sufficient for the Prosecuting Attorney to convince the minds of three Justices of the Peace and to get the defendants held to the District Court for trial on the charge. The Prosecuting Attorneys in their desire to be successful in a case too often secure such results, not giving evidence the analysis which all trial lawyers, with skilled minds should, and usually do.

The defense was begun by calling as the first witness Thomas Jeans, a resident of Labette County, living in Osage Township during the time that the Benders were at Bender house. He lived less than three-fourths of a mile southeast of the Bender place:

Fifty-six years of age . . . knew Benders when building frame house . . . four in family . . . old man, old lady, John, Jr., and Kate . . . knew all when saw them . . . lived in neighborhood all time they lived there . . . often at Bender place . . . saw all together one Sunday . . . another time saw old man, old lady, and Kate there . . . sold them wood all the time they lived there . . . when they got acquainted with anyone they stuck to that one . . . was at Benders perhaps a dozen times . . . saw Kate at old man Hill's . . . would recognize women when met them . . . old man Bender was about sixty years old . . . John, Jr., twenty-five to twenty-six . . . old lady fifty to sixty . . . Kate about twenty-one or twenty-two . . . very fair . . . fair skin . . . dark-red hair . . . five-feet, four or five inches tall . . . believe would know her if see her now . . . believe would know old lady Bender . . . old man Bender was very rough . . . observed these defendants . . . talked with them . . . old lady Bender talked language I could not understand . . . don't recognize the voice of these defendants as any one I ever knew . . . can understand this old lady defendant . . . old lady Bender was too Dutchy for me . . . never saw either of these defendants before I saw them at Lansing . . . upon my best judgment, don't think either of these defendants are the Bender women.

Cross-examination by Prosecuting Attorney Morrison for State:

Kate was medium sized girl . . . stood up straight . . . talked similar to other girls . . . dark-red hair . . . think her eyes were blue . . . fair complexion . . . five-feet four or five inches tall . . . about average height of women . . . old lady Bender was a little old woman . . . under ordinary height . . . quite small.

Re-direct examination:

Never had any conversation with Kate . . . heard her talking with Mrs. King . . . have used spectacles for fine sight five or six

126

years . . . before that my sight was good.

The second witness for the defense was Silas Toles, of
Peru, in Chautauqua County, Kansas:

*Lived in Osage Township, Labette County, 1871 to 1879 . . .
knew Bender place . . . lived about half mile from Bender house .
. . Benders there when I went there to live . . . was near them
eighteen month . . . knew family well . . . never spoke with old
lady Bender . . . went to Bender store with my brother for groceries . . . saw John, Jr., . . . Kate and old lady . . . living so close
often passed there . . . saw Kate and John as they came from
camp-meeting ground in 1872 . . . Saturday afternoon . . . had
long conversation . . . frequently saw Kate and old lady as
passed house . . . Kate had light blue eyes . . . light hair . . .
sandy order . . . slight build . . . five-feet two inches tall . . . old
lady dark hair and eyes . . . maybe hair little grey . . . she was
slender . . . from acquaintance at that time think would recognize them . . . they may have changed some . . . it is my judgment I would recognize them . . . have seen and talked with defendants . . . examined them with view to identify them . . . it is
my judgment that these defendants are not the Benders.*

Cross-examination by Prosecuting Attorney Morrison:

*Am forty-nine . . . was present at discovery of bodies . . .
with Liam Pierce first discovered condition of Bender premises
after they left . . . had not been near for some time before this
discovery . . . had only two conversations with Kate.*

The Court took a recess until one o'clock in the afternoon.
When the Court convened after recess, Silas Toles was on the
stand for further cross-examination and the Prosecuting Attorney showed him two letters:

*Witness admitted that the handwriting was his . . . had two
conversations with Kate Bender . . . can't tell how often he saw
her when he didn't converse with her.*

The third witness for defense was Mrs. Vesta Green:

*Reside in Oswego . . . lived in Shiloh Township, Neosho
County, Kansas, before came here . . . was acquainted with a few*

persons in Osage Township, Labette County . . . know where the Bender place is located . . . have been at that place . . . was there in 1871 . . . was in house three times . . . took dinner there . . . was perhaps five or six months between my visits . . . was there twice on month . . . four members in the family . . . have conversed with Bender women each time was there . . . never saw them anywhere else . . . two man and two women . . . girl's name Kate . . . boy, John, Jr., . . . think remember how Kate looked . . . was twenty . . . had auburn hair . . . medium height . . . freckled face . . . old lady Bender tried to talk to me . . . could not understand her . . . thought she was German by her talk . . . when bodies were discovered I was in Illinois . . . stopped there two or three years . . . think would be able to recognize the women . . . especially old lady . . . her eyes were close together . . . too close to look nice . . . they were particularly peculiar in appearance . . . it is a long time since I saw them . . . think would know them . . . have seen defendants . . . once before the come into court room . . . have talked to them . . . do not recognize in them either of the Benders . . . think these defendants are not same women I saw as Benders.

Cross-examination by Prosecuting Attorney Morrison:

They do not look like the Benders . . . old lady Bender was German . . . this woman is a Yankee . . . saw defendants next day after they came . . . went on my own responsibility . . . was in DeKalb County, Illinois, at time of publication of Bender crimes . . . had been there only short time . . . went once to Cherryvale . . . twice to Independence when we stopped at Benders . . . old Mrs. Bender tried to talk English but could not understand her . . . she was fifty-five or sixty . . . eyes close together . . . grey hair . . . Kate had auburn hair, between red and brown.

Mr. Morrison asked witness to tell just what she meant by auburn. Witness pointed to Mr. James, one of the attorneys for the defense, and said his mustache was auburn as witness meant by that color.

Kate was of good form . . . round, full face . . . nice looking . . . talked some with defendants at Lawson's house . . . remained ten minutes, told them if they were Benders they must know me . . . said they did not know me.

128

Re-direct examination:

Only two rooms in Bender house that witness observed . . . canvas partition.

The fourth witness for the defense was Dr. E. W. Wright:

Practicing physician . . . reside in Oswego . . . lived in La-bette County twenty-two years . . . Oswego been home . . . know geography of the County well . . . was here when bodies of murdered persons were exhumed . . . 1872 lady came to my office to get medicine for chills . . . was told she was Kate Bender . . . she was here ostensibly to lecture . . . was of sandy complexion . . . five-feet four or five inches tall . . . high cheek bones . . . in my office in 1872 as near as I can recollect . . . younger defendant is not Kate Bender . . . Kate Bender was taller than this defendant . . . defendant is not the woman who called at my office as I think.

The fifth witness for the defense was H. G. Miller of Cherryvale:

Lived there over a year . . . before that at Oswego ten or twelve years . . . knew Bender place . . . have been there several times . . . saw members of family when I stopped to buy things as passed . . . have seen two old people and two young people . . . old man, old woman, young man and young woman . . . can't say ever heard either talk . . . can't describe either woman . . . can't recognize either of those women in defendants.

The sixth witness for the defense was A. Stewart of Coffey County, Kansas:

Was in law business 1871, 1872, 1873 . . . passed through Labette County . . . stopped at Bender house four times . . . met old gentleman, old lady, and girl . . . old woman called her daughter . . . think saw enough of old lady to describe her . . . came into court room out of curiosity to see the Benders . . . as to younger women, can't say . . . old lady is older then Mrs. Bender was then . . . never saw two parties resemble more than this old lady and Mrs. Bender . . . don't know whether was there

129

in 1873 . . . was there in 1872 . . . took dinner . . . thought Benders were out of existence . . . other times just stopped . . . bought some things . . . talked with old woman . . . Mrs. Bender talked considerably broken.

Cross-examination by Judge Atchinson for State:

Can't swear was there any time in 1873 . . . am very poor on time and name . . . think was there in Fall of 1872 . . . old man Bender looked older than old lady . . . she was about my age . . . German's age hard to tell . . . think if she were living would be about sixty-five or seventy . . . call her German from her talk . . . thought she was German . . . told old lady the girl was not her child as she was not German . . . can't remember that girl was called Kate . . . can't say that I said anything to girl . . . don't think ever passed Bender place before 1872 . . . passed twice . . . was there four times . . . first time stopped and watered horses . . . went to door to go in . . . saw only old lady and gentleman . . . can't say what time in year . . . second time about month later . . . first time was going southwest . . . second time coming back . . . third time coming from Parsons . . . old lady there every time . . . girl once . . . all four once . . . old man talked broken . . . more so than old lady . . . if old lady was here to-day would be seventy years old . . . was rather heavy set . . . stout woman . . . hair turning . . . didn't think there was such a things as the Bender women now . . . old lady Bender didn't speak plain English . . . her German tongue was natural . . . it was not put on . . . this woman is more fleshy . . . has whiter hair than Mrs. Bender5 . . . am not swearing that this old lady is Mrs. Bender.

The old lady defendant was requested to talk with witness which she did in open court for several minutes. After having the conversation with the defendant the witness said, "This woman does not talk as broken as Mrs. Bender did."

Re-examination by Judge Webb:

Having heard this woman talk I think it is different from what it was then . . . this woman has not the broken accent that Mrs. Bender had . . . otherwise there is a similarity.

Re-cross-examination by Prosecuting Attorney Morrison:

Germans talk all English at home with families and learn it thoroughly . . . those without children do not improve.

Mrs. Elmira Griffith (Monroe) was called as seventh witness for defense, and on her own behalf she testified as follows:

Name is Elmira Griffith . . . maiden name Elmira Hill . . . father George Hill . . . he was born on Long Island in 1790 . . . mother Charlotte Hill . . . maiden name Charlotte Marshal . . . was born in Rhode Island in 1800 . . . I was born Saw Mill Run, Little Valley, Cattaraugas County, New York in 1821 . . . married Simon Mark, a Frenchman, December 21, 1839 . . . at my place of birth . . . had by him twelve children . . . James N., Simon, Charles, Caroline Elizabeth, Sarah Eliza, Mary Ann, William Henry, Rosette, Emmett A., Elsie Adeline, Myron A., and Myra A. . . . Simon Mark died February 13, 1866 . . . had three brothers, John, Marshall, and Washington, and four sisters, Cornelia, Louisa, Mahala, and Dority.

Cross-examination by Prosecuting Attorney Morrison:

Had two names . . . Mark and Van Alstein . . . never had name Flickinger . . . never knew Peter Flickinger . . . never testified how many times was married . . . never married Bartlett . . . he boarded with me in 1867 . . . was a widow with family . . . Mark was dead . . . am sixty-eight . . . married Van Alstein when seventeen . . . was divorced rom him in Cattaraugas County, New York . . . he had wife . . . married Simon Mark . . . lived with him until his death at Portland, Michigan in 1866 . . . Ionia County . . . married Monroe at Carlton, Michigan in 1872 . . . lived in Michigan from 1866 to 1874 . . . March 1869 went to National Hotel, Ionia, Michigan . . . remained four weeks . . . April, went to Hardcastle, six miles north of Milwaukee, Saginaw County, Michigan . . . at once took my mother to Hancock City . . . lived in McFadden's house three months . . . last of July moved to St. Charles, Saginaw County, Michigan . . . lived in Mr. Howe's house one year and five months . . . December, 1870 moved to Grass Lake, Michigan . . . lived in house for which Mr. Nicholson was agent ten months . . . moved to Saginaw in October, 1871 . . . rented Louis Gonsinmonger's house in Colton, a suburb . . . lived there until October 1872 . . .

131

married Josiah Monroe here . . . went with him to Berlin, Michigan . . . remained about four weeks . . . Monroe's first wife appeared . . . left Monroe went to Tekousha, Calhoun County, Michigan . . . lived at Tekousha until April 1874 . . . went to my sister at Martinsville, Ohio . . . remained until September 1874 . . . went to concord, Michigan . . . live in Mr. Ink's house through horn-husking . . . about November, 1874, moved to Saginaw . . . rented George Munger's house of his nephew, Hiram Yakel, his agent . . . house stands close to lutheran church . . . lived in that house until April 1876 . . . moved to Claflin's house on Genesse Street, East Saginaw . . . remained four weeks . . . May 1876 went to my brother at Hardscrabble, Michigan . . . he was an old man . . . went to take care of him . . . remained until July . . . moved to Dundee, Michigan . . . remained until November . . . moved to Niles, Michigan and have lived there ever since . . . married William Stephen Griffith at Howard City, Michigan, Montcalm County, July 3, 1880 . . . lived together until May 1882 . . . he left in search of work . . . he went to Illinois . . . has never returned . . . went Illinois myself in 1866 . . . to Aurora . . . went to look for my daughter, Rosa . . . never had a Kate in my family . . . can't even talk German . . . can't under-stand it . . . had no conversation with Leroy F. Dick in German . . . never knew any of the Dick family . . . never saw any of them until met him in Niles, Michigan . . . never had a Dutch husband . . . had not connection whatever with old man Bender . . . do not understand the "goose language" that Dick told about . . . was in Detroit House of Correction for commit-ting an abortion . . . the other defendant in this case is my daughter Sarah Eliza Davis . . . she is not Kate Bender.

Sarah Eliza Davis was called as the eighth witness for de-fense, and on her own behalf testified as follows:

Was born June, 1845 . . . maiden name Mark . . . earliest re-collections are of Cattaraugas County, New York . . . married man by name of Japhet at Salmonca in 1868 . . . he worked for Morrison . . . first kept house at Port Crissen in 1871 . . . lived at Salmonca, 1869 . . . than at lumber camp . . . husband worked in mill of Walter Hume . . . went to Wild Fowl Bay 1872 . . . he worked for same company, Mr. Hume . . . on farm from Spring to 1872 to Fall, 1873 . . . he chopped cord-wood for George Taylor from October 1873 to April '74 . . . moved to Caro, Buscola County . . . was there until May 1896 . . . went to Oran,

Oakland County, Michigan . . . worked on farm there . . . he changed hame to Hiram Johnson when we came to Michigan . . . remained until Spring, 1876 . . . went to my mother at Dundee . . . was divorced from my husband at Pontiac, Michigan, September, 1876 . . . remained with mother at Dundee until last October or first of November 1876 . . . we moved to Niles . . . lived with mother there until Fall 1877 . . . mother has made her home in Niles ever since we moved there . . . went to Battle Creek, March, 1877 . . . lived in J. H. Wuldo's house . . . moved to Bellevue, Eaton County, Michigan July 1877 . . . married Levi B. Madison at Belleview, July 23, 1877 . . . by Justice Bouton . . . went to Madison's farm to live . . . was there until Fall . . . he traded for farm in Cedar County, Missouri . . . he went there and remained until Summer 1878 . . . I went to Missouri, June, 1878 . . . stayed on farm there seven months . . . we went to Elmore, Michigan . . . I began washing . . . my husband was sick . . . could do nothing . . . lived at Elmore two years . . . in David Jones' house . . . moved to Jackson, Michigan . . . washed to maintain family . . . worked in Weaver Laundry by the day . . . my husband died in 1882 . . . remained at work until 1884 . . . moved to McPherson, Kansas, left Michigan February 1884 . . . remained at McPherson two years and five months . . . returned to Michigan, July 1886 . . . washed by day in McPherson . . . was mother of three living children.Gussie May, Lillie Elmira, and Freddie Albers . . . children went with me to Adrian, Michigan . . . remained until February 1887 . . . went to Emporia, Kansas . . . John Feenay went with me and children to Emporia . . . had married him at McPherson . . . went to Quincy, Illinois, September 1888 . . . went to Jackson, Michigan, with my four children, February 2889 . . . this child is mine by Feenay . . . was two years old May 12th . . . Feenay was brought home dead while we lived at Emporia . . . went to St. Johns, June 1889 . . . went to Lansing, July 1889 . . . was larger place . . . Hoped to get more work . . . September 1889 went to Niles on telegram that mother was about to die . . . returned in four days . . . was arrested on charge of larceny soon after . . . taken before magistrate and discharged . . . then was arrested as Kate Bender . . . have been in jail and custody of officer ever since . . . married James Davis in Mason, Michigan, August 12, 1889 . . . was arrested about middle of September . . . Davis was at Lansing when I came away . . . he is a stonecutter . . . is thirty-nine years old . . . has refused to live with me, or support me, until this charge is cleared up . . . have three living children in Poor House at Berrien County, Michigan . . . they were never a

133

*charge upon the public until since my arrest . . . have no know-
ledge of the German language . . . never had the name Bender . .
. I am not Kate Bender . . . I never said my mother was old Mrs.
Bender . . . I did say that if she would have her daughter arrested, she would be none too good to be old Mrs. Bender . . . In the
name of God, I say I never bore the name of Kate Bender and I
am not one of the Bender family.*

There was no cross-examination of Mrs. Davis by counsel
for the State. Upon completion of Mrs. Davis' testimony the
defense rested.

Prosecuting Attorney Morrison for the State in rebuttal,
offered in evidence a letter from Silas Toles to Mrs. McCann
about aiding her to identify the Benders which without objection was read. This closed the case so far as evidence for
either party was to be considered. It was five o'clock in the afternoon of November 19, 1889. The arguments of counsel
were then begun by Judge Atchinson for the State. He was followed by Judge Webb and J. T. James for the defense. Prosecuting Attorney Morrison closed for the State. Two hours was
given to the discussion of the case by respective counsel.

The court room was packed with an eager populace, waiting breathlessly and anxiously for the decision. The three
Justices had a long conference and then Justice Kiersey announced the decision, which was that the evidence was sufficient to identify the defendants as the Benders, and to justify
their being held for trial in the District Court of Labette
County, Kansas upon the charge of having murdered Dr. William H. York.

Accordingly, they were held without bail for that murder
and committed by the Court to the custody and keeping of the
Sheriff of Labette County, Kansas to await the further action
on the case in the District Court.

CHAPTER XVII.

After that preliminary hearing, the paramount inquiry
among the people of Labette County and elsewhere was, "Are
those women Mrs. Bender and her daughter, Kate Bender?"

To prove that Doctor York was murdered, and that the

134

Benders were his murderers, was not a hard or difficult thing to do. To prove that Mrs. Elmira Griffith was old Mrs. Bender and that Mrs. Sarah Eliza Davis was Kate Bender would be very difficult.

Many of the people in Labette County believed that the Benders were killed by the posse soon after the discovery of their horrible deeds nearly seven teen years before this preliminary hearing.

The feeling in favor of the defendants largely prevailed in the community. They were women, and there was that little girl. Labette County jail offered very uncomfortable quarters for the defendants who had been committed to the custody of the Sheriff, to be held for trial in the District Court, possibly at the February, 1890 term, which was several months after this commitment.

Many people became aroused and indignant about keeping the women and that little girl in such a place as was afforded in that jail. They gave decided expression to that opinion to the Sheriff. He was a very kind-hearted and sympathetic man, and to meet the situation and allay the feelings of the people in this matter, arrangements were made and the prisoners with that little girl were kept at the residence of Thomas Lawson.

Prosecuting Attorney Morrison and his associate in the case, Judge Atchinson, now became confident that these defendants were the Bender women and were determined to prosecute with all their ability notwithstanding the serious difficulty of identification with confronted them.

Judge Webb and J. T. James were certain that their clients were not the Bender women, but they fully realized the danger ahead of them, and the necessity for positive proof that they were not the Benders when the case would come before a jury for trial. With so many reputable and respectable citizens t4stifying that they were the Bender women, the State might get a verdict convicting their clients of that murder. They at once began to prepare for the hard legal battle now confronting them, and it was one of fact.

Mrs. McCann said that in all of her work bringing these women to Oswego as the Bender women, she had been guided solely by her intuitions, or impressions made on her mind by some mysterious influence. She had not seen her family for six months, but she certainly had followed her theory faith-

135

fully. She admitted that the confession which she had obtained from one of the defendants would not convict. She was, however, determined to find out and punish the murderer of her father, Mr. John W. Sanford.

If this little detective had not brought to Oswego old Mrs. Bender and her daughter, Kate, she had surely unearthed a family some of whom were criminals, guilty of crimes almost as atrocious as those which were committed by the Benders, provided the evidence and many statements of Sarah Eliza Davis were to have full credence.

Mrs. McCann had made up her mind that the influence had guided her aright, and if every old settler and former neighbor of the Benders had sworn that the defendants wee not the Bender women and looked nothing like them, she would yet insist that she could not be mistaken. It has been said of her that she had more determination concealed about her small body than was usually vouchsafed to a whole community of women.

Leroy F. Dick, the special Deputy Sheriff, who had brought these defendants to Oswego from Michigan, was confident that the Bender women were in custody. He was a neighbor of the Benders when they lived in Labette County, and knew the Bender women personally. He was certain that these were the identical Mrs. Bender and her daughter Kate Bender. He said that their testimony in the preliminary hearing at Oswego did not correspond with the story told on the trial of Mrs. Davis for larceny at Niles, Michigan. He had heard the old lady defendant tell two or three different stories. In making investigation he visited towns where the old lady told him that she had lived during the time the Benders were committing the outrages in Labette County, and he found that she was mistaken. She had lived at those places at other times. He found that wherever she had been, she bore a hard name and he said she had been driven out of several communities.He said that Mrs. Davis testified in Niles that her mother had committed murders in Michigan. She said that at one time when she was a child of seven, her mother killed an old beggar woman with an ax-helve, who had made her angry. That in the night her mother hitched an old grey horse to a care, put the body of that woman in it, drove to a creek a few miles distant, tied a rock to the body, and sunk it in a deep hole. Mr. Dick found old residents, in his investigation of these facts, who remembered

136

that old grey horse and that cart.

Mrs. Griffith swore at Niles that she never had a German husband. When asked concerning one Flickinger, deceased, about whom Dick had learned in making his search for evidence to satisfy his mind that she was in fact old Mrs. Bender, she replied that she, " . . . had made a mash on so many in her time, that it was hard to remember them all."

Mr. Dick said that this Flickinger answered every description of old man Bender. That he is supposed to have committed suicide by drowning himself in Lake Michigan in the year 1884. He had followed closely the lives of both Mrs. Griffith and Mrs. Davis, and from his personal acquaintance with the Bender family, he asserted positively that eh right parties were under arrest and now held at Oswego as old Mrs. Bender and her daughter, Kate Bender.

The trained legal mind will not be very highly impressed by the work that Mr. Dick had done in this case as a detective and an officer for the State of Kansas.

CHAPTER XVIII.
New Phase in the Bender Case

A dispatch dated November 20, 1889, at East Saginaw, Michigan, threw some light on the history of Mrs. Davis. It read:

"A new phase in the Bender case has been developed. The sheriff of Oswego, Kansas, wrote a letter to the Sheriff of Huron County, Michigan, in behalf of the woman suspected at Kate Bender. In it he states that she alleges she lived at Wild Fowl Bay, now known as Bayport, with her husband in 1873 and 1874. She gives her husband's name as Hiram Johnson. On investigation, the Sheriff found the incidents mentioned by her, including her child's death and burial were corroborated by people now living at Bayport who state such a family did live there at that time."

A Mistake.

During the time that the defendants were in custody at Os-

137

wego, one of the papers in that town published the following article:

Mrs. Davis, now in custody in this city as the alleged Kate Bender, may not be the veritable Kate, but she is a "gay deceiver" all the same. Sometime since she informed her custodian that she was about to become a mother and it would be necessary to have an "outfit" suitable for the occasion. The kind hearted Sheriff at once procured an elegant wardrobe for the prospective heir, and everything passed along in the "even tenor of its way" until a few days ago, Dr. George S. Liggett was called in. His interview revealed the fact that Kate has no present need of "baby clothes" and was not likely to have while she remained in "durance vile." This was possibly a little scheme to enlist sympathy in her behalf, but she instituted proceedings a little too soon and it failed. If you mention the matter to Sheriff Wilson, do so at long range.

More Detective Work.

The Independence Reporter of Independence, Kansas, published an article entitled, "The Benders" while Mrs. Griffith and Mrs. Davis were held awaiting trial in the District Court at Oswego. It read as follows:

A mysterious stranger visited Independence last Friday, who seemed very much interested in regard to the Benders. He was anxious to talk with any old citizen, who might know the most about the Benders. He had been at work for some time, and had interviewed Rudolph Brockmann, the man who was hung by the Vigilantes on suspicion of being a confederate, and had also spent some time at Cherryvale in search of information. He was very reticent as to his object and could not be induced to tell any more about his business than was necessary.

He was particularly interested in learning everything possible about Shennowaldt6, the desperado, who attracted so much attention at Independence in old times by his boldness, stealing Sheriff Brock's horse when Brock was hunting him, and standing off with his gun persons who tried to arrest him. Just why he wanted to learn about this desperado he would not disclose, but intimated very closely that he was one of the

138

Bender Gang. He acted a good deal like a detective seeking on his own hook for evidence of the identity of the supposed Benders, with a view to securing a good slice of the large rewards offered for their apprehension.

It is very probable, unless something occurs to show that the suspect now under arrest are not the Benders, that the trial will prove exceedingly interesting. There will be a tremendous effort made by the State to identify and convict, while the defense will be able and determined. Between now and then, a good deal of close detective work will be done, and the occurrences of sixteen and seventeen years ago closely scrutinized.

After the preliminary hearing, and before the February, 1890, term of the District Court to be held at Oswego, the attorneys for both State and defense were making every investigation that could be made to secure evidence about the Benders as well as about these defendants. It was generally believed that large rewards were outstanding for the arrest and conviction of the Benders. The attorneys for the defense had detectives at work gathering evidence. The foregoing articles show that detectives were at work.

Old settlers who knew the Bender family not only did not identify either of these women as Bender women, but many wee outspoken in the belief that they were not the Benders. A prominent physician of Oswego declared that Mrs. Davis bore no resemblance whatever to Kate Bender. He also declared that Mrs. Bender was a German and that Mrs. Griffith was a typical New York Yankee; that there should be not doubt about it that she was not old Mrs. Bender.

The *Oswego Independent* contained the following:

HOPE GONE.

The Alleged Bender Women do Not Greet Any Labette County Acquaintances — Mrs. McCann, the Inspired Detective, Gets Revelations from the Wrong Spirits.

The Benders in town, is a dead topic with Oswego, and it is a lonesome few who entertain any hope that the suspects now under arrest, and held by the strong arm of the law, in Oswego, belong to that notorious Bender Family. No old residents have as yet been able to positively identify the prisoners, and a majority think there is no resemblance whatever to the famous family of butchers.

Said a prominent physician of Oswego to an *Independent* reporter: "Kate Bender was a slender woman, with red hair, fair complexion, high cheek bones, and a prominent nose. This women, alleged to be Kate, is a short, heavy set woman, with regular features, black hair, and very dark complexion. She bears no resemblance whatever to the festive Kate. Old Mrs. Bender was a German, could speak only broken English. The woman under arrest has every appearance of being a typical New York Yankee."

Popular sympathy goes for the women under arrest and there is but little doubt, that they will be discharged at their trial.

Very few of the old settlers who called to see Mrs. Griffith and Mrs. Davis as the Bender women, could see any resemblance whatever, and the others laughed at the idea that they were the Benders.

CHAPTER XIX.

Prosecuting Attorney Morrison had a very difficult place to fill, and was himself much in doubt about these women being the Benders.

The attorneys for the defense did much hard work to get the case ready for trial, which would probably be held at Oswego during the February, 1890, term of the District Court. The true situation for the defendants and the facts with which the attorneys for the defense were confronted and compelled to cope with are fully set forth in the following article which appeared in the *Oswego Independent* at that time:

CONFIDENT OF ACQUITTAL

"In a conversation with Mrs. Elmira Griffith and her daughter, Mrs. Eliza Davis, the two prisoners charged with being the Bender women, an *Independent* reporter finds them apparently confident that no semblance of evidence can be produced against them when they come to trial and that they will be cleared without delay. Mrs. Griffith has been ill for a couple of weeks, looks weak, and has lost some flesh, but is now convalescing."

"Mrs. Davis, the alleged Kate, while elated over her prospective freedom, is considerably depressed over her children, a boy and girl, aged respectively eight and ten years, whom she left behind in Niles, Michigan. She is afraid they will be put in the State Orphan Asylum, and forever taken from her reach. She said that her son, Charles Johnson of Bayport, Michigan, who is now twenty-three, will arrive in the city this week and stay with her until the close of the trial. He will bring with him affidavits showing his mother's marriage and her place of residence from 1869 to 1874. Also, a certificate showing the date of his birth. These affidavits, she said, will show that Mrs. Davis first lived in Canada, then Chautauqua County, New York, and afterwards moving to Ft. Crisen and Bayport, Michigan, living in these places up to the time of 1874."

"As the witnesses testified on the stand that Kate Bender was eighteen to twenty years of age, which would make her about thirty-five now, and as Mrs. Davis claims to be forty-five and had a son aged seven at the time Kate lived in this country, she regards this as a strong point to establish her innocence."

"The old lady Griffith, while there seems to be some delay in getting important testimony, is still of good cheer, and announces that she will have conclusive evidence to prove she was never west of Illinois until brought here for trial. She denounces Mr. Dick, the special officer, who arrested her on this charge, a scoundrel of the basest kind. She says that at Niles, Michigan, her son-in-law, Henry Hogue, offered to pay the expenses of herself and Dick, to travel around to the places where she had lived during the critical period of 1870 to 1874 but this officer refused to so, as she claims."

"Both women also assert positively that Dick did not visit these places on his own account to satisfy himself of the correctness of their statements, but they are evidently mistaken on this point, as Dick recited in his testimony the different places he had traveled in the hopes of finding something reliable about the careers of the women, his evidence showing that he failed to locate Mrs. Griffith during the time that the Bender outrages were committed in this County, although he claimed to have traced their whereabouts before and after this time."

141

"Mrs. Davis, the alleged Kate Bender, is a good talker and expresses herself well pleased with her treatment in Oswego. She was brought here with only one change of clothes, but this week she was given ten dollars to purchase necessary wearing apparel."

"Mrs. Davis showed the reporter a letter from their attorney, J. T. James, in which he tells them that he has secured a great deal of information and is daily getting more and says he will have the evidence necessary to prove they are not the Benders. He also tells Mrs. Davis not to fret about her children as they are being kindly cared for and that while she is being held prisoner, the authorities will not permit them to be removed. He suggests that they have no money as yet to secure important evidence so that it will be impossible to secure their release on Habeas Corpus proceedings."

The people were carefully considering the facts about the arrest of these defendants as the Benders, and holding them in custody for so long a time, and insisted upon knowing what was the basis for the action of the authorities in this case.

Declarations were made that these defendants were arrested without cause; that the charge made by Mrs. McCann was flimsy, based upon her dreams; that she had told a very weak story, a queer tale, on which to jeopardize the lives and liberty of these defendants. The expressed determination to hang these women, if possible, made by this woman detective, convinced people that there was malicious action, and it looked very much like persecution instead of legal and legitimate prosecution.

Mrs. McCann and Leroy F. Dick had been instrumental in having these defendants arrested in Michigan and brought to Oswego as the Bender women, and they were determined that the State should prosecute them as Benders. Together they were going about Labette County industriously working to arouse a public sentiment against these defendants.

Attorneys for the defense found their task of securing evidence and preparing the defense a very difficult one. Either the defendants were not able or not willing to tell one truth about themselves and their lives. Dates, events, and places when given would almost invariably be found to be erroneous.

It was not difficult to find people in Michigan who could testify as to where and when the defendants were living

142

among them and what events in their lives transpired from 1870 to 1874. But, invariably, it would be found to differ from what the defendants had told their attorneys and that made them double work. These defendants had lived very hard lives, and by some people it was said that they belonged to the criminal classes.

Attorneys, in preparing the defense had to sift the prejudice out of the facts presented to them, as obtained, and get to the truth about where they were living and what they were doing during the time the Benders were in Kansas, so as to be able to show that they were not in Kansas at that time and could not be Benders.

Both women had been married several times, had lost marriage certificates, and could not give proper dates, so they could not help the attorneys determine under what name they were known at various times and in different localities. Mrs. Griffith had married a man by the name of Shearer and was convicted and punished for manslaughter under that name. She either forgot that name or would not tell it to her attorneys. However, step by step, these attorneys unraveled the thread of their lives and secured information very much needed for the defense.

They secured official information by certified copies of records of the arrest, trial, conviction, sentencing, and commitment of Mrs. Elmira Griffith, under the name of Elmira Shearer, to the House of Correction at Detroit, Michigan, in April, 1872, and her receipt at that institution in May, 1872, and her discharge from it in March, 1873.

They also secured the testimony of a witness who saw her in that institution in October, 1872, and who identified Mrs. Griffith — the defendant alleged to be Mrs. Bender in the case pending at Oswego — as the woman who was committed and served in Detroit House of Corrections as Elmira Shearer from April, 1872, to March, 1873.

An alibi was thus established for the defendant, Mrs. Elmira Griffith.

143

George Evans Downer

Mrs. Frances McCann

Mrs. (Monroe) Griffith

Sarah Eliza Davis and Baby

CHAPTER XX.

The Statesman, published at Oswego, gave an account of the situation in the defense of these women at that time as follows:

"Mr. J. T. James, one of the counsel for the Benders, the two women alleged to be members of the Bender family, has been in the city this week. He has a pocket full of affidavits to prove that these women were living in Michigan during all the time that the Benders were committing those atrocious murders in this county."

"It is reported that the County Attorney is satisfied that it is a "gone case," but he has no power to order the discharge of the defendants until the case is called in the District Court, and no further proceedings will probably be taken until the meeting of that body. The court will convene on Tuesday, February 4, when the matter will be determined."

"The Statesman has believed from the first that this was a false alarm, and all developments so far tend to strengthen its conviction."

To get the depositions of witnesses residing in Michigan would require the expenditure of a large sum of money for both sides. The women had no money nor property. All expenditure on their behalf must be paid by their attorneys. The State had been at a very heavy outlay to arrest and bring the defendants from Michigan, keep them in custody, hold the Preliminary, and prepare the case for trial in District Court.

The taxpayers were complaining of the expense to the State of which the Prosecuting Attorney was informed, so he desired to expend just as little money as possible and faithfully perform his duty in the prosecution of the case.

It was agreed between the Prosecuting Attorney and attorneys for the defense to waive all formalities that could be legally waived and to make the money expenditure as small as possible. The attorneys for the defense were anxious that this should be done for the reason that they were paying hundreds of dollars in preparing the defense and were receiving nothing from any source on behalf of the defendants to meet that outlay.

It was agreed that affidavits should be considered in so far

148

as could be legally done, in lieu of depositions to be used as evidence. All affidavits when procured were first to be submitted to the Prosecuting Attorney, before any use would be made of them by counsel for defendants, and it was decided that they were to be admitted as evidence, then copies were to be furnished counsel for the State.

Attorneys for defendants submitted some affidavits to the Prosecuting Attorney, but they were not satisfactory to him and his reasons were given to the newspapers, for not permitting them to be used as evidence for the defense. These were published without the knowledge or consent of the attorneys for the defense.

The Oswego Independent published the following:

The Bender Women.

"J. T. James, of Kansas City, Mo., one of the counsel for the alleged Bender women, was in the city this week. He presented to Mr. Morrison, the County Attorney, affidavits of parties in Michigan, to prove an alibi for his clients."

"Maria Chapman of Berrien County, Michigan, avers that she saw and knew Mrs. Monroe during the Spring and Summer of 1873. That she lived in Michigan at that time."

"Myra A. Hogue of Niles, Michigan, alleges that she is the daughter of Mrs. Monroe and in a general way states that her mother lived in Michigan during the years 1870 to 1874, inclusive."

"The County Attorney could not dismiss the case upon such a showing, and very promptly informed Mr. James so."

"Mr. Morrison desires us to state that the report sent out from this city, to the *Kansas City Times*, that the long confinement, and excitement of the trial had affected the mind of Mrs. Monroe, is absolutely untrue. She is, perhaps, not the most amiable woman in the world, and does not get along with her daughter as pleasantly as might be desired, but she is perfectly sane and bears her confinement with Christian (?) fortitude."

"The statement also, that this case would be brought before the Grand Jury, is not correct. The case is already on the Criminal Docket of the District Court and the State will be ready for trial, unless the defendants should be discharged upon a writ of habeas corpus, which is not at all probable."

149

Another Oswego paper, the same week, contained the following:

The Bender Women Still in Custody

"J. T. James, of Kansas City, attorney for the women charged with being the Benders, was in the city this week, with affidavits concerning the lives of the Bender women."

"Mr. Morrison regards the evidence present not sufficient to warrant the discharge of the women. Unless evidence more convincing is presented to the County Attorney, the women will be tried at the February Term of the District Court. Mr. Morrison did say to Mr. James that at any time satisfactory proof be made that the prisoners are not the parties wanted, the State would be glad to discharge them and would not be technical with regard to how the testimony should be made, meaning that matters of form in taking the evidence would be waived."

"By their conflicting stories, the women do much to injure their case, if innocent, and make search for evidence perplexing and difficult. The change for Kate's acquittal is good and she had repeatedly said in private conversations that the old woman is as innocent as a new-born babe, and yet the reporter saw a letter this week, she had written to Governor Humphrey, asking him to intercede in her behalf, in which she states that her mother had at one time acknowledged that she was Mrs. Bender. She states in her letter that Mrs. Monroe told her that they escaped to No-Man's-Land in the Indian Territory, where they had a quarrel over the disposition of the money, a stocking full. That at night, the old man shot Jane, meaning Kate. That they went to Denver, where the men deserted her, leaving her penniless."

"Mrs. Davis, the alleged Kate, says that her mother wrote from this place, asking for money to come home, but that she had none to give her. If this evidence could be relied upon, it would be a strong point against the old lady."

"Mr. Morrison is very doubtful whether sufficient evidence can be gathered to prove the women guilty, but he feels it his duty to let a jury decide the question."

"The people were informed by a sensational dispatch sent to the *Kansas City Times*, the first of the week, that old Mrs.

150

Monroe had gone crazy, on account of worrying over the confinement and the awful crimes charged against her, but if she is insane, the attending physician has failed to discover it. She is a woman of nervous temperament and possessed of a violent tempter, and she has occasional "spells" that sometimes last two or three days, but if she loses her reason, it is only temporary."

The case was the most important one that was to be heard at the February, 1890, term of the District Court, and much interest was taken in it, not only in Labette County, but elsewhere in the State.

The *Star* and *Kansan* of Independence, Kansas, published the following:

"Among the cases that will come before Judge McCue, for trial at his first term of court in Labette County, is that of the State of Kansas against the alleged Benders. If the State makes any sort of a case, this will one of the most interesting trials that has taken place in Kansas, and will occupy, no doubt, a full month's time. The selection of a jury for this trial will prove to be no easy matter."

CHAPTER XXI.

Sheriff Wilson retired from office and was succeeded by the newly-elected sheriff, William Cook, on January 8, 1890, to whom was transferred the custody of the alleged Bender women. For some time, there had been ill feeling between Mrs. Griffith and Mrs. Davis, while they were held at the house of Tom Lawson. Sheriff Cook decided to get another place in which to keep these prisoners and arranged with Mr. and Mrs. Lawrence to keep and guard them. Mrs. Griffith informed Sheriff Cook that she feared Mrs. Davis would kill her. To make certain that nothing of that kind would be attempted, the sheriff had Mr. and Mr4s. Lawrence put Mrs. Griffith in one room and Mrs. Davis and her child in another, then to keep careful watch over them and see they did not get together. This was a wise move and insured no trouble with the prisoners.

151

The Prosecuting Attorney wrote the following letters:

Oswego, Kansas, Jan. 28, 1890.
Mr. J. T. James,
Kansas City.

Dear Sir: — It is my intention now to move in the Bender case at the earliest possible moment when Court convenes. Will have the Clerk send you a copy of information. Please govern yourself accordingly, as I want to dispose of this matter at the earliest possible moment.

Yours very truly,
J. H. MORRISON

Oswego, Kansas, Jan. 28, 1890.
Hon. H. G. Webb,
Parsons, Kansas.

Dear Judge: — I desire to move in the "Bender" case at the earliest possible moment after the Court convenes. My present impression is we will not want to try the Osborn case again. Will have the Clerk send you a copy of information in the Bender Case.

Yours very truly,
J. H. MORRISON

Upon this letter is written in Judge Webb's handwriting the following:

Mr. James: You better come so as to be on hand. I do not wish to act without consulting you.

H. G. WEBB

These letters, and a copy of the information, were received by J. T. James at Kansas City, MO., January 31, 1890. The information was in words and figures, as follows:

INFORMATION

State of Kansas) ss. In The District Court
County of Labette) For Said County
THE STATE OF KANSAS)
        Plaintiff,)
        vs.)
ELMIRA GRIFFITH, *alias*)
    Kate Bender, Sr., and)
SARAH ELIZA DAVIS, *alias*)
    Kate Bender, Jr.,)
        Defendants)

State of Kansas, Labette County, as:

I, J. H. Morrison, the undersigned, County Attorney of said County, in the name, and by the authority, and on behalf of the State of Kansas, come now here and give the Court to understand and be informed, that on the 25th, day of April, A.D., 1873, in said County of Labette and State of Kansas, Elmira Griffith, alias Kate Bender, Sr., and Sarah Eliza Davis, alias Kate Bender, Jr., did then and there unlawfully, feloniously, with force and arms in and upon one William York, willfully, deliberately, premeditatedly, and with malice aforethought, make an assault; and said Elmira Griffith, alias Kate Bender, Sr., and the said Sarah E. Davis, alias Kate Bender, Jr., did then and there with a certain heavy iron hammer, a deadly weapon held in the hands of one John Bender, Sr., aided and abetted and assisted by the said Elmira Griffith alias Kate Bender, Sr., and the said Sarah E. Davis alias Kate Bender, Jr., purposely, willfully, deliberately, premeditatedly, with malice afore thought, unlawfully and feloniously, with intent to kill and murder the said William York, then and there unlawfully, willfully, feloniously, purposely and of their deliberate and premeditatedly, did strike, thrust, then and there, giving to the said William York, with the heavy iron hammer aforesaid in and upon the head of him, the said William York, one mortal wound, of which said mortal would, he, the said William York, then and there instantly died; and the said Elmira Griffith alias Kate Bender, Sr., and the said Sarah E. Davis alias Kate Bender, Jr., did then and there in the manner aforesaid, unlawfully, feloniously, purposely, and of deliberate and premeditated malice kill and murder the said William York.

Contrary to the form of the Statute in such case made and provided, and against the peace and dignity of the State of Kansas. J. H. MORRISON
County Attorney

State of Kansas, County of Labette, as:
I, J. H. Morrison, being duly sworn on oath, say that I am County Attorney of said Labette County, in the State of Kansas, and that the allegations set forth in the within Information are true, to the best of my knowledge and belief. So help me God. J. H. MORRISON.
(SEAL)
Subscribed in my presence and sworn to before me by J. H. Morrison, County Attorney, this 30th day of January, A.D. 1890. COLIN HODGE.
Clerk of the District Court.

No. 925
State of Kansas, *Plaintiff.*
vs.
Elmira Griffith *alias* Kate Bender, Sr.,, *et al.*

INFORMATION
A True Bill
Files January, 1890, Clerk of District Court.
Witnesses: L. F. Dick, William Dick, J. H. Hanley, Delia Dick, T. B. Smith, Delia Keck, G. W. Gabriel, Joseph Story, C. W. Booth, Morris Sparks, David Monahan, William Clair, Martin Shive, Chris Apeck, J.P. Carpenter, Geo. Frease, Frances McCann, E. D. Kiersey.

Upon the back of this copy is written:

Received by mail, Jany., 31, '90 at 10:30 a.m.
Attest: J.T. James
D.M. Gurnea Attorney

Another letter:

Oswego, Kansas, Jan. 30, 1890.
J. T. James, Esq.
Kansas City.

Dear Sir:
I see I am quoted in the newspapers as agreeing to admit your "affidavits" upon the trial of the alleged Benders.
I do not want any mistake about this. I did not so agree. I said they might go in for what they were worth in a *habeas corpus* proceeding.
Your were to get depositions of the parties you desired to use upon the trial — I said I would waive application to the Court, and would only ask reasonable notice of the time and place of taking them.

Yours very truly,
J. H. MORRISON

When the District Court convened at Oswego February 4, 1890, because the time of Judge McCue would be so taken up with holding Court at different places in his District, and the admission of the Attorneys for State and defense in the Bender case that it would take several weeks to try the case when it was taken up, the Court continued the Bender Case to the May, 1890, term of the Court to be held in Oswego, and the defendants remained in the custody of the Sheriff.

CHAPTER XXII.

During the months of February and March, 1890, the attorneys for the defendant, Elmira Griffith, secured certified copies of the Court records of Ionia County, Michigan, showing the arrest, arraignment, trial, conviction, sentencing, and committal to Detroit House of Correction, of Elmira Shearer on a charge of manslaughter. Also, the certified copies of the records of the House of Correction at Detroit, showing that she was received into that Institution on May 13, 1872, and was discharged from there on March 24, 1873. That record also showed that she was sixty-two years old, born in the State of

155

New York, and by occupation, was a housekeeper. Certified copies of the marriage certificates of Elmira Mark to Shearer, Griffith, and Monroe were also procured as evidence in the case.

The testimony of Mrs. John Garged, residing at Saginaw, Michigan, a daughter of Mrs. Griffith, was procured showing that while Mrs. Griffith was in the House of Correction at Detroit in 1872, during the month of October, Mrs. Garden visited her, that she Mrs. Shearer then in that institution and visited by Mrs. Garden, was the identical Mrs. Elmira Griffith held at Oswego, Kansas, as Kate Bender, Sr., and that she was not old Mrs. Bender, nor a member of the Bender family.

A writ of habeas corpus was taken out for her and upon its return, the District Judge was absent from Labette County and a hearing was had before the Judge of Probate Court of that County, in April, 1890. At that hearing, the certified copies of the records, testimony of Mrs. Garden, and the evidence of Mrs. Griffith, and Mrs. Davis, were presented for the consideration of the Court. Attorneys for both the State and defense made arguments.

The Judge fully considered the evidence and arguments in the case and upon the showing made was convinced, as was the Prosecuting Attorney, Mr. Morrison, that this defendant was not old Mrs. Bender. He made the order discharging Mrs. Elmira Griffith from the custody of the sheriff as being held without warrant and as the wrong person. After more than five months of prison life at Oswego, this old woman was now free, but without any means, far from friends and acquaintances, and there was no redress for her against any reliable or responsible source.

Prosecuting Attorney Morrison was now convinced that these women were not the Bender women. In the District Court, he dismissed the case against both of the defendants, and Sarah Eliza Davis, held as Kate Bender, Jr., was also discharged from custody.

The abnormal desire to be known as a notorious criminal and the unbridled tongue of Sarah Eliza Davis — whom one of the attorneys for the defense in his address to the Court said was the "colossal liar" of his experience in criminal practice — had caused these defendants all of this trouble, and laid the base for the enormous expense which had been made to arrest and prosecute them as the alleged Benders.

156

Having been held in Labette County as prisoners for more than five months, at an expense of many thousands of dollars to taxpayers, these women were set free, paupers in a land of strangers, far from home, relatives, friends, or acquaintances, unable to compensate their attorneys and without any means of support. The Labette County authorities instructed Sheriff Cook to purchase railroad tickets for them from Oswego to Niles, Michigan, which he did, and sent them over the M. K. & T. railroad via Parsons.

Mrs. Griffith told Sheriff Cook that she was afraid to travel with Mrs. Davis, because she believed Mrs. Davis would kill her. They would change trains at Parsons, Sheriff Cook arranged to have Mrs. Griffith taken secretly to a hotel at Parsons and kept until the next train. Mrs. Davis and her child went on the first train and Mrs. Griffith followed on the next train. They were thus separated and a tragedy avoided.

The people of Labette County were glad indeed when these defendants had departed from Oswego and the expense to taxpayers stopped.

A few weeks after Sheriff Cook had sent them away from Oswego, Mrs. Davis returned with three children and rented a house near the Lawrence residence. They lived there for some months. Mrs. Davis did washing to support them. They then left Oswego and have not been seen since.

At the time of their discharge from custody, Mrs. Griffith was nearly seventy years and Mrs. Davis almost forty-six years of age. Both have since deceased.

Many Benders have been located at different times in many places. Mrs. Griffith and Mrs. Davis were the only persons placed under arrest, by officers, identified by former neighbors, and taken to Labette County for trial.

CHAPTER XXIII.
The Benders Spirited Away.

Colonel Triplett believed the Benders were probably living at the time he gave this interview in 1889. When these women were in custody at Oswego, he said, "Perhaps singly, by confederates, through the Indian Nation, into Texas. That the family drifted to Leadville and started their "murder mill" there. In the early days of Leadville, it is a well known fact that many men were disappearing almost daily."

"Many of those so mysteriously spirited away were strangers from the East, staid businessmen, who's habits and associations were not such as to subject them to the ordinary claims of midnight assassination. The work look very like that of the Benders, and Leadville was, for a time, at least, their refuge."

"No man could have so exulted himself in the minds of the people of Kansas at that time, as by killing the Benders. They never met their fate in that way."

All of the Benders Returned to Michigan.

Leroy F. Dick said, "The Benders drove their team into the timber and left it tied to the wagon: that the team had eaten the wagon-bed nearly up and were almost perished when found: that the Benders bought tickets to Humboldt and went Southward, dived into two parties, and rounded up and came together at Denison, Texas. From thence into New Mexico, or the unpopulated country in Western Texas. They were followed, at every turn they made were discovered, but always too late to apprehend them. When they reached the Western wilds, all trace of them disappeared, and for several years it was lost. Finally, a clew was given by a lady, led to the suspicion that they had returned to Michigan."

The Benders Were Not Captured.

J. J. Johns located in Osage township during the year 1869, and lived there for twenty years. He was a neighbor of the Benders and a frequent visitor at the Bender house. Once when he called there, he was refused admittance. This aroused suspicion.

Mr. Johns was with Colonel York and the searching party on May 5, 1873, when the bodies were exhumed. He was a member of the Vigilance Committee. He joined the posse and went in pursuit of the Benders. He said: "They did not capture nor kill the Benders."

The Benders Were Killed.

George Evans Downer, a member of the Vigilance Committee, who lived at Independence, became one of the posse in pursuit of the Benders.

On his death-bed at Downer's Grove, Illinois, he made the statement that he was present, gun in hand, when father, mother, son, and daughter of the Bender family were sent to death by the posse. He said an oath was taken which has made the fate of the Benders a mystery during all of the years since they were killed. The Vigilance Committee of which Mr. Downer was a member was organized at Independence.

In those days of lawlessness in that county, such organization was the only means of keeping order and protecting life and property.

Several members of the Vigilance Committee besides Mr. Downer, were Colonel York at Bender house that day when the discoveries were made and the bodies of the victims exhumes.

The Benders Captured and Shot.

In the Fall of 1876, only three and a half years after the Bender house discoveries and disclosures, in a camp in New Mexico, near the Arizona line, a man on his death-bed made the following statement, "I was living in the State of Kansas, near the town of Cherryvale, at the time the Bender family escaped from their claim and the officers of the law. Forty-eight hours after they started for the South, I and six others, well mounted and armed, started at midnight in pursuit. We found that they had abandoned their team, which they first started with, and had taken up with a freighter going to the Sac and Fox Agency. The freighter was made acquainted with the circumstances. The Benders were taken one mile south-west of the ford and laid under the ground."

"Among their effects was found seven thousand dollars, which was divided into eight parts. The amount was a great surprise to all of us, and considering that we had done a great service to the country and community, we — each of us — there took a solemn oath, never to divulge any part or parcel of the night's work. Never give away any names of the parties that I now give to you."

The dying man then directed that his effects be sent to his

159

sister at Independence. His grave was made in a beautiful valley in the south-western part of New Mexico. There he sleeps his last long sleep. The names of those who formed that posse, which he gave, have never been made known by publication.

At the time the alleged Bender women were in the custody at Oswego in 1889, the statement was published that four of that posse were dead, one then lived in Seattle, and another was a prominent business and stock man at Sherman, Texas. The other one was still following the business of furnishing supplies to Indians and emigrants in the Southwest Territory.

The following dispatch was published as sent from Little Rock, Arkansas, November 4, 1889, "A gentleman who arrived here from New Mexico, stated that he was in possession of evidence to show that the notorious Bender family had all been killed and buried in the west end of the Cherokee Strip, their executioners being the party which started in pursuit immediately after the butcheries were discovered. The entire family was exterminated. L. T. Stephenson, a resident of Independence, and a member of the Vigilance Committee, became one of the posse which pursued and killed the Benders."He helped dig the graves in which the Benders were buried."

CHAPTER XXIV.

When Judge Webb and J. T. James had their first conference as the attorneys for the alleged Bender women, Judge Webb said: "They are not the Benders. We will have a long, hard fight, but we are defending innocent clients, in this case."

Judge Webb was a stranger to Mr. James, but the manner of his saying that they were not the Benders, indicated that he knew. Mr. James had left Minneapolis in the month of May, previous, and had been looking after some business in the Indian Territory, keeping a temporary office at Fort Smith, Arkansas. Upon a telegram received at Wagoner, he went direct to Oswego over the M. K. & T. Railway. It was the first time that he had seen either of the defendants, or had met Judge Webb and he had never heard of either of the defendants until the receipt of that telegram which was sent to him by a

160

former client.

Mr. James, in his law practice up to that date, had refused to defend any person on a murder charge, and before he would enter this case as one of the attorneys, he wanted to be sure that the women were not the Bender women. Colonel York, who was then living at Fort Scott, Kansas, not very far from Oswego, was not pushing the prosecution of this case and seemed to take no interest in it whatever. This was significant.

After a talk with some members of the posse, including the Captain, Mr. James became convinced that these were not the Bender women. With Judge Webb, he entered into the defense and the record tells of the faithful, hard work done by these attorneys in that case. To make this defense, secure better detective service, and be near the place of the trial, Mr. James changed his office from Fort Smith to Kansas City, where he had an office in the Sheidley Building.

Levi B. Madison, a former husband of the defendant, Mrs. Davis, had owned 320 acres of land in Cedar County, Missouri. This land he left to her at his death in Michigan, in the year 1882. Mrs. Davis now agreed to convey that land to Attorney James to be used to obtain money with which to secure evidence and conduct the defense of both Mrs. Davis and her mother, Mrs. Griffith. Investigation of the title to this land at Stockton, Missouri, disclosed the fact that a mortgage had been foreclosed, the land sold, and Judge Stratton, living at Nevada, Missouri, had bought the land in the year 1882, the very year that Madison died. Judge Stratton sold this land to Rookins R. Moore, who was living on it in 1889.

Under date of December 14, Judge Stratton wrote as follows:

Nevada, Mo. Dec. 14, '88.

J. T. James, Esq.

Dear Sir: I am requested by an old friend of mine to write to you regarding certain land in Cedar County, Mo., formerly owned by one Levi B. Madison. The land was mortgaged to one John Vanderburg and sold under the same in 1882 —

161

bought by me and sold to Rookins R. Moore who is now in possession and at whose request I write this.

Yours truly,
D. P. STRATTON
Judge 25th Judicial Cir., Mo.

The envelope bears the following: Return to D. P. Stratton, Box No. 134, Nevada, Mo. If not delivered within 10 days. Postmarked Nevada, Mo. Dec. 14, 1889. Addressed, J. T. James, Esq. Ft. Smith, Ark.

On the back of this envelope in Mr. James' handwriting appears: Ans. Jany 6, '90. That farm was not available for the defense.

CHAPTER XXV.
Reminiscences of H. L. McCune, of Kansas City, Mo., Formerly a Resident of Oswego.

In the spring of 1872, Dr. William York of Independence, Kan., while returning on horseback from a visit to his brother at Fort Scott, stopped at a store in Parsons to make some purchases and then continued on his journey.

Failing to reach his destination, his brother, Col. A. M. York, organized a searching party and started on the road from Parsons to Independence; not far from Cherryvale they found a man sitting by the road reading a Bible. In answer to their inquiries he informed them that he himself had been attached by bandits and believed that York had fallen a victim to the same outlaws.

York went on in pursuit and the Bible student, who proved to be John Bender, Jr., of the notorious Bender family, returned to his home and gave the alarm and the Benders disappeared.

Whether they were overtaken and exterminated by a posse under command of Colonel York, or whether they succeeded in making their escape is still a mooted question in Southeastern Kansas.

A few days later, the body of Doctor York was found buried

in the orchard on the Bender place, naked, face down, throat cut, and skull broken. Further search disclosed seven other bodies buried in the garden and another body was found near Cherryvale.

An examination of the house proved it to be a veritable slaughter pen. It was a small frame structure about sixteen by twenty feet in dimensions with a door at either end and was divided into two rooms by a canvas partition drawn tightly over upright standards. Under the house was a small, deep cellar.

In the floor of the east room, over the cellar, was a trap door. It was the custom of the Benders to decoy into the house the unwary traveler who had stopped to drink at the well or to buy at the little store. He would be seated in a chair with the back of his against the canvas partition.

At a given signal, some member of the family generally believed to be Kate Bender, would strike the victim from behind the screen with a large hammer. The drop was them sprung and the body fell, chair and all, into the cellar, where the work of robbery and mutilation too place at leisure.

The details of these horrible butcheries were published everywhere and were still familiar to the public. Naturally, they created intense excitement and indignation in the locality where they were committed, and every effort was made to apprehend the guilty ones and bring them to justice, but with avail, and to this day all attempts to locate them have proven fruitless and their fate is unknown, unless it be to the surviving members of Colonel York's band, who many believe overtook and slew the fugitives as they fled into the Indian Territory, and who have ever since guarded their secret well.

In the fall of 1886, having obtained a diploma from a law school and desiring to make myself eligible to distinction, I decided to locate in Kansas. An old friend was practicing at Oswego, Labette County, and by invitation I went there and formed a partnership with him. Soon after my partner was elected Prosecuting Attorney of the County and entered on the duties of that Office.

In the summer of 1889, he received information from the town of Niles, Michigan, that two women were living in that vicinity who were known to be criminals and who were believed by the authorities there to be Mrs. Kate Bender and her daughter, Kate.

163

After some correspondence with the Michigan officers, the County Commissioners of Labette County, to whom the matter was referred, decided to send Mr. Leroy F. Dick of Parsons, formerly Sheriff of the County, and in earlier days a neighbor and acquaintance of the Benders, to Niles to investigate the matter.

Mr. Dick went to Michigan and saw the women, and on his return reported that they were, beyond question in his opinion, the guilty parties, and upon the strength of his identification the necessary steps were taken and in November, 1889, the two women were brought to Oswego charged with the murder of Dr. York.

News of the apprehension of these noted criminals was widely published in the newspapers. *The Kansas City* snitch, I believe, had not come into existence at that time.

However, the second day after the arrival of the women, a Kansas City lawyer appeared on the scene and called at the hotel where the women were being kept temporarily and volunteered to defend them.

They had no money and he asked no compensation and was therefore no snitch, but a worthy young lawyer who saw an opportunity to gain a reputation honorably in the defense of two women charged with a great crime. And it may not be out of place to say that he received ample reward, for so well did he acquit himself that one of the most estimable young ladies of the town fell in love with him and they were married soon after and I am sure have lived happily ever since.

The legal battle took place at the preliminary examination. The complaint charge John Bender, Sr., Kate Bender, Sr., Kate Bender, Jr., and John Bender, Jr., with having on the 5th day of June, 1872, in the County of Labette and State of Kansas, murdered one William York, and the records of the Justice of the Peace recite that the warrant was returned and filed November 2, 1889, with Kate Bender, Sr., and Kate Bender, Jr., in court.

The examination took place in the circuit court room beginning on November 18 and continuing two days. The venerable Justice of the Peace who had issued the warrant associated with him two other Justices, and these three sat together and heard the evidence.

The trial, as I recall it, was remarkable and at times exceedingly dramatic. The court room was crowded with people

164

from all parts of Labette and adjoining Counties. Friends of the victims were present and interest in the proceedings was intense.

Seventeen years had passed since the commission of the crime, but the laps of time had not blotted out the memory of the bloody deeds that had been committed nor dulled the desire for vengeance.

The only question in the case was, of course, that of the identity of the prisoners, an exceedingly difficult matter owing to the time that had intervened since the commission of the crime, and especially difficult in the case of the younger woman, who had in the interval passes from girlhood to middle age.

The State produced fifteen witnesses who had know the Bender family and who identified the prisoners, with more or less certainty, as the female Benders, while the defense put eleven witnesses on the stand equally credible and equally positive that they were not the supposed criminals. The case was tried with ability on both sides.

The Prosecuting Attorney was a shrewd and resourceful trial lawyer, but he succeeded in discrediting one witness in a wholly unexpected manner. The witness had proven a valuable one for the defense. He had known Kate Bender and he remembered her face, height, and general appearance distinctly, and was positive that the woman on trial could never have been the girl he had known.

In the course of his direct examination, he stated that Kate Bender's hair was red. On cross examination the prosecutor said, "You say that Kate Bender had red hair — when did you see her last?" The witness answered, "Seventeen or eighteen years ago."

The prosecutor — "Now, please close your eyes — now what color is this woman's hair?" The witness answered that it was brown.

The woman's hair was in reality of a dark shade, but with a decided tendency to red.

"Now, please state to the Court, the color of my hair?" The witness answered without hesitation, "Your hair is grey."

The prosecutor was possessed of a luxuriant growth of sandy hair and the answer of the witness provoked a laugh in the court room.

"Now, please state to the Court, please open your eyes and

165

look at my hair and tell the Court what color it is?" All eyes were centered on the witness to see his discomfiture, bur he calmly looked at the lawyer's head and said, 'Your hair is gray, sir.' "

Thereupon it developed that the witness was color-blind and wholly incompetent to distinguish colors, and that the defect was in his eye rather than in his memory, but he was effectively discredited nevertheless.

When the examination was closed, the Justices put there heads together for a time and then announced their finding that the crime charged had been committed and that there was probably cause for believing the defendants guilty of its commission. The bond of the prisoners was fixed at $10,000, and as they were minus over 999 percent of that amount, they went to jail.

The county bastille was, however, unfit for women prisoners, and they were soon after placed under guard at the home of a Deputy Sheriff to await trial.

One morning on arriving at my office, I found the Deputy Sheriff awaiting me. He stated that Mrs. Bender, Sr., had taken violently ill during the preceding night, and believing herself about to die she had sent for the Prosecuting Attorney to whom she desired to make a confession. The deputy informed me that the Prosecuting Attorney was away from home and he desired me to go with him and take the old woman's statement.

You can imagine with what feelings I gathered up paper, pen, and ink and followed the officer. I was about to hear from the lips of this dying woman the true story of these great crimes — possibly to learn the whereabouts of the other members of the family. Truly, it promised to be an unusual experience and I commented to myself on the circumstances which had resulted in placing me, for the moment, in the place of the Prosecuting Attorney.

I found the woman apparently in a dying condition. She seemed to breathe with difficulty, her voice was scarcely audible, at times her mind wandered, and her speech became incoherent. She urged me to make haste and take down her statement before it was too late.

Then, with great difficulty and frequently interrupted by paroxysms of pain, she made a statement which I took down in writing and which was in substance as follows:

166

"A few years before, she had met and married a widower in the State of Michigan. He had a daughter by a former wife. After their marriage, he confessed to her that he was living under an assumed name. That he was old man Bender and his daughter was the notorious Kate. That after the murder of Doctor York, the family had fled south into the Indian Territory. That John Bender, Jr., had the money that had been taken from their various victims."

"One morning, as they were camped beside a little stream, the father and son quarreled and the old man brained the younger with a neck-yoke. The remainder of the family then worked their way north until they reached Michigan, where Mrs. Bender died."

"My informant further stated that her husband had been drowned shortly after their marriage and that she and her step-daughter, Kate Bender, had lived together thereafter until they were arrested and brought to Kansas. That the young woman downstairs was undoubtedly Kate Bender, the only surviving member of that family. That she, my informant, was a Bender only marriage and an innocent and much abused old lady."

She signed this statement, using the name under which she had been living in Michigan. She then asked me if I did not think this confession sufficient to clear her if she should recover and she appeared much disappointed and also much stronger physically when I informed her that I did not thing a dying statement would be competent evidence for that purpose.

As I was leaving the house, Kate Bender requested an interview and informed me that she would like to turn State's evidence, as she could tell some very damaging things about the old woman upstairs. But I had enough for one day. The old lady decided not to die and was as well as ever in a few days.

During the next few weeks, the Prosecuting Attorney began a careful investigation of the history of our prisoners, which ultimately disclosed that the older woman had served a term in the penitentiary at Jackson, Michigan, and on examination the records of that Institution it was found that in 1872, when the Bender murders were committed in Kansas, this woman was in the Michigan prison serving a sentence for manslaughter, she having struck one of her daughters in the abdomen with a stick of stove wood.

Here was conclusive proof that the prisoners were not members of the Bender family, but undoubtedly they were just as bad. Mother and daughter, and yet either would have sent the other to prison or the gallows to save herself.

And now, like the man who caught the bear, we endeavored to let loose. By suggestion of the Prosecuting Attorney, habeas corpus proceedings were instituted before the Probate Judge, and the prisoners were released on condition that they would return to Michigan at once.

Through-tickets were furnished them and they were placed on a train for St. Louis. At Columbus, Kansas, the first stop, they got off, sold their tickets, and the next day were back in Oswego, saying they liked Kansas better than Michigan and intended to remain with us, and here we will leave them and here the reminiscence ends.

I have told the story as accurately as I can recall the facts. If there are any lessons to be drawn from it, you must find them yourselves. I believe that no further attempt has been made by Labette County to catch the Bender family.

Travelers who visit the locality where they formerly lived say a curse seems to rest upon what was once the Bender farm. No one will live upon the place. The house and barn have been carried away in pieces by relic hunters. The fences have disappeared. Weeds and thistles cover the ground and the traveler hurries on to gaze on more attractive landscapes; for all about are cultivated and appealing farms and comfortable homes, transforming what once was a flat and treeless waste into a rich and attractive farming country.

CHAPTER XXVI.
Bender Gossip

(Interesting stories told on the witness stand in Niles, Michigan by Mrs. Davis against her mother.)

The Alleged Mrs. Bender.

During the examination of the larceny case at Niles, where Mrs. Monroe had become enraged at the actions of her daughter, Mrs. Davis, she had her charged with burglary and arraigned in court.

The Sheriff went to Lansing with a warrant to bring Mrs. Davis back. This made her so mad that she began to charge her mother with crimes, murder, and almost every crime known.

It finally developed to the suspicion that Mrs. Monroe was the real, old Mrs. Bender devil that was connected with the terrible murders in this County a few years ago. No stolen good were found in her possession, and the prisoner alleged that it was a trumped-up charge by her mother to get her into State Prison so she could not testify as to the various crimes committed by her mother.

After the conclusion of the testimony of Mrs. Monroe and her daughter, Mrs. Hogue, Mrs. Davis took the stand and was proceeding to give a history of her mother, of her various murders, etc., when the Public Prosecutor, Mr. Bridgman, called for a pause, alleging that the testimony of Mrs. Monroe must first be signed. This was considered by some bad policy, for Mrs. Davis appeared to be in the right mood to make rich developments.

In the meantime, the mother and daughter became reconciled to each other and started on foot to escape. They were arrested, and finally brought to Oswego charged with being old Mrs. Bender and her daughter, Kate.

"Bender Gossip" was published by a paper at Oswego, Kansas, from which is obtained the account of the trial at Niles, Michigan.

Larceny Case.

A preliminary hearing was given, in this case, in Michigan. *The Daily Star*, published at Niles, in the issue of October 22, 1889, gave a review of Mrs. Davis' testimony, as follows:

The case against Mrs. Eliza Davis has been postponed so often that the people are very tired in waiting for results. Yesterday afternoon the trial was resumed before Squire Barron, at his office in the American Block, a little room twenty by fifteen feet. People crowded into the place and packed it on short notice. The air became stifling and people gasped for fresh air. In due time, the examination commenced.

Mrs. Davis commenced her testimony by stating that there were various reasons why she could not give further testimony against her own mother. She had been convinced now that she was her own mother.

"If I told all that I know, it would imprison her, and I do not wish to do it."

Attorney Hamilton: "Have you been threatened if you proceeded?"

Witness: "Yes, threats have been made. Henry Howe called out and said if I continued to testify as I did he would fill me full of holes. There were other reasons. It was pretty hard to testify against my own mother."

Bridgman: "Then she is your own mother?"

Witness: "She has convinced me that she is my own mother. All I swore to when I was on the stand before was absolutely true, but I do not want to give further testimony against my mother. If I would give a true statement it would send her to the penitentiary and I do not wish to do it."

"We lived a mile and a half from Portland in '62. I have never been welcome at home. I was a little girl at home sleeping upstairs. I heard in the night a baby cry. I jumped up, and looked down between the cracks and saw my mother roll the back-log forward and thrown the child behind it and burn it up.

This was 1859, at North Shade, in Gratiot County, Michigan.

"My oldest sister, Elizabeth, had a mishaps and this was done to save disgrace."

"Saw her kill a woman who asked her for something to eat. She did not give meals away. A dispute arose and she struck with an ax-helve on the back of the neck and killed her. It was afternoon. She took the body to a manure pile and buried it until evening, when she took it to a slough hole and sunk it. I was made to go with her. Her husband was in town to sell ax-helves.

"I don't think Mother ever lived in Canada; she got into trouble with brother George's wife and was arrested in 1868 and sent to the Detroit House of Correction one year."

"I have lived in McPherson, Kansas; then at Emporin. I received letters with Mother's name signed, from Kansas, Colorado, and Texas; she wrote me for money. I sent her some to

Colorado; she had told me at different times that she was in Kansas and had seen all that country she wanted to see; she never mentioned any names."

"In 1872, I think she was in Howard city; had a letter from her in 1872 from Kansas; all these were stolen from me on my late visit to Niles, as I can prove by my daughter."

"November 16, I had a letter from her in Texas; 1874, in the latter part of the year; all were stolen from me; it was dated at Dover or Doliver — some such name."

"She said: 'My Dear Daughter: Send me some money. Ten dollars if no more; I am deserted."

"I do not know who was with her in Kansas; never heard her tell what business she was in; she took up land and was farming, but didn't like the country; had a letter from Hutchinson and Florence, Kansas; her name was on the letters."

"Ed Stokes, the fellow who went to prison for killing a man in New York, married Mrs. Monroe's daughter; she then married a man in Canada named Wm. Sanford; he was killed at Windsor; I was in the house when it happened, and was between eight and nine years old when it happened. It was a large two-story brown house just outside of the city. There was Mary Gordon, a little girl five or six years old; he was roped down in the cellar, and his throat cut with a razor; Mary was down cellar."

"I was so abused and pounded by Mother that I ran away and stayed in Detroit two or three weeks, when I was taken to Portland, insensible; don't know how I came so; the killing was done at three or four o'clock in the morning."

"Mother tole me what became of Griffith at Dowagle; Myron Monroe and Griffith got into a fuss; Myron cut him on the back of the neck until he was dead, and he was thrown in a well."

"I heard Mother talk about the Benders seven or eight years ago, telling what crimes they had committed, killing so many people and burying one child alive; told how they were killed by being struck with a hatchet or hammer, springing a trap door and then carrying them through the window, and the whole thing."

Bridgman: "Did you go down to Kansas to get married?"

Witness: "That is none of your business. I will get married again sometime."

"The Bible containing records of birth was sent with

Mother's trunk to Muskegon, and those matters of importance are in the trunk."

Bridgman: "Do you think your mother is crazy?"

Witness: "Crazy with the devil. She lied about me and has owned up to it, and has the goods she charged me with stealing. She praises God when she don't praise the devil."

Bridgman: "Mrs. Monroe, can you sing?"

Mrs. Monroe: "Yes, I can sing to Mr. Hamilton, lull-a-by-baby, on the tree top."

Witness: "Lived in Lansing when my mother broke me up. Don't know which of us wakes up the spirits."

(Mrs. Monroe raps under the table.)

Witness: "Bring in the battery. I have been told that Mr. Bridgman has threatened me with the penitentiary."

Bridgman: "For telling the truth?"

(This garrulous child is an innocent nuisance.)

"My mother said she was in Kansas since we separated. In 1899 she went to Kansas. Hardscrabble and dozens of other places."

"I have received letters from her and they were taken from me only lately by my mother; they were lost last in my valise at her house; one was asking for money; it was from Texas, asking me for ten dollars. I dot not send it; I feel sure it was from D; it commenced with a D; I'm sure; there was one from Denver asking me for money; I sent her three dollars; this was in July, 1874; I sent it from Cairo."

"She never described her farming in Kansas, nor never told me who was farming with her; it was at Hutchinson — prairie land."

"I was with her when she was here."

Here Stokes, who murdered Fisk, is sworn to have married a daughter of Mrs. Monroe, and Mrs. Davis still swears she heard he was "sent up" in New York. This was Elizabeth who married Stokes.

Mrs. Davis then says her sister Mary murdered her husband in the cellar.

"This made me run away from my mother; after this man was killed I became insensible to all and everything; this murder occurred at four in the morning; I can remember the husband's name."

"Mrs. Monroe frequently told me of the murders by the Benders in Kansas. I am either forty-four or thirty-eight, or

172

thirty-seven; my mother has three different ages for me."

"I believe my mother is devilish crazy and is always doing something against her children."

(Mrs. Davis insinuates Mrs. Monroe dare not get up and deny before God she is anything but a liar. Here Mrs. M. does get up amid the roars of laughter of spectators. She put up her two hands and declared she was innocent.)

"My name has been Davis since July last — Mrs. James Davis; I was married at Lansing; my husband is not there. I don't know where he is; I lived at Jackson, this State, three years ago."

Bridgman: "Do you know Jud Crouch?"

Mrs. Davis: "You ask questions when your mouth should be shut."

(Boisterous laughter, which Judge Barron was obliged to subdue with stern voice and countenance.)

"This is a larceny case, and my knowing or not knowing Jud Crouch has nothing to do with this case," said Mrs. Davis, "and I tell you, Mr. Bridgman, the way to get along with women is to mind your own business and leave theirs alone."

Mrs. Davis continuing, said: "I have another witness; my eldest daughter knows my mother had possession of the very property which she charges as having been stolen by me."

Mrs. Davis thought her mother had gotten her into a scrape, and she should punish her for it in the courts.

Adjourned until Tuesday, Oct. 29.

CHAPTER XXVII.

The *Kansas City Star* reporter gave the following account of his visit to Oswego:

Old settlers who were expected to identify Mrs. Elmira Monroe and Mrs. Sarah E. Davis as Mrs. John and Kate Bender have seen the women since their arrival here. Two say the right people have been captured, but others laugh at the idea and the Prosecuting Attorney is in great doubt now.

Public opinion is fast molding itself into favor of the two women. The attempt at identification has proven a dismal failure. The witnesses on whose opinions the most reliance has been placed by Prosecuting Attorney Morrison have declared

173

in a few words that the wrong parties have been arrested.

Silas Toles, now of Chautauqua County, and his younger brother were the first to discover the fact that the Benders had fled the country. He was sent for by the Prosecuting Attorney and arrived in Oswego Saturday afternoon.

"If Toles does not identify Mrs. Davis as Kate Bender," remarked Prosecuting Attorney Morrison, "I shall believe we have the wrong parties. He knew her intimately and lived on an adjoining farm to the Benders, the two houses being not more than a quarter of a mile apart."

Toles was admitted in the room in which the prisoners are being kept and talked with them for half an hour. On his return to the Prosecuting Attorney's office, he said, "You have the wrong parties. Kate Bender and Mrs. Davis correspond fairly in height, but there the similarity ends. Kate Bender's h air was lighter and her face much thinner than Mrs. Davis'. In the color of the eyes a great difference can also be noticed. The old woman does not resemble Mrs. Bender."

Thomas Jeans, a resident of this County, who owned a farm adjoining that of the Benders, declared that Mrs. Monroe did not look like Mrs. Bender and that Mrs. Davis bore no resemblance whatever to Kate.

The Prosecuting Attorney Blue.

Joseph Story, a policeman of Parsons, was the only person who saw the prisoners to-day and discovered any resemblance between them and the criminals for whom they were taken.

He said that there was no doubt whatever in his mind, that Mrs. Davis and Kate Bender were identical. He claims to have seen Kate Bender only half a dozen times, but tells a long-winded story to show that he would never forget her face.

The Prosecuting Attorney admits that he is badly discouraged, but declares that he will probe the mystery to the bottom.

It is very different with Mrs. McCann. She has made up her mind that the influences guided her aright, and if every old settler in Labette County would swear that the two women looked no more like the persons for whom they were arrested than they do like Queen Victoria, she would still insist that she could not be mistaken.

They do not look like criminals, and, as their history shows, have devoted most of their lives to getting married and raising children.

Mrs. Monroe claims to have been married three times and to have been the mother of twelve children.

Mrs. Davis acknowledges having been married three times and having partially raised seven children.

Mrs. McCann says she can prove that Mrs. Monroe has been married eleven times, and Mrs. Monroe charges Mrs. McCann with having stolen her marriage certificates.

Mrs. Davis Tells Her Story.

With her two-year-old babe in her arms, Mrs. Davis told the story of the persecution of Mrs. McCann. The "influence" exerted by Mrs. McCann over the ignorant woman is the most remarkable feature of this most remarkable case. Mrs. McCann believes she has a mission to perform, and that mission is to discover the whereabouts of her father's murderers and bring them to justice. She thinks impressions lead her in the right direction, and Mrs. Davis is ignorant and superstitious and believes that the alleged detective is a Spiritualist who has absolute control over her.

"Mrs. McCann first came to my home in McPherson about six years ago. I was sick from child-birth and Mrs. McCann followed my little girl home. She professed a great sympathy for us and for several weeks made frequent trips to our house claiming it was being done for charity's sake. I was sick for three weeks and as soon as I could sit up in bed, she began talking to me."

"One day she brought an instrument to the house which she said would write my name and place of birth. I took it and sure enough, it wrote Sarah Eliza Mark, Cattaraugus County, New York."

"I did not know what it all meant, but from that time, Mrs. McCann could do anything with me she pleased. She would ask me questions and I would answer them just as she wanted me to."

"Finally, I fell sick and remained in this condition for three weeks until Dr. Smith of McPherson was called to see me. During all this time, I was sick, Mrs. McCann would ask me questions."

175

Mrs. Davis told me several other stories, showing that Mrs. McCann had mesmeric influence over her. She said she did not remember having sworn in Michigan that her mother was Mrs. Bender, but said that she testified just as Mrs. McCann wanted her to and could not help it.

Neither of the women have any means with which to make a defense.

They claim that they will be able to prove that Mrs. McCann offered one of their relatives twenty-five dollars to swear that they are Mrs. John and Kate Bender.

Mrs. Davis claims that Mrs. McCann offered her fifty dollars to swear that Mrs. Monroe was Mrs. John Bender, and Mrs. Monroe said that she was offered fifty dollars to swear that her daughter was Kate Bender.

Mr. James, attorney for the defense, expects to prove that Mrs. Elmira Griffith, or Monroe, is sixty-eight years of age. Her maiden name was Elmira Hill and she was born in Cattaraugus County, New York. She was married three times and was the mother of twelve children, six of whom are living.

In 1839, she was married to Simon Ward, a Frenchman living in Cattaraugus County, who was the father of all of her children. He died in 1866 and in 1872 she was married to Joseph Monroe, and in 1880 married William Stephen Griffith of Howard City, Michigan, who now lives in Muncie, Indiana. She lived with her last husband only a few months, and was known in the community as Mrs. Monroe.

Mrs. Sarah E. Davis claims to have been born in Cattaraugus County, New York, in 1844 and moved to Michigan in 1852.

She was married to Levi B. Madison in 1863. In 1879 he died, and in February, 1884, she went to McPherson, Kansas, a widow with three children, all of whom are now in the poor house. Within three months after arriving in McPherson, she was married to John Thompson, who died in 1886.

She went to Niles, Michigan, where she remained until 1886 when she returned to Emporin, Kansas. She remained in Emporia six months, returning to Niles, Michigan, where she remained until her arrest.

CHAPTER XXVIII.

The *Kansas City Journal* contained the following:

THE TWO ALLEGED BENDERS

A Journal Representative Interviews the Prisoners — The Prosecution Seems to Have Been Made at the Instance of Spooks. — Three Men Fail to Identify Them, While the Fourth Man is Positive the Younger Woman is Kate Bender.

Oswego, Kansas. — To-days's developments go far toward establishing the innocence of the alleged Benders. Three men, at least, J. W. Jeens of Montana, Dr. McKenale of Oswego, and another man, all of whom knew the Benders, have failed to identify them.

Public opinion, as moulded by reports that come from interviews, is that these are innocent parties, and that the authorities have been misled by the delusive chattering of Mrs. McCann, the "detective." Even the County Attorney has fears of establishing their identity.

Mr. James, their attorney, has ordered the women defendants not to talk to reporters, but the *Journal* correspondent had an interview with them this morning at the residence of Tom Lawson, within a stone's throw of the hotel where Mrs. McCann is stopping.

The reporter was taken upstairs into a low room and upon the bed sat Elmira Griffith, and near her, on a chair, sat Sarah Eliza Davis, the alleged "Kate Bender," holding upon her lap a curly-headed little girl about two years of age. They stoutly protested innocence. In response to a question of her life, the older woman said:

"I was born in Cattaraugus County, New York, in 1821. My maiden name was Elmira Hill. I was married there in Sawmill Run in 1839 to a Frenchman named Simon Mark and twelve children were born to us. He died in 1866 and I married a Scotchman by the name of Josiah Monroe, in 1872, in Michigan. I had my marriage certificate until Mrs. McCann stole it from me."

"We moved to Niles, Michigan, in November, 1874. I was divorced from Monroe and married a third time to William Steven Griffith, at Howard City, Michigan. He deserted me in

1887 and is now in Muncie, Indiana."

"I have never lived in Kansas and know nothing about the Benders. I have made a living peddling, washing, and anything I could find to do."

Mrs. Griffith is rather fleshy and is sprightly for her age, and joked about the writer seeing the famous Benders.

Sarah Eliza Davis was then interviewed. She is about five-feet, two-inches tall, has brown hair and is minus an upper incisor. She was poorly clad and was nursing her little girl at the breast and bears the marks of age, that maternity of seven children would naturally occasion.

Almost the first thing she said was, "That woman," meaning Mrs. McCann, the detective, "has power to do anything with me. Why, she brought a magnet shaped like a harp, which had a frame on it. When I would grasp it, my hand would write anything Mrs. McCann wants it to write. When she came into the house, I was completely under the influence. She mesmerized me. One time I was under influence for two weeks. I am afraid of her. Everywhere I go, she follows me."

"When were you first married, Mrs. Davis?" was asked.

"I was first married to Levi B. Madison in Michigan in 1863. He died in 1879."

"In 1884, I moved to McPherson, Kansas. There I married John Thompson. He lived eighteen months. About this time I made the acquaintance of Mrs. McCann and in a short time, she had me under her influence. I lived in McPherson two years."

"If I ever made a confession to Mrs. McCann, I don't know it, but all the time she was trying to surprise me and coax me into a confession."

"I moved back to Niles, Michigan, in 1887, and lived there one year. I went to Emporia, Kansas, in 1888 and Mrs. McCann came there and watched me. I moved back to Niles in six months."

"I have three children; Gertrude, aged sixteen, Lillie, aged thirteen, and Freddie, aged eleven. The two youngest were put in a poor house, and the oldest went to work."

When asked about her marriage certificates, she claimed that Mrs. McCann had stolen them and other papers from her.

When interrogated as to her mother's career, she admitted that she had served a term in the Michigan penitentiary for infanticide.

Mrs. McCann was seen by the *Journal* reporter this evening and she said that in all of her work in this matter, she had been guided solely by her intuitions or impressions made upon her by some mysterious influence.

She says she will go to McPherson and visit her family whom she has not seen for six months.

She certainly has followed her theory faithfully, though she admits that the confession she has obtained will not convict them.

Uncle Joseph Story of Parsons, who knew the Bender family, will come down this evening and says that if the younger woman is not Kate Bender, she is her exact counterpart.

CHAPTER XXIX.

The *Kansas City Times* contained an article entitled:

BASED ON DREAMS.

Mrs. McCann's Charge Flimsy. — The Alleged Benders Arrested Almost Without a Cause. — Decidedly Weak Story Told by Female Detective. — The Big Sensation Very Much Like a Persecution Now. — Determination to Hang the Two Women, if Possible, Expressed by the Accuser. — Queer Tale on Which to Jeopardize Lives.

Oswego, Kansas, Nov. 2. — Mrs. Frances E. McCann left Oswego on the evening train for Parsons, where she will remain for several days, the guest of Deputy Sheriff Dick, who brought Mrs. Monroe and Mrs. Davis from Niles, Michigan.

Mrs. McCann and Mr. Dick are about the only persons who think that Mrs. John and Kate Bender have been captured.

In an interview at the depot this morning, the lady said: "If I have not captured Mrs. Bender, I have succeeded in bringing from Michigan the ugliest woman ever seen in Kansas."

Then the little woman shrugged her shoulders and laughed heartily at her attempt at a joke.

"I did not expect," Mrs. McCann continued, "that many persons in this part of Oswego would be able to identify the pris-

179

oners, for few of them knew the Bender family, by sight. I cannot say that I will be satisfied even if at the trial they are turned loose. It depends altogether on how the investigation is conducted. If they are turned loose on this charge, the murder of my father, John W. Sanford, at Windsor, Canada, remains to be disposed of."

"Mrs. Davis swore on the witness stand at Niles, Michigan, that her mother was instrumental in the murder of John W. Sanford."

"It is a matter of public record, and whether it is competent evidence in the preliminary hearing or not, it will furnish grounds for another investigation. I propose to see that the investigation is conducted by the State in such a manner that the whole truth will arrived at."

Based Entirely on Dreams.

The second charge is based on a dream. Supplementing the dream are confessions of Mrs. Davis made, she claims, while under a mesmeric influence.

Hobgoblins and ghosts figure even more prominently in the Stanford murder investigation than they do in the Bender fiasco.

Mrs. McCann had a dream which revealed the murder of an old man, by an old woman and her daughter. The little daughter of the murdered man was spared. The story preyed on her mind and she told it to Mrs. Davis at McPherson.

Mrs. Davis "interpreted" the dream.

"Yes, there was a murder," said Mrs. Davis, "the murdered man was John W. Sanford, of Windsor, Canada, and you are the daughter who escaped. My mother was the murderer."

Mrs. McCann did not know her parentage, and so impressed was she with the interpretation that she made a pilgrimage to Kentucky, where she visited an orphan asylum in which she was raised.

There she discovered that she had been received as Emily Sanford.

Her next visit was to Windsor, Canada, where she discovered that a man by the name of John W. Sanford had been murdered.

Mrs. McCann returned to McPherson, determined to prosecute her search for the murderer of her father. She began by shadowing Mrs. Davis.

How the Bender Idea Began.

"There was one thing," said Mrs. McCann, in relating her story, "which Mrs. Davis said she would never tell me. I kept thinking the matter over and these words came to my mind, 'these people are the Benders.' "

"One day, I asked Mrs. Davis point-blank if her mother was not Mrs. Bender. She became indignant at once and fiercely tole me never to refer to that subject again.

"On the following day she was busily engaged in washing over a washtub. 'How many were there in the Bender family?' I asked in and off-hand way and she was caught napping. 'Well, let me see,' she said, 'there was Mother — ,' She stopped in an instant and throwing her hands up exclaimed, 'Now you have the secret. I have told you all!' "

"She warned me on fear of death never to refer to the subject again, and I believe that the only the reason she had in telling me further of the many murders committed by her family, was to intimidate me."

The dream and the confession which followed it, form the ground-work of all subsequent investigations.

No attempts at identification were made to-day and the curious were refused admittance to the room in which Mrs. Monroe and Mrs. Davis are guarded.

The attorneys for the two are collecting evidence to establish the identity of their clients.

A dispatch from Portland, Michigan, states that a deputy sheriff of the County had received a letter from Mrs. Monroe requesting him to procure affidavits from prominent citizens regarding the manner of her husband's (Mark's) death.

A dispatch from Portland published in the Detroit Free Press corroborates, in part, the story told by Mrs. Monroe, in regard to her Michigan life.

The dispatch says, "Mr. and Mrs. Monroe came to Portland in 1870, shortly after the Windsor tragedy, and occupied the old block house on the west side of Grand River. They were generally regarded as a quarrelsome, dangerous set and were seldom molested by the townsfolk. The facts connected with the death of Mark cannot now be recalled, but the husband and wife were certainly disagreeing. The family had some

181

trouble here over the alleged drowning of a baby, but no arrests were made."

CHAPTER XXX.

State of Michigan, County of Berrien:

Marian Chapman, being duly sworn in, says, " . . . that in the early Spring of 1873, she became acquainted with Mrs. Elmira Monroe, now under arrest on suspicion of being one of the Bender family and connected with the murders of that family in the State of Kansas. That she worked for my next neighbor in planting corn and other work in the house, that Spring and Summer.

This woman lived a mile from me and worked for a Mr. Lankston on an adjoining farm.

She fixes the date at which she first knew Mrs. Monroe by the birth of her child, the child being born in the Spring of 1872. She saw and knew this Mrs. Monroe during the Spring and Summer of 1873 and more or less often each year to the present time."

MARIAN CHAPMAN

Sworn and subscribed before me this 16th day of November, 1889

(SEAL)   DAVID BACON, *Notary Public*

State of Michigan, County of Berrien, as:

Myra A. Hogue, being duly sworn, says: " . . . that she is a resident of Niles, Michigan, and she has been for fourteen years last past. That she has been a resident of the State of Michigan for twenty-five years. That during the years 1870, 1871, 1872, and 1873, she was well and intimately acquainted with Elmira Griffith, formerly Elmira Mark, now under arrest and held at Oswego, Kansas, as the noted Mrs. Bender, and charged with the murder of Doctor York, and others in Labette County, Kansas. That affiliant, Myra A. Hogue is the daughter of said Mrs. Mark. That during the year 1870, Mrs. Mark lived in David Perry's house, in Concord Township, in Jackson

County, Michigan. That in the year 1872, she lived in Carlton, a suburb and adjoining South Saginaw, Michigan, in a house owned by one Louis Gonsinminger. That in 1873 and 1874, Mrs. Mark, then known as Mrs. Monroe, lived at Tekousha, Calhoun County, Michigan. That affiliant was well acquainted with Mrs. Griffith during said time and of her own knowledge says that she was living during said years at the places above set forth.

MYRA A. HOGUE   *XXX*

Her Mark

Sworn and subscribed before me, 13th day of Jan., 1890.
(SEAL)   DAVID BACON, *Notary Public.*

One of the Oswego weekly papers contained the following:

J. J. Johns of Oswego Township spent Saturday with his mother-in-law, Mrs. I. W. Patrick. In 1869, Mr. Johns located in Labette County and was a neighbor of the notorious Bender family. When asked his opinion regarding the fate of this family, he stated positively that they were not captured and killed by a vigilance committee, as he was a member of that organization. He was a frequent visitor at the house and one time was refused admittance, which aroused his suspicions.

CHAPTER XXXI.

The *Parsons Palladium*, dated June 12, 1907, contained an article which read as follows:

Following close upon a story recently published that Kate Bender had been discovered in Oklahoma and had been denounced by a man who wanted to marry her daughter and had been refused; now comes a story from a Kansas City woman who formerly lived in Montgomery County and who claims her father-in-law was a member of the avenging party that slaughtered the Benders after finding of the evidence of the murders.

She mentions Judge Webb, formerly of this County as one

183

of the party who discovered the notorious trap door through which the victims of the Benders were thrown after being struck on the head.

(This article then quoted part of an article which was published in the *Kansas City Star* dated June Second 1907, and was as follows:)

HELPED SLAY THE BENDERS

A County Treasurer Is Said To Have Aided Avengers.

Apropos of an article in last Sunday's *Star*, in which John Keepers related the story of what many persons believe to have been the tragic end of the notorious Bender family of Kansas, Mrs. E. L. Stephenson of Kansas City offers some testimony tending to corroborate Mr. Keeper's theory.

Mrs. Stephenson declares that her father-in-law, L. T. Stephenson, at one time Treasurer of Montgomery County, Kansas, was one of a party of men who pursued and killed the Benders, in the manner described by a Cherokee Indian, who witnessed the execution.

"In the party of avengers," she says, "were many prominent citizens of Montgomery County, nearly all of whom are now dead."

"After the disappearance of Doctor York and his little daughter," said Mrs. Stephenson, "a search was made for them, which resulted in locating them finally in a grave on the Bender Farm, together with some sixteen other bodies all of whom had been killed on the same manner."

"Doctor York had been killed by being struck in the back of the head, but the little daughter, from all appearances, had been buried alive in her father's grave."

"Everything indicated that the premises had been but lately vacated, scouts having evidently gotten wind of the fact that the avengers of Doctor York were headed that way and the trail was taken up and followed for three days."

"At the end of that time, the wagons, which had broken down and had been abandoned, were found, and soon after the entire party was overtaken and dispatched without mercy."

"Kate Bender, who seemed to be the leading spirit of the party, is said to have fought for her life viciously."

"At a time when reports being circulated that the Benders had been found and arrested, knowing that my father-in-law had been living in the country at that time, I asked him if he thought it was true, and his reply, quietly given was that he knew it was not, for he had helped to dig their graves."

"Later, he tole me of an experience he had himself had with the Benders."

"In the early days of Montgomery County, Kansas, he had held the position of County Treasurer, banking funds at Oswego, some sixty-five miles away, to which place he made trips overland by private conveyance."

"On the occasion spoken of, he was accompanied by H. G. Webb, the District Judge of the County, who was going to Oswego to hold his regular term of court."

"Father owned the finest team of horses in the County of Arabian and Hambletonian stock, with harness silver-mounted and a find covered buggy."

"On the way, they stopped for dinner at the Bender farm, which was the only inn along the route. Driving into the barnyard, they ordered that the horses be fed without unhitching, as they were in haste."

"Being ushered into the front room of the house, carrying with them the valise containing the funds, they were confronted by Kate Bender, who came to take their orders."

"They were forcibly struck by her evil face, the Judge remarking after she left that he wouldn't care to be compelled to face her in close quarters without weapons of defense."

"While waiting for their meal to be brought, Father walked out to see that the horses had been attended to and discovered that his orders to feed them without unhitching them had been disregarded, the horses having been taken from the buggy, and locked inside the barn."

"Returning to the house, he told this to the Judge. Both regarded it as a suspicious circumstance and they began to look about them."

"The room in which they sat was divided from a rear room by a thick curtain, and on closer examination, it was found that this curtain and the table covered a long, closely fitting trap door."

"In a short time, Kate Bender reappeared with their meal, and placing it on the table, drew two chairs to one side of the table, with backs to the curtain, and invited them to "draw

185

up," immediately leaving the room"

"Quietly lifting the table over to the other side of the room, they took their places at it, facing the curtain."

"Scarcely had they done so, when a vigorous blow was struck on the other side of the curtain in such a way that had they been sitting in front of the curtain, one of them must have been killed."

"Simultaneously with this blow, the trap door in the floor flew open downward, revealing a hole large enough to have taken in table, chairs, and their occupants."

"Realizing that they would probably be outnumbered, Father and the Judge drew their revolvers, rushed out of the house to the barn, broke in the door, and while one stood on the defensive, the other hitched the horses to the buggy."

"They drove out of the place as fast as they could, followed by several shots from the house."

"On returning to Independence a few days afterward, carefully avoiding the Bender farm on his way, Father learned of the disappearance of Doctor York and his little daughter, who had left Independence some days precious."

"It was the information given by him of his adventure at the Bender farm which led the avenging party to make straight for that place."

CHAPTER XXXII.
He Knew the Bender Family.

In May, 1907, the *Kansas City Star*, in its Sunday edition, contained the following:

John Keepers Aided in the Search for the Murderers

Periodically the report goes over the country that the notorious Bender family has been found. But always the rumor is found to be false.

"They will never be found," said John Keepers, an ex-Kansan, now living at 2113 Belle Fontaine Avenue. "When the Benders left their farm in Crawford County, Kansas in 1873, after their after their crimes had been committed and discovered, they are supposed to have gone into the Indian Territory."

"It is almost an absolute certainty that the Benders were all killed and buried by outlaws like themselves."

"The Benders knew too much — that's why they were killed."

"I was one of the party of men that went to the Bender home when a search was being made for Doctor York of Independence, a brother of Col. A. M. York of Fort Scott.

"We met old man Bender at the gate and told him our errand. He said he had been shot at by highwaymen a few days before on the Verdigris River, six miles distant. That led us off on a false scent."

"When we came back ten days later, the Benders had disappeared. The discovery of their flight was made by a neighbor named Pierce. He told others and a search of the premises was begun."

"First, we went through the house. We found a trap door in the floor, and below it in the cellar, the gravel flooring was stained with blood."

"In the garden we found several places where the earth had sunk. The most recent appearing of these we dug into and found there the body of Doctor York. We sounded all the other depressions with an iron rod and found in that way sixteen bodies. If I remember rightly, a total of 104 persons were reported missing in that neighborhood."

"Of course, we never knew whether the Benders had killed them all, for the bodies were not found."

"But, I believe if we had made a closer search at the time we could have found more graves."

"All of the murders occurred in the Fall of 1872 and the Winter and Spring of 1873."

"The Benders kept a store and hotel for travelers, though I don't believe they ever had more than ten dollars worth of goods in the store at any one time."

"And I don't believe any traveler who stopped there ever lived to continue his journey. If he wasn't murdered in his sleep, he was killed at the dining table."

Mr. Keeper does not credit the story that the Benders were killed by a lynching party not far from their home.

"If they had been," he said, "I would have known about it. There was a large reward for each member of the family, dead or alive, and if they had been killed, someone would have

187

claimed the reward."

"There is more probability in the story of a Cherokee Indian, who while fishing along the tributary of the Verdigris, about twenty-five miles south of the Kansas line, witnessed what many people believe to have been the finish of the Benders."

"The Indian said he saw an old man and an old woman, with a younger couple, camped around a covered wagon."

"A band of twenty men came upon them suddenly and killed everyone, burned the wagon and outfit, and then left."

Another paper published in Kansas, near the Bender farm, contained, among other things, the following:

The question as to what became of the Benders has been revived. Most people for years have believed that the Benders escaped from Kansas and are still living somewhere.

Kansas has had many revolting crimes with her borders, but none ever equalled the Bender crimes, except possibly the sacking of Lawrence.

The Benders lived on the main road about half-way between Thayer and Cherryvale. That was in the early 'seventies. There were four in the family. Old man Bender and his wife and a sone and his wife. The son's wife claimed to be a Medium and had great influence over other members of the family. They ran a sort of a country tavern. They sold refreshments and fed travelers who happened along about meal time.

Their house consisted of two rooms and the partition consisted of a calico curtain.

In the early spring of '73, people began to suddenly disappear around that section of the country. They would start out on the Thayer-Cherryvale road and that would be the last seen of them. They would drop completely out of sight.

In march of that year, William York, a brother of Senator York, who played an important role in the Pomeroy Senatorial Scandal, started from Fort Scott to independence. He also dropped out of sight. Shortly afterwards, the Bender family disappeared. The first time they were missed was when a neighbor found a calf tied to a tree in the yard dead. The calf had died of starvation.

The people then became curious and an investigation followed. They found a trap-door in the house and it opened to a pit about six feet in diameter. The ground floor of it was soaked with blood. It smelled of decayed human flesh.

Out in the garden, some sunken holes were discovered. A neighbor thought he would dig down and see what would turn up. He discovered a human corpse. When it was removed, it was discovered to be that of William York. The investigation then continued and seven more bodies were afterwards discovered. They were all identified with the exception of one.

Those identified were: George W. Longcohr and his daughter, three months old; Longcohr had lost his wife and was taking the little girl back to Iowa to live; George Brown, of Cherryvale; William McCrotty, of Howard County, who left home with two thousand dollars in his possession; H. T. McKenzie, of Indiana, who had come west with a little money to relocate; M. R. Boyle, of Montgomery County, and an unknown man.

It was afterwards brought out that all of these people were killed in the Bender home at different times, with the exception of Longcohr and his daughter.

The victim would stop for a meal. He would be seated at the table with his back near the calico curtain. Then one of the Benders would slip up and hit him on the head with a hammer, crushing his skull. His body would drop through the trap into the hole and to make sure of his death, one of the Benders would then cut his throat from ear to ear.

Every victim was treated in this fashion. Their heads were all crushed and their throats cut. In due time, the body would be taken to the garden and buried.

On April 7, 1873, the four Benders drove away. They left their team about a mile from Thayer and took the train for Humboldt. At least that is the story. They have never been seen since.

A posse was after them about this time. After skirmishing all around, the members of the posse returned home, saying they had given up the hut. They dropped the subject quickly.

The whereabouts of the Benders never seemed to bother them after that. But, other people were curious and are curious to this day. The posse never preached. That they got rid of the Benders has always been suspected by many.

CHAPTER XXXIII.
Story of the Benders.

It was our rare good fortune to have as our guest over night recently, with the Banner folks, Mr. Leroy F. Dick, of Parsons, who was a near neighbor of the Benders at the time of their murders here; who was Township Trustee of that Township at that time; who exhumed those corpses in the Bender graveyard; who had charge of those corpses after they were exhumed; had charge of the Bender premises after the Benders left; and participated in all the leading scenes and incidents connected with the discovery of the crimes.

He was the first to point out the correct clew to the missing Doctor York; had charge of the posses in the search; and who was afterward Deputy Sheriff in the efforts that were made to track, follow, and apprehend the Benders.

It was last Thursday night at nine o'clock, after we had finished printing and addressing the Banner while sitting around the fire, in company with Brother Dick, that a casual remark made by one of the family relative to the Bender murder, which happened after we came to Jewel County, Kansas, sprung the subject and turned his attention to it.

From nine o'clock to one o'clock in the morning we sat entranced with that thrilling story — thrilling in its horridness — thrilling in the manner in which it was told — thrilling in its minutiae and incidents and all of the details of which Brother Dick is so fully cognizant, and to which he was an eye witness, and in which he was compelled to be a participant at that time.

From him we learned that the *New York Ledger* story that old man Bender, old woman Bender, Kate, and John were overtaken by Colonel York and his party and all shot to death, down on Cow Creek (or some other creek) was the veriest fiction.

They had been gone seventeen days before they were missed from the premises. A calf that they had left tied up at the stable had perished for water or starved to death, and their team that they had driven into the timber and left tied to the wagon had eaten the wagon bed nearly up and were almost perished when found.

They therefore did not drive off, according to the *Ledger's* beautiful legend, but bought tickets to Humboldt on the rail-

190

road, went Southward, divided into two parties, rounded up and came together at Denison, Texas. From there they went to New Mexico, to the unpopulated country in Western Texas.

They were followed. Every turn they made was discovered, but always too late to apprehend them. When they reached the western wilds all trace of them disappeared and for several years was lost.

Finally, a clew, given by a lady, led to the suspicion that they had returned to Michigan. Brother Dick was appointed Deputy Sheriff to track this clew. He traveled all over eleven thousand miles, found the old lady, found Kate, and found two other daughters of Mrs. Bender, but John and the old man he could not get track of.

Old Mrs. Bender had been married thirteen times, the other two daughters were living with their eighth or ninth husband, andKate had a baby in her arms and had been muchly married, but was at that time without a husband.

He brought Kate and the baby and old Mrs. Bender back to Oswego and lodged them in jail, thereby performing his part in the drama as fully and successfully as possible.

This was in 1889, seventeen years after the murders were committed. Kate from a trim, well proportioned girl had grown corpulent. The old woman had become haggard, wrinkled, and skinny.

Identification here was not complete. The necessary evidence and witnesses from Michigan, and other places, would have cost the State a large sum.

A lawyer appeared on the scene from their old haunts to defend them, presumably the father of Kate's child.

The difficulty of fastening the crimes upon these two women — in the absence of John, Jr. and the old man Bender — added to the improbability that a jury would do so, and various other considerations led the County Attorney to doubt the propriety of prosecuting the case. Another problem was the expense of the case on an over-burdened and, at that time, debt-ridden County.

This decision to dismiss the case had led many to doubt the real identity of the parties apprehended; but the facts, as given by Mr. Dick, must forever dispel any doubt of that kind in the mind of anyone who should hear the evidence; and this decision of the County Attorney, and dismissal of these wretches from justice, is by far the most unsavory and unsatisfactory part of this great Bender episode.

Brother Dick has in his possession the hammer and other implements of death which the Benders used to dispatch their victims. He has kept track of the history of his prisoners since they were released from custody here. He has also been enabled to get some information with regard to the other members of the Bender family.

Kate Bender is now dead. Old man Bender is also dead. He went mad and committed suicide by drowning himself in Lake Michigan.

He was kept for a time in a private asylum. The old lady went to see him, and at the sight of her, he became raving and frantic. His real name was not Bender, but Flickinger.

John is still, at last accounts, living someplace in the pineries of northern Michigan. The old woman is still alive.

None of them ever went by the name Bender after they left Labette County, but Mr. Dick is well acquainted with their assumed and often changed names, or was until recently.

All of this may not read so prettily as the published romance of the fate of the Benders, but it is a great deal more correct.

Crime sometimes becomes so great and appalling in its magnitude as to defy justice. This seems to be the case with the Bender murders here.

Eight bodies were exhumed from the Bender orchard; one a little child that was laid in a hole alive, with its murdered father, and so buried up, alive. The bodies were buried seven feet deep. Their heads were smashed with a hammer and their throats were cut to bleed them well.

There was a prepared receptacle under the house to catch the blood. Every vestige of the subsoil was removed from where the bodies were buried, and hauled to the barnyard and carefully covered over by manure. The ground was kept nicely burrowed over, and was set in apple trees.

Other bodies and skeletons were afterwards found along the bottoms and in the timber that were no doubt also Bender murders. In fact, one was discovered at some distance from their home, in a creek or pond, that first gave a clew to foul play going on in that vicinity. From this it is known that they did not put all of their victims into their private grave-yard at home.

They secured several thousand dollars from their victims.

An old German lady just from the old country whom they did not murder was robbed of fifteen hundred dollars in gold, two thousand dollars in jewelry, and had two checks on the bank for large sums taken from her while stopping a few days at their house while her son-in-law was looking for a home. The money and jewelry were never recovered but payment was stopped on the checks and that money she afterward received.

From two others of their victims they received over three thousand dollars. One young man who died and was buried with the rest had only forty cents, although they expected to get a large sum from him. From their first victim they obtained over fifteen hundred dollars, and it was no doubt this good luck, and the feverish thirst for gain that followed, that seared their consciences and steeled their hearts to the enormity of their crimes.

The bodies were stripped naked before being buried and the men were mutilated by having the private parts cut off.

CHAPTER XXXIV.
Old Man Bender

The theory of L. F. Dick of Parsons, who went to Michigan and brought back two women as old Mrs. Bender and Kate, is that old man Bender is dead, having committed suicide in Michigan. This theory, however, is not accepted by everybody, and there are many who believe the old man is yet alive, despite Dick's belief in the suicide theory and the belief of others that he and the remainder of the infamous family were disposed of years ago by the vigilantes.

A Columbus, Ohio newspaper of last Saturday printed a sensational story that old Man bender is still alive and was recently paroled from the Ohio penitentiary.

Photographs are given of the man recently paroled, and old man Bender as he looked when he disappeared. As the story goes, this suspect was received at the penitentiary from Cincinnati under the name of C. S. Miller, July 12, 1886, on a seven year sentence for grand larceny.

He drifted into Cincinnati from where, no one knows, shortly prior to his arrest, and absolutely refused to divulge any portion of his past history or give his place of residence.

While in the prison at Columbus, Ohio, Miller claimed to be worth a considerable sum of money but would never tell how he came in possession of it.

Although repeated efforts were made by the officials at the State Prison, to learn something of Miller's past life, not one syllable of his history was ever given by him.

Previous to the date of his release, he met the requirements of the parole law by securing employment from a farmer in Morgan County, Ohio.

Miller, however, only remained with his employer two days, leaving one night for parts unknown after the farmer and his family had retired, and no clew to his whereabouts has since been learned.

This action of the prisoner constitutes a violation of his parole and fifty dollars reward has been offered by the penitentiary authorities for information that will lead to his capture.

Miller is now seventy-two years old, and his mysterious disappearance from Morgan County certainly bears some significance, for it is hardly reasonable that a man of his age would care to expose himself to a return to the penitentiary by violating the condition of his release unless there was a fear that he would be taken up on some graver charge.

And to forge another link in the chain of circumstances which seem to reasonably establish the claim that old man Bender and Miller are one and the same man, and also account for Miller's strange disappearance since his release from the penitentiary, it is said that since this investigation has been instituted it has been learned that some of the officials at that institution accused Miller of being old man Bender.

Phipps, a member of the board of managers from Cincinnati, was heard to remark that there was a great many people in this city who had seen Miller, and who were also familiar with the newspaper cuts of old man Bender, that thought there was a remarkable resemblance between the two.

It is also said that there are many persons who have come in contact with Miller who agree with the foregoing opinions, yet their confidence in the resemblance was not sufficiently strong to arouse suspicion, think, as many others yet think, that all the Bender family were killed by the posse of armed men who pursued them some sixteen years ago.

CHAPTER XXXV.
Mrs. Garden's Correspondence.

Mrs. John Garden of Saginaw, Michigan, was a daughter of Mrs. Griffith. The following letters were received and written by her.

DETROIT HOUSE OF CORRECTION
Office of the Superintendent

Detroit, Dec. 27, 1889.

Mrs. John Garden,
200 Hermanson R. Saginaw, Mich.

Madam:

In reply to yours of 24th inst., would say upon referring to our records, we find that no person by the name of Elmira Marks or Bartlett was committed here between January 1st, and January 1st, 1874.

We do find, however, a record of one Elmira Shearer having been sentenced to one year's imprisonment here on May 13th, 1872, from Ionia Co., Michigan, for the crime of manslaughter. She was discharged from here March 24th, 1873.

When received here, she stated she was sixty-two years of age, was born in New York, and her occupation as housekeeper. This is all the information we can find in this case.

Yours truly,
JOS. NICHOLSON, Supt.

Saginaw, Jan. 25, 1890.

Mr. J. T. James,

Dear Sir: — Your letter is just received so hasten to answer. This is the first straight account I have had on the whole case. Mother is wrong as to dates in the time she was sent to prison for you can see by the letter I send you that it was in '72 she was in Detroit.

I shall go Monday to Jackson to get her marriage certificate if it is there. I am almost a stranger to my mother and her doings for I left home in '62 at the age of ten years and have not been home only three or four times since, and then not to

195

stay only a few hours so you see, I know less about them than you do. I think if you write to Detroit workhouse they will make out a regular certificate of her imprisonment and discharge. If you think I ought to go there, I will go and get it myself. I do not know what name mother was married under to Mr. Shearer. I wrote her to send me her name and she does not answer my letter. After my father died in '65, I was not home for over ten years so I do not know any of my stepfather's names or which was first or last, only Griffith. I know him. I have been to Carlton and find out it was in '74 she lived there so that will do her no good but I can swear she was in Detroit in '72 for I went there to see her myself and I think that will be all that is needed. Please write me if you think that will be all right. Mr. James, I will be truthful with you. I have not got the money or I would not be idle as I have been but will do all I can.

Yours respectfully,
MRS. MARY GARDEN,

Saginaw, Jan 31, 1890

Mr. James,

Dear Sir: — I sent you to-day a copy of the marriage of my mother to Monroe. Also will send you a letter I just received from Jackson. I will send the money to-day to get a copy and I will send to you just as soon as possible. I think all will be well with her for I know she is innocent. Please excuse this short letter for I am so tired I can hardly stand up. I have traveled all day on foot to find Mr. Robinson and found him sick in bed with La Grippe. Give mother my best wishes and love. Write if there is more to do.

Yours truly,
MRS. MARY GARDEN,

Saginaw, Feb. 10, 1890.

Mr. James,

Dear Sir: — Your letter is just now received so I hasten to answer. Do you think there is any justice in holding my mother there when you know she is not Old Mrs. Bender? Is there any way by which we can make the State pay her for all this?

196

There ought to be. It is not possible for me to get the fifty dollars nor is it possible for me to be there at court, although I should like to be. But you can speak some words of cheer to my mother from me. Did you get the paper from Detroit? And do they still hold Mrs. Davis? Or have they let her go? God only knows what punishment to put on her for the terrible lies she has told. Sometimes I think she is in some way, connected with those Benders. Do you know what has been done with her little children that were left in Michigan? Mother wrote me they was sent to Cold Water school. I wrote to Mother this morning before I got your letter and gave her good cheer and I know it was no use. If it was possible to send you the money I would, but I cannot. My husband will not let me have it not even one-tenth part of it for he says they brung it on themselves. But if there is anything I can do please let me know and I will do it if in my power. I remain yours to command.

Yours truly,
MRS. MARY GARDEN

CHAPTER XXXVI.
The Benders Bound Over.

A Difference of Opinion Still as to Their Identity. — Seven Witnesses Declare That the Two Michigan Women Are the Benders, While Seven Others Equally as Reliable Declare They Are Not. — The Triune Court Give Justice the Benefit of the Doubt and Holds the Prisoners Without Bail.

Oswego, Kansas, Nov. 19. — (Special) — After the examination of sixteen witnesses, seven of whom declare the prisoners are the Benders and seven of whom say they are not, and two having no opinion, the three justices decide that there is probable cause for holding them for trial in the District Court without bail.

The court room has been packed with citizens of Labette County for two days, and never was such interest manifested in a trial in Labette County. The decision was given at ten o'clock to-night.

One witness for the State and six for the defense were on

197

the stand to-day, besides the prisoners who were placed on the stand in their own defense.

Mrs. McCann thinks now that she will reap her reward while County Attorney Morrison believes he will convict them.

Judge Webb and Mr. James, the attorneys for the defense, laughed at the idea of their ever being convicted, while the great crowd of people are equally divided in opinion. The prisoners accept the situation and seem not to be affected.

Leroy Dick was the last and most important witness for the State and testified as follows: "I have lived in this County for twenty-one years; lived from 1869 to 1878 two miles south and two miles east of the Bender farm. I knew the Benders, all of them; saw the young people at Sunday-school and singing; saw the men in the timber; tried to swap horses with them. I was with York when his brother's body was found. I have the hammers and the clock in my possession. One of the hammers is a six-pound collier's hammer, another an Alaskan hammer, and the third a small hammer. I was the Township Trustee at the time. The election was at my house. The Bender men came there to vote; was at Niles, Mich.; heard preliminary examination. The younger woman testified that her mother was the veritable Mrs. Bender and was not her mother, but her step-mother."

"She admitted to me several times that her mother was Mrs. Bender. Kate Bender had a small wart or mole under her left eye. I believe these women are the Bender women. I conversed with Mrs. Bender in 1872 in English. I spoke to the elder prisoner in Berrien Springs, Mich., in German, She replied in German."

Cross-examination elicited the following testimony: "I went to Michigan to bring back the prisoners, if I identified them. I first saw them in the Berrien Springs jail. The old lady asked me to talk to her privately in an inner room of the jail. She asked me to intercede with the authorioti3es to haver her and her daughter separated, as her daughter had threatened her life. She said she believed her daughter was Kate Bender. She said that she believed Mrs. McCann was her long-lost daughter Rosa, and didn't know what she was doing."

Question by Mr. James — "What was your exact language to her in German?"

He replied: "I asked her, 'Kann Ich nicht verkaufen in Deutsch?' She replied, 'Das Kann du nicht.' "

Q. "Can you interpret?"

A. "Yes, it is 'Can I sell you in Dutch?' 'That you can't,' she replied."

Mr. Dick was on the stand all forenoon and as he detailed the conversation with the women in Michigan, and the charged they had made against each other, the prisoners became very much excited and muttered constantly: "Oh, what lies; did you ever hear such stuff?"

Mr. Dick replied to repeated questioning that he was still satisfied that these are the Bender women.

His evidence showed that by their own testimony, these women are hard cases, if they are not the Benders.

Witnesses for the Defense

(As the testimony of each of these witnesses has been given fully in the Chapter which rehearses the calling of witnesses and evidence given as called, in this report of that case, as given in the paper, all evidence is omitted except particular points made in the trial. The State rested and the defense called as their first witness, Thomas Jeans.)

Question by Judge Webb, "On your best judgment are either of these women old Mrs. Bender or Kate?"

A. "I don't think that either one of them is Mrs. Bender or Kate."

On cross-examination the witness was considerably confused. He said, "That Mrs. Bender was a very small woman weighting about one hundred and ten pounds." He was confused and failed to describe the prisoners with his eyes shut.

Silas Toles of Peru, Chautauqua County, Kansas, was called.

In closing, he said, "My judgment is that these are not the Bender women."

Mrs. Vesta Green was called as a witness by the defense.

Question by Judge Webb, "Are either of these women the Benders?"

A. "I believe they are not. They don't look like them at all. Mrs. Bender had a peculiar look out of her eyes. Her eyes were very close together."

On cross-examination, witness said, "I have seen these people before to-day, and I saw as quick as I looked at them that they were not the Benders. I can't see that Eliza Davis has the first look like her."

The old lady, whom several people have said was Mrs. Bender, went on the stand in her own behalf and all eyes were strained to get a look at her. She had the story of her life down pat, and give it glibly.

"My father's name was Hill. I had three brothers and four sisters. I married three other men beside Griffith. One by name of Mark and one by name of Van Alstein and one by the name of Monroe. I am sixty-eight years old, I was married at seventeen to Van Alstein. At twenty-one I married Mark, a Frenchman. Mark died in 1866. I was in Michigan from 1866 to 1872. I was in Detroit in the House of Correction for committing an abortion. I got out in 1869."

She then enumerated six or eight places where she went.

"In 1869," she said, "I lived at St. Charles a year and a half, or until 1871. Then I went to Charleton, and married Mr. Monroe, in 1872."

The witness then enumerated about ten places where she lived from 1872 to 1876. She said she went to Niles in 1876, and had been there since. She said she had her daughter arrested for larceny.

A labored and odious cross-examination followed, in which the old lady questioned the County Attorney several times, causing laughter.

Sarah Eliza Davis was then sworn and gave the straightest story the writer has ever heard, in all instances giving exact dates and names of places where she had lived from 1860 to 1889. She married four men, Gilbert Juphet, alias Hiram Johnson, at Lansing; James Madison at Belleview; John Feenay at McPherson, and Mr. Davis at Mason, and had lived in several places in Illinois, Michigan, and Kansas. She told of her four children and broke down crying while giving their names. She said, "In the name of God, I am not a Bender."

On cross-examination she said, "I do not know where my mother lived from 1869 to 1871. In my examination at Niles I did not say that my mother was Mrs. Bender, but I said that she was none too good to be Mrs. Bender."

The cross-examination failed to shake her, and in it she gave the names of parties in Wild Fowl Bay and other places in Michigan, where she had lived from 1869.

Her story was one that showed a life of hardships and

200

trouble, of marrying and bearing children, and of the many removals she had made in order that the wolf might be kept from the door.

This in the *Kansas City Journal* report of the Case Made on the night that the case was closed and the decision of the Justices made to hold the defendants without bail, and the same night the following was sent from Oswego and appeared in the *Journal* with the foregoing report of the case:

Description of the Benders.

Oswego, Kas. Nov. 19. (Special) — The *Journal* correspondent was shown by J.A. Wells, of Erie, Kas. A very interesting relic which he has kept for sixteen years, in the shape of one of the original proclamations of Ex-Governor Osborne, of Kansas, dated May 17, 1873, or twelve days after the bodies were found, which after reciting that "Whereas, several atrocious murders have been recently committed in Labette County, Kas., under circumstances which fastens beyond doubt the commission of these crimes upon a family known as the Bender family," offers a reward of five hundred dollars for the capture and delivery of either of the parties to the Sheriff of Labette County.

The chief interest attached to this handbill is the fact that in it are given descriptions of the Benders as obtained from the best sources at the time. They are as follows:

John Bender, about sixty years of age, five-feet eight-inches in height, German, speaks but little English, dark complexion, no whiskers, and sparely built.

Mrs. Bender, about fifty years of age, rather heavy set, blue eyes, brown hair, German, speaks broken English.

John Bender, Jr., alias John Gebhardt, five-feet eight or nine inches in height, slightly built, grey eyes with brownish tint, brown hair, light mustache, no whiskers, about twenty-seven years of age, speaks English with a German accent.

Kate Bender, about twenty-four years of age, dark hair and eyes, good looking, well formed, rather bold in appearance, fluent talker, speaks good English with very little German accent.

One of the strange things shown by the testimony in the trial is the idea people have of what is auburn hair.

They all swear that Kate Bender had between a light and a dark auburn hair, and then say that what they mean by auburn hair is that of the color of the younger prisoner, who has a dark brown hair.

The descriptions given above of the two women are strikingly similar to the prisoners, with no exception, unless it is the lack of German accent in the old woman.

CHAPTER XXXVII.
Thinks The Benders Located.

Near Echo, Montana. — Discoverer Lived in Kansas Once Upon a Time. — Will Bet hisRanch That It is Kate. Gives Minute Directions How He Can Be Found. — Is Living in a Log Cabin with Tar Paper Roof.

Every once in a while, someone writes to the Labette County authorities that they have discovered the whereabouts of John and Kate Bender, members of Labette County's famous family of murderers.

Each informant is positive that he has the right parties. Already, the County has spent hundreds of dollars in trying suspects and in the following up of alleged clews. No longer than last year, the people were excited over the reported discovery in Colorado and some money was spent by the County to make an unsuccessful investigation.

The following is the latest communication. It will not be acted upon.

"To the Sheriff of Labette Co., Kansas."

"Dear sir: — There is a party here that we have strong suspicions of being the Benders. And I am a Kansas man myself having lived in Kansas at the time the Benders done their work there. It cause me to believe these are the Benders. This woman is forty-six to fifty-six years old, weighs about one hundred and eighty pounds, is about five-feet ten-inches high. She claims her folks live in Missouri. She has lived in Michigan and moved from there to Iowa and from Iowa to here. As I hear it, she was run out of Iowa as a fire-bug. She has six chil-

202

dren (all blonds) and a husband. He is about six-feet two-inches high and not very fleshy. If this is Kate Bender, her eyes are steel blue with light brown hair.

It has been over a year since I read in the *Kansas City Star* about the Benders. There has been something here very mysterious, and I have been a year deciding what to do. She has threatened people here. They are talking of going to Canada. If you think of sending a man, send one that knows them for sure. If not, send me a description of Kate and John Bender and a photograph if you have them. Write to box (6) six, Echo Montana, and if you sent a man, tell him to come to Echo and go about one-half mile south on the main road and very near one mile east and he will find the writer of this on the right of the road in a little log house with tar paper roof, or inquire of the postmaster at Echo about box six.

I have a ranch here and if these are the parties I suspect, would like to have it kept quiet after. Write and let me have a good description of the Benders if you don't send a man here right away. If you send a man here let him pretend to be wanting to buy a farm. We surmise this woman colors her hair. We think it is white and curly. You had better be careful as these people are on the lookout. The postmaster will tell you my wife and I are all right, but it would be better to inquire as it might cause suspicion by these parties if they are the Benders. I will bet my ranch on it.

July 18, 1902.

CHAPTER XXXVIII.
Frank Ayers Dead.

Man Who Claimed to be Kate Bender's Husband, Murdered.

Fort Collins, Col. April 4 — Frank Ayers, who about two years ago, gained considerable notoriety by charging his wife with being a member of the notorious Bender family, of Kansas, was found shot through the head and mortally wounded near his home in Owl Canyon, twenty miles northeast of here. A ranch hand who reported the case the authorities said that he was riding by and heard the shots.

Upon investigation he found Ayres lying on the ground

with a rifle and revolver beside him. He has been detained pending investigation by the coroner.

Ayers led the authorities of Kansas on a long wild goose chase in 1901, when he claimed the standing reward offered for the arrest of the Benders. He said he had married Kate Bender and she had tried to kill him after she had confessed that she was really Kate Bender.

Further concerning the case, the *Kansas City Journal* of April 3, says:

The coroner left for Owl Canyon to-night and will hold an inquest. It has not been learned whether the shooting was done by Ayres or not.

Frank Ayres, about two years ago, acquired some notoriety by appearing in Kansas City dressed in woman's clothes. He gave his name and address, and was released by police.

He later caused the arrest of his wife, charging her with being a member of the notorious Bender family, of Kansas.

A couple of years ago, Ayres created a sensation in this County, the scene of the notorious Bender murders, and was given much publicity at the time.

He clothed himself with mystery and was evasive in statements. However, he succeeded in enlisting the Commissioners in his tale and as a result, a trip was made to Fort Collins by E. L. Burton, representing the County, and V. Monyhan, Frank Dienst, and M. E. Sparks, the three latter were residents formerly of Oswego township, and acquainted with the Benders at the time the crimes were committed.

The trip was fruitless as investigation revealed that the parties suspected were not the ones wanted, and the Ayres' statements were not to be relied upon.

CHAPTER XXXIX.
Story of the Fate of the Bender Family Told by
Man Who Helped Pursue Them.

Special Dispatch to the *Globe-Democrat.*

Chicago, Ill., July 12 — George Evans Downer, of Downer's Grove, who on his death bed has lifted the veil of secrecy from the fate of the infamous Bender family of Kansas, as was told exclusively in Sunday's *Globe-Democrat,* is a grandson of Pierce Downer, who founded the settlement of Downer's Grove in 1833, and for over thirty years has lived the life of a respected and honored business man of the Chicago suburb.

Hundreds of stories of the fate of the Bender family have been told, and at frequent intervals men and women have been accused of being members of the murderers. Several confessed that the charge was true, and two were tried on it, but in every case it was proved conclusively that the persons were either unjustly accused, insane, or notoriety seeking cranks.

Downer's wonderful story, however, is not from hearsay, not from rumor or "reasoning," but is the recital of an eye-witness who watched the fiends at work, who helped to organize the posse which pursued the flying murders, and who was present with gun in hand when father, mother, son, and daughter were sent to death.

And then an oath was taken that has made the fate of the Benders a mystery all these years.

Wife Was to Reveal Story

To his wife, Downer has told the story a hundred times since their marriage twenty years ago, and it was understood that she — who knew the story by heart — should give it to the world after his death.

But for many months he has been lying on a sick bed waiting for the end, brooding over his wild Western Life in the 'sixties and early 'seventies. The weight of his secret has been an ever greater burden to him, and at last he expressed the desire to have the matter settled before his death.

After this decision, he became rapidly weaker, and when the time came to take down the story, it was only possible for his wife to tell it in his presence; in his words as she remembered them, with occasional corrections and additions by the dying man.

While living in Independence, Kansas, he became a member of the vigilance committee, as in those lawless days such organizations were the only means of keeping order and protecting life. He had considerable success in several criminal cases, and when people began to disappear on the road from Osage Mission to Independence, he had a desire to solve the mystery. This desire was increased when Dr. W. H. York disap-

205

peared, and he with several other members of this vigilance committee, set themselves about to find the murderers.

How Clew was Secured.

His first clew came from a woman canvasser who had appealed to a lawyer to recover some goods in the possession of the Benders.

She had reached the Bender house in the afternoon and after selling some goods to Kate, she was invited to spend the evening with them, and after supper the family insisted that she remain for the night.

While Kate was washing the dishes, her brother John came into the room and started to sharpen an ugly looking knife. This was too much for the woman, who was already terrified by the evil looks exchanged by the family, and insistence that she stay all night.

She fled to the woods and hid in a creek while the Benders hunted for her. Later, she made her way to Independence. The lawyer thought there was nothing in the story, as the goods were returned, but it proved the clew that led to the end of the family of butchers.

CHAPTER XL.
Kate Bender Reported Dead.

The *Globe-Democrat* published the following dispatches:

Californian Says Woman Known as Mrs. Peters
Confessed to Him.

Rio Vista, Cal., May 5 — Kate Bender, of the notorious family of Kansas murderers, is dead here, according to a statement made to-day by John Collins. The woman was known as Mrs. Gavin and later as Mrs. Peters. Collins declares the woman gave him a detailed account of many murders which she and her brother committed in the Bender home at Cherryvale, Kansas, in the 'seventies.

Many Crimes Committed.

Kansas City, Mo., May 5 — It is not known how many murders the notorious Bender family committed while living in Kansas.

The family consisted of Wm. Bender, aged 60; his wife, aged 55; Kate, aged 25; and John, aged 23 years. Kate and John were children of Wm. Bender by a former wife. The Benders kept a little store, which is believed, however, to have been maintained only as a decoy for travelers.

Kate Bender professed to be a magnetic healer. Her role was to make love to the unfortunate wayfarers who sought shelter at the Bender house and lure them to a corner of a room where her brother, concealed behind a curtain, would crush their skulls with heavy clubs. Robbery was the motive of the crimes. After the family fled, the bodies of nine victims were found on the Bender place.

The *San Francisco Examiner*, dated May 6, 1910, published the following dispatch:

NINE BODIES FOUND IN BENDER CELLAR.
How Many Persons the Family Slew Never Known; Gang's Fate a Mystery.

Kansas City (Mo.,) May 5 — It is not known how many murders the notorious Bender family committed while living the early '70s in Labette County Kansas. The family consisted of William Bender, sixty years old; his wife, aged fifty-five years; Kate, twenty-five years old; and John, twenty-three. Kate and John were children of William Bender by a former wife.

Kate Bender professed to be a magnetic healer. The Bender house was situated on the main highway between Independence, Kansas, and the Osage Mission. The Benders kept a little store supplied with food for men and beast, but it was said to have been a decoy for weary travelers rather than anything else.

The Benders lived in a frame house, about twenty feet long and sixteen feet wide. The one room was divided by a canvas

207

partition drawn tightly over upright scantlings. This partition was the death trap.

The victim was decoyed to a seat near the canvas. Kate, behind the canvas, would render the victim senseless with a hammer. If the blow was not fatal, the old man followed with blows on the temple. Then the throat was cut. After the body was robbed, it was thrown into the cellar through a "blind door."

After the family fled, nine bodies were found on the place.

The murder of Doctor York, of Independence, led to the undoing of the murderers. His brother, A. M. York, of Fort Scott, instituted a search and found nine bodies on the Bender place, including that of his brother.

The fate of the Bender family has never been definitely known. At various times, persons who have claimed to have been members of a posse that pursued the family have given out statements. Some have said that the entire family was killed. Others have stated that Kate escaped.

NEWSPAPER COMPILATION

THE BLOOD-STAINED BENDER BAND
More Facts Concerning the Horrible Tragedy in Kansas.

A reporter of the Kansas City Times, who returned from the scene of the murders on Monday night, makes the following statement, which contains many facts of interest in addition to those already published:

The devil's kitchen, otherwise the Bender house, is a small, rude frame shanty, without lath or plaster or intervening substance between its floor and the rafters of the pointed roof. In size it is 16 by 24 feet. Small uprights 2 by 4 inches are set to mark the house into two compartments, but no wall had ever been made other than a white cotton cloth hung in the rear apartment and against these uprights. The front apartment had in it a counter over which the butchers once pretended to sell groceries. In the rear room was a rude bed, a table, a stove, and three chairs.

The table to which the guests of the fiends were seated, was placed directly over the trap door so that the guest's back was to and against the white curtain. In this position it was an easy thing for the male villains in the front apartment to strike the form clearly lined and resting against the white cloth and when the blows of the sledge and the hammer had knocked the victim, with a crushed and broken skull, senseless and helpless to the floor, for the female fiends in the back room to cut their throat. The execution was as simple as it was dreadful, but, though it would seem resistance to such well planned murder of the trusting and unsuspecting was impossible, the walls gave silent evidence that some of the murdered ones had not been sent to their doom without an effort to defend themselves. No less than a dozen bullet holes in the sides and roof of the house attest that armed men, when struck down so relentlessly, had attempted to shoot their murderers, but, unfortunately, the aims had been wild and the murderers are reserved for the hempen halter.

The Situation.

This building is located just on the rising edge of a beautiful narrow valley, circled on the south, east and west by a

209

range of mounds of the valley. The hills are distant from the house from a half mile to a mile, the closest being on the south to the rear. The house fronted to the road just in the bend, sitting back about its own length from the roadway.

From this point of the road can be had a full view of everything for half a mile in every direction, but not another house is within sight. It is about seven miles from Cherryvale, ten miles from Thayer, eight miles from Ladore, and two miles from Morehead, and just in the northwest corner of Labette county.

Pistols And Knives For A Supper.

One of the most marvelous stories ever heard, but which is vouched for by reliable men is the following: One evening about three months ago, a poor woman, footsore and weary, traveling to Independence, without money, stopped at the Bender den and asked for some supper, and for the privilege of resting awhile.

She was invited in and being nearly exhausted she took her shoes and scanty wrappings off and lay down on the bed in the back room. She soon fell into a troubled doze, from which she was awakened by the "touch of the old hag of the den, who pointing to an array of pistols and double edged knives of various sizes, lying on the table, said in the spirit of hellish malignity: "There, your supper is ready."

The woman was motionless and breathless with terror, and as she sank back on the bed, the devil dame picked up the knives one by one and drew her finger along the sharpened blades at the same time glancing fiendishly at her intended victim. How long this terror lasted the woman could not tell but at last she, in the very desperation of fear, arose, as though not alarmed and made a private excuse for going out.

She was permitted to do so and moving around to the shelter of the stable, barefooted and scarce half clad, she darted off on the wings of fear and ran two miles to the house of one who protected her and gave her shelter. As she was running away, she turned frequently to see if she was pursued but no one followed her, though she saw the light from the opened doorway several times, as though the devils inside were awaiting her return.

Even this story seems not have aroused more than the before existing suspicion that the Benders were not exactly the right kind of people.

Strange Disappearances

In May 1871, the body of a man named Jones, who had had his skull crushed and his throat cut, was discovered in Drum Creek. The owner of the Drum Creek claim was suspected, but no action was taken.

In February 1872, the bodies of two men were found who had the same injuries as Jones.

By 1873, reports of missing people who had passed through the area had become so common that travelers began to avoid the trail. The area was already widely known for "horse thieves and villains", and vigilance committees often "arrested" some for the disappearances, only for them to be later released by the authorities. Many honest men under suspicion were also run out of the county by these vigilance committees.

In the winter of 1872, George Newton Longcohr and his infant daughter, Mary Ann, left Independence, Kansas, to resettle in Iowa and were never seen again.

In the spring of 1873, Longcohr's former neighbor, Dr. William Henry York, went looking for them and questioned homesteaders along the trail. Dr. York reached Fort Scott, and on March 9 began the return journey to Independence but never arrived home. Dr. York had two brothers: Colonel Ed York living in Fort Scott, and Alexander M. York, a member of the Kansas State Senate from Independence who, in November 1872, had been instrumental in exposing U.S. Senator Samuel C. Pomeroy's bribery of state legislators in his bid for re-election. Both knew of William's travel plans and, when he failed to return home, an all-out search began for the missing doctor. Colonel York, leading a company of some fifty men, questioned every traveler along the trail and visited all the area homesteads.

On March 28, 1873, Colonel York arrived at the Benders' inn with a Mr. Johnson, explaining to them that his brother had gone missing and asking if they had seen him. They admitted Dr. York had stayed with them and suggested the possibility that he had run into trouble with Indians. Colonel York agreed that this was possible and remained for dinner.

On April 3, Colonel York returned to the inn with armed men after being informed that a woman had fled from the inn after being threatened with knives by Elvira Bender. Elvira allegedly could not understand English, while the younger Benders denied the claim. When York repeated the claim, Elvira became enraged, said the woman was a witch who had cursed her coffee, and ordered the men to leave her house, revealing for the first time that "her sense of the English language" was much better than was let on.

Before York left, Kate asked him to return alone the following Friday night, and she would use her clairvoyant abilities to help him find his brother. The men with York were convinced the Benders and a neighboring family, the Roaches, were guilty and wanted to hang them all, but York insisted that evidence must be found.

Around the same time, neighboring communities began to make accusations that the Osage community was responsible for the disappearances, and a meeting was arranged by the Osage township in the Harmony Grove schoolhouse. The meeting was attended by seventy-five locals, including Colonel York and both John Bender, Sr. and John Bender, Jr.. Following discussions concerning the disappearances, including that of William York, it was agreed that a search warrant would be obtained to search every homestead between Big Hill Creek and Drum Creek. Despite York's strong suspicions regarding the Benders since his visit several weeks earlier, no one had watched them, and it was not noticed for several days that they had fled.

A Bungling Business.

Although for the past three years this section has been infested with horse thieves and murders, and this known to every one about the country, it is probable the same state of affairs might have continued for an indefinite period had not the murder of Dr. York, a man of family, friends and reputation, led to the exposure.

Men have been missed and bodies found of murdered men for three years past, and vigilance committees have hunted and driven some men from the country but it would now seem as though the leaders of these "regulators" were themselves the villains and honest men had been falsely and foully sus-

212

pected and driven from their homes. Known villains have for that time been sent to the Penitentiary only to be pardoned out by Governors.

And even the band of seventy-five armed and honest men who scoured the country in search of Dr. York when it was learned that he was missing seem to have had very little judgment or discretion.

On the 28th of March last, Col. York and Mr. Johnson visited the Bender House, to which place they had tracked Dr. York, and endeavored to coax some information from them, but they would tell nothing. On the 3d of April, this armed band visited the house with the sole object of finding the murderers of Dr. York, yet they did not notice the bullet holes in the house, and allowed themselves to be fooled by an assumed stupidity which was the disguise of most hellish cunning. The old hag sat mum and gloomy, pretending she could not understand nor speak English, old man Bender said nothing; Kate, she of the evil-eye, denied all knowledge of the lost individuals, and the younger male villain fooled them with a well made up story.

He said that at about the time they said Dr. York was missed, he, Bender, had been shot at in a lonesome place near Drum Creek, one evening, and it must have been by those who killed the doctor. He described the place minutely and then took them to it, and it was found as he said, and they half believed his story, and returned with him.

Col. York repeated the story given above, of supper and pistols and knives offered to the lone woman, when the old hag soon found her sense of the English language improved. She understood all that had been said, and flew into a violent passion. She denied the story of the supper, but said that that was a bad and wicked woman whom she would kill if she ever came near them again; that the woman was a witch and had bewitched Kate's coffee, and then she ordered the whole band away. While going and coming from the creek John told Col. York that his sister Kate could do anything, that she could control the devil, and that the devil did her bidding. When they returned to the house, Col. York tried to induce this wonderful mistress of the devil to reveal where the body of his brother was. She positively and persistently refused her Satanic aid at this time, giving as her reason therefore that she could not do so in the daytime and while there were so

213

many men and so much noise about.

This pretended sorceress and true fiend then told Col. York privately that if he would come the next night, Friday — when best she worked her spells — and bring only one man with him, she would take him to the grave of his murdered brother. Had the Colonel been so foolish as to believe this mysterious power of the creature there is no doubt she would have proved her promise good.

The whole band then left the house. They visited the houses of Roach, Smith. and Harness at Ladore, and made many threats, but accomplished nothing. Their intent was good, but they lacked an experienced detective for a leader. So strong was their conviction, however, of the guilt of the Roach's and the Benders that they would have hung them then if it had not been for the persuasion of Col. York and a few others, who were determined that none but the known guilty should suffer. Of course this visit alarmed the Benders, and they fled.

More Carelessness.

It seems strange that no watch was put upon the suspected Benders and still more strange that they should have been gone three weeks before anyone knew of it. When they went to Thayer they left their team, wagon, and dog on the public street of the town. On the street the team and wagon remained for two days without a claimant when they were taken charge of by a livery firm there — Bears & Wheeler.

No notice, other than a notice in the *Head Light*, the local journal, was given of the finding of the team and no description of the horses published, though they were peculiarly and similarly marked. Had such description been given, it must have led to the speedy pursuit of the fleeing criminals. It is not suspected that there was any guilt in this neglect, but only carelessness.

There Must Be A Gang.

No doubt is entertained that the Benders have not been

alone in their damnable villainy. They must have had confederates to dispose of the stock and clothes of the murdered men, and suspicion has readily pointed to a number of men, living throughout that section, in different directions, and to none with more evidence of justice than to one Mit Cherry.

This fellow lives about three miles south of Parsons, and when Col. York was making search for his brother he tried to influence the Colonel to employ him as a detective. Luckily the Colonel would have nothing to do with him. This man, it is said by two men who are generally credited, at different places and times, and separately, told him he was a member of a band of "Regulators" in the county, and that when they found a criminal they never troubled him with the law, or put the county to any expense about him; that the band always knew their own work when they saw it, for every man they put out of the way laid with his throat cut, his left arm across his breast, and his right by his side. In all such condition and position were found nearly all the Bender victims.

As a further evidence against this fellow, it is known that soon after McCrotty's disappearance was known, and when there was about to be some action taken to look for him, he pretended to have a letter from McCrotty, telling of his safe arrival in Illinois, at his intended destination.

The other suspected parties who have been arrested are men of bad repute in general and believed for some time to be horse thieves, if nothing worse. On Sunday, Sheriff Stone brought into Independence, under arrest, Addison Roach, of Ladore, and William Buxton, a son-in-law of the elder Roach, both fond near Cedarvale. This makes the number under arrest now on suspicion, so far as known, twelve. The names of the others have been published in the Times.

Sunday At The Graves.

On last Sunday there were about one thousand men, women and children at the Bender grounds, gazing with mingled emotions of horror and curiosity. The graves even yet sent forth a sickening stench, and women held their noses as they peered down into the now tenantless holes. Two special trains were run, one from Independence and one from Coffeyville, to a point on the railway line about two miles from the house and teams were busy running to and from the grounds, while

215

the greater portion of the crowd were compelled to walk. The trains brought three hundred persons there from all parts of the surrounding country, in wagons, carriages and on horseback.

The curiosity of many seemed to master their repulsion and hundred brought away some memento of the dreadful place. The bloodstained bedstead was smashed to pieces and divided in the crowd, all the shrubbery and the young trees were broken or torn up and carried away and pieces of the house borne off by the curious. Such another raid would not leave much of the shanty. It was supposed that the grounds would be plowed and scraped again this day to search for other bodies but the intent was abandoned and it is not probably that any further search will be made until it is done regularly by the county authorities.

Rewards Offered.

Rewards to the amount of $5,000 have been offered for the capture of the murderers, and there is not the slightest doubt that they will be recovered. On last Saturday the detectives were on the trail of the Benders, with the expressed certainty of effecting their speedy capture and it is more than probable they are already taken. With the number under arrest and the others watched, no doubt someone will reveal the whole truth, when Kansas will be rid of the worst scoundrels that ever infested and cursed this country.

Arrests

Several weeks after the discovery of the bodies, Addison Roach and his son-in-law, William Buxton, were arrested as accessories. In total twelve men "of bad repute in general" would be arrested including Breckman. All were thought to have been involved in disposing of the victims' stolen goods with Mit Cherry, a member of the vigilance committee. Cherry was additionally implicated for forging a letter from one of the victims, informing the man's wife that he had arrived safely at his destination in Illinois.

Breckman would be arrested again twenty-three years later for the rape and murder of his own 18-year-old daughter

Many stories say that one vigilante group actually caught

the Benders and shot all of them but Kate, whom they burned alive. Another group claimed they had caught the Benders and lynched them before throwing their bodies into the Verdigris River. Yet another group claimed to have killed the Benders during a gunfight and buried their bodies on the prairie. However, no one ever claimed the $3,000 reward.

1884 an elderly man matching Pa Benders description was arrested in Montana for a murder committed near Salmon, Idaho where the victim had been killed by a hammer blow to the head. A message requesting positive identification was sent to Cherryvale but the suspect severed his foot to escape his leg irons and bled to death. By the time a deputy from Cherryvale arrived, identification was impossible due to decomposition. Despite the lack of identification, the man's skull was displayed as that of "Pa Bender" in a Salmon saloon until prohibition forced its closure in 1920 and the skull disappeared. Whether or not John Flickinger was really John Bender is unknown.

Based on an inscription in a Bible recovered from the Bender home, it was believed that John Jr. was born John Gebhardt although no other proof of his identity exists. Some of the Benders' neighbors claimed that John and Kate were not brother and sister, but actually husband and wife.

No Evidence.

Several parties who lived near the Benders were supposed to be implicated with them in their crimes, and some of them were arrested, but upon examination they were discharged, there not being sufficient evidence to hold them for trial. One or two of those thus arrested brought suit for false imprisonment, and obtained a verdict for a small amount of damages.

The Band Formerly From Indiana.

The sickening details of the terrible Bender murders in Kansas, come to us with fearful emphasis in view of our discovery, of the fact that the inhuman murderers were probably for some time residents of the neighborhood of this city, and that circumstances in connection with the recent developments in Kansas, strongly point them out as the authors of a mysterious murder, which happened in our midst some year

217

and a half ago.

Our readers will remember the circumstances attending the murder of a German and his wife by the name of Bandle, and the burning of the house over their bodies. The mystery has never been removed from that terrible tragedy and up to this time no person has ever been accused, or even suspected, of the commission of that crime. We believe that the bloody trail leads us to the Kansas fiends. At the time of the Bandle tragedy, there was resident, near this city a family by the name of Bender.

The family consisted of two men and two women. The men were employed on the McCulloch farm on Silver Creek at the time of the Bandle murder, and it will be remembered that this identical farm was the scene of that homicide. Soon after the occurrence of that shocking affair, the Benders left and went to Kansas. It seems that on reaching Kansas they entered upon a career of crime which is without parallel in the history of our times.

Taking up their residence near Cherryvale, Kansas in an unfinished house, standing on the roadside and out of view of any other human habitation, they constructed, with devilish ingenuity a regular trap for any traveler whom they could inveigle into their den. They placed the table from which their meals were taken near a curtain of cotton cloth, so that the victim would sit with his back against the curtain. A candle placed on the table, would of course, shadow the form of the person sitting against it on the cloth and a blow with an ax or hammer given by a man on the opposite side of the curtain would fell the sitter to the floor, and then the cutting of his throat could be easily accomplished.

The number of their victims is as yet unknown. Eight bodies have already been disinterred and recognized by their clothing or by marks upon their persons. These monsters had buried their victims in the garden attached to their premises. In one instance they had buried a man and in the same grave was found the dead body of his infant child, with every evidence of its having been buried alive. The circumstantial evidence which connects them with the murder of Bandle and his wife may be summed up thus:

The identity of the names: The description of the Kansas murderers answers exactly to the Benders who lived here; their manner of living in Kansas — the two men and the two women living as one family, is exactly as they lived here; the Benders left this city for Kansas, the place we find them now; the time of their departure from this point corresponds with the time of their arrival in Kansas, the residence of the Benders on the farm on which Bandle and his wife were murdered, and their immediate departure from the scene.

The Benders fled from Kansas when they discovered the suspicions of the people there; but we are informed by telegraph that the entire brood of devils were arrested this morning near Dallas, Texas. We predict that before they all swing from the scaffold, someone of them will confess their complicity with the Bandle tragedy near this city.

Sheriff Saves a Man Who Murdered His Own Daughter.

A German named Breckman has been hurried to the Oswego jail from the Bender settlement, north of here, to prevent his being lynched for having ruined and murdered his 18-year-old daughter.

The neighbors yesterday found the girl in the Breckman barn, unconscious and nearly dead.

Her father, it is alleged, had ruined her and then beaten her into insensibility.

Later in the day she died, and, the facts becoming known, an angry mob sought to lynch Breckman. The sheriff took him from the town lock-up, where he had been temporarily placed, and hurried to Oswego with the prisoner.

Breckman has a hard name, and during the Benders horrors, in 1873, he was charged with being implicated in several murders committed by that gang. On one occasion he was strung up several times, but would not confess, and was finally liberated.

Known Victims in Kansas

1871: The body of a Mr. Jones. was found in Drum Creek with a crushed skull and throat cut.

1872: Ben Brown from Howard County, Kansas went missing while carrying $2,600.

1872: Two unidentified men found on the prairie with crushed skulls and throats cut.

1872: W. F. McCrotty was buried in the Bender orchard. His

wagon, team of horses, and $38 cash were missing.

1872: Henry McKenzie, was buried in the Bender orchard. His matched team of horses and $753 were missing.

1872: Jack Bogart went missing.

1872: Johnny Boyle was thrown into the Bender well. His pacing mare, saddle, and $860 cash were missing.

1872: George Newton Longcohr and his 18-month-old daughter, Mary Ann were buried together in the Bender orchard. His skull was crushed, she was burned alive.

1873: Dr. William York was burned in the Bender orchard. $2,000 cash was missing.

John Greary was buried in the Bender orchard.

Unidentified male No. 1 was buried in the Bender orchard.

Unidentified male No. 2 was buried in the Bender orchard.

Various body parts, not belonging to victims listed above, were discovered indicating the possibility of at least three additional victims buried in the Bender orchard.

1873: During an expanded search, bodies of four more unidentified males were found in the Drum Creek area. All four had crushed skulls and slit throats. One victim might have been Jack Bogart who went missing in 1872.

Speculation indicates that recovered body parts not matched to any other bodies may represent remains of at least 20 victims.

Henry McKenzie's and William York's remains were reinterred in Independence, Kansas.

George and Mary Ann Longcohr's remains were reinterred in Montgomery County, Kansas.

W. F. McCrotty's remains were reinterred in Parsons, Kansas.

None of the other bodies nor remains were claimed and all were reinterred at the base of a small hill one mile southeast of the Bender's orchard. The burial ground is called "The Bender Mounds."

Made in the USA
Monee, IL
26 January 2021